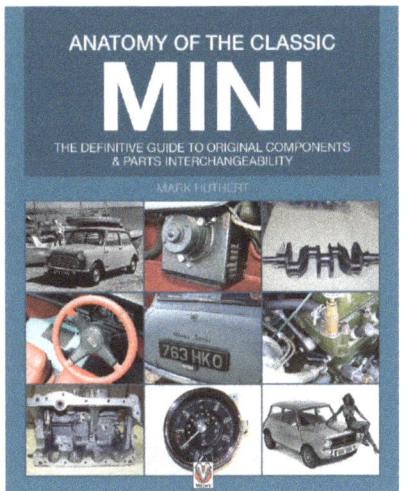

First published in January 2017, reprinted May 2019 and 2025 by Veloce, an imprint of David and Charles Limited. Tel +44 (0)1305 260068 / e-mail info@veloce.co.uk / web www.veloce.co.uk.

ISBN: 978-1-84584-223-9

© 2017, 2019 & 2025 Mark Huthert and David and Charles. All rights reserved. With the exception of quoting brief passages for the purpose of review, no part of this publication may be recorded, reproduced or transmitted by any means, including photocopying, without the written permission of David and Charles Limited.

Throughout this book logos, model names and designations, etc, have been used for the purposes of identification, illustration and decoration. Such names are the property of the trademark holder as this is not an official publication. Readers with ideas for automotive books, or books on other transport or related hobby subjects, are invited to write to the editorial director of Veloce at the above email address. British Library Cataloguing in Publication Data – A catalogue record for this book is available from the British Library. Design and DTP by Veloce.

ANATOMY OF THE CLASSIC
MINI

THE DEFINITIVE GUIDE TO ORIGINAL COMPONENTS & PARTS INTERCHANGEABILITY

MARK HUTHERT

Contents

Introduction 6

Chapter 1 Bodywork 7
Chapter 2 Braking 33
Chapter 3 Breathing 37
Chapter 4 Brightwork 41
Chapter 5 Camshafts, cam followers, etc 54
Chapter 6 Cooling system 60
Chapter 7 Crankshafts & connecting rods 70
Chapter 8 Cylinder heads & rocker gear 79
Chapter 9 Crankshaft pulleys & dampers 87
Chapter 10 Distributors & drives 89
Chapter 11 Engine block & upper stabiliser bars 92
Chapter 12 Exhaust & inlet manifolds 108
Chapter 13 Hydraulics & pedal box assemblies 115

CONTENTS

Chapter 14 Fuel system 121

Chapter 15 Gauges & mounting pods 128

Chapter 16 Glass & lighting 131

Chapter 17 Oil system 136

Chapter 18 Steering 143

Chapter 19 Subframes & suspension 148

Chapter 20 Transmission & lower stabiliser bars 156

Chapter 21 Wheels 180

Chapter 22 Handbuilt 621 AOK & 1959 Mini 763 HKO 184

Useful contacts & museums 187

Index 190

Introduction

They say that you never forget your first Mini. Mine was actually a Fiesta Yellow 850cc Austin Seven, bought for me by my father, Norman Huthert, in 1975. It had been involved in an accident and came with a replacement distributor as a spare part. This first car cemented my interest in the little automotive icon.

Why a whole book about original Mini parts? Well, why not? I don't think this type of thing has ever been attempted before for the classic Mini. I must admit that researching it did become something akin to an archaeological dig spread over several years!

I have been attending Mini shows since 1995, and always learn more about classic Minis during such events. To this day I'm still coming across new information about a car that went out of production in 2000.

The purpose of this work is to enable the reader to identify important parts correctly, and help source replacements from other vehicles from the same manufacturers, particularly engine and gearbox components.

The engine fitted to the classic Mini was originally called the AS3. It then became the A-Series in 1952 when Austin and Morris came together to form the British Motor Corporation. The engine was built between 1951 and 2000, and there were literally millions of them produced.

Anyway, above all, I hope this work will enable people to keep their classic Minis running.

I'd like to thank everyone at Veloce Publishing for their help along the way (especially Kevin Quinn).

Happy Mini Motoring!

Mark Huthert

Chapter 1
Bodywork

All vehicles from October 1961 to 2000 each floorpan quarter has two pressings (originally for fastening carpets). See also 'Separate inner sills, 1959 to October 1961' (page 13).

SALOON BODYSHELL FLOORS

Only the first type of floor was non-production line. All the rest used lifting shoes.

Early models

The first three floors listed here were all of one-piece construction. I think it was just the large front floorpan vehicles that had captive nuts attached to the toe board. The bolts that fit into captive nuts had part number HZS0505.

• Chassis numbers A-A2S7-101 to 17987 (Austin) and M-A2S4-101 to 22441 (Morris) had captive nuts in the front floorpans (one in each floorpan) – for locating the front subframe. I believe these vehicles were built with the wrong overlap between the front floorpans and toe board.

• The east-west box section to which the front seats are bolted extends below the upper sill steps on the first three floor types.

• All three floor types without separate outer sills have an external seam running from just behind the front subframe turret all the way to the apex panel. Pic 1 (shows inner front wheelarch behind offside front wheel)

First type (hand-built cars)

Pics 2 (near-side front AOK with stamped in reinforcing channels), 3 (off-side front AOK with stamped in reinforcing channels) & 4 (fabricated floor starter button mounting)

• Floor and outer sills all one panel.
• Two large flat front floorpans, without stamped-in reinforcing channels.
• Four brackets welded to east-west box section to take seat mountings. Pic 5
• Fabricated floor starter button mounting.
• Battery solenoid cable held to floor by individual metal tags.
• No blind bolts for lifting shoes fitted to the floor.
• One large hole stamped in each front floorpan, and fitted with alloy blanking plugs. Two large holes stamped in each rear floorpan, and fitted with alloy blanking plugs. Pics 6 & 7
• Two stamped holes in the rear tunnel (the north/south tunnel that takes the exhaust pipe). Pic 8

Second type

Pics 9 (near-side front), 10 (near-side rear), 11 (off-side jacking point) & 12 (off-side outer)

• Floor and outer sills all one panel.
• Two large flat front floorpans, without stamped-in reinforcing channels.
• Four brackets welded to east-west box section to take seat mountings.
• Fabricated floor starter button mounting.
• Battery solenoid cable held to floor by individual metal tags.
• Eight blind bolts fitted to floor, two in each floorpan, for the attachment of lifting shoes.
• One large hole stamped in each front floorpan, and fitted with alloy blanking plugs. Two large holes stamped in each rear floorpan, and fitted with alloy blanking plugs.

ANATOMY OF THE CLASSIC MINI

BODYWORK

• Two stamped holes in the rear tunnel for handbrake cables.

Third type
The third type of floor was fitted with inner sills inside the rear companion bins, and the space between the inner and outer sills filled with foam.

Also see Second type: Nearside front, Offside rear.
• Floor and outer sills all one panel.
• Two smaller front floorpans – this floorpan size was standardised up until the deep floorpan models. Pics 13, 14, & 15
• Four brackets welded to east-west box section to take seat mountings.
• Floor starter mounting now part of floor pressing. Pic 16
• Battery solenoid cable held to floor by individual metal tags.
• Eight blind bolts fitted to floor, two in each floorpan, for the attachment of lifting shoes.
• One large hole stamped in each front floorpan, and fitted with alloy blanking plug. Two large holes stamped in each rear floorpan, and fitted with alloy blanking plugs.
• Two stamped holes in the rear tunnel for handbrake cables.

Separate outer sill models
Front subframe secured to floorpan and toe board by nuts and bolts. Austin chassis number A-A2S7 17988 onward. Morris chassis number M-A2S4 22442 onward. Bolt part number HZS0507, nut part number FNZ105.

By UK law, all cars built from 1st June 1961 had to have seatbelt anchorages.

It is my personal opinion that BMC took this opportunity to redesign the floor of the saloon models.

Fourth type
• This floor is the first with separate outer sills.
• The floor incorporates the inner sills, which also have captive nuts for seatbelt mounting. Pic 17

Pic 18

Pic 19

Pic 20

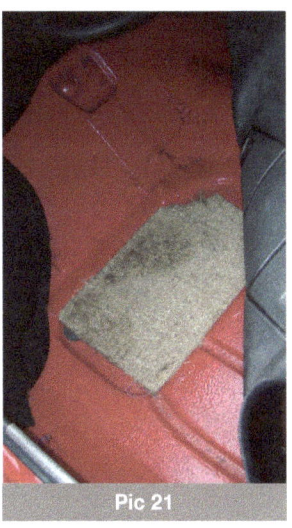
Pic 21

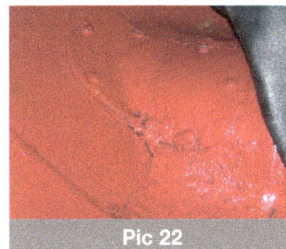
Pic 22

• Two smaller front floorpans. This floorpan size was standardised up until the deep floorpan models.
• East-west box section has eight captive nuts to take seat mounting brackets.
• Floor starter mounting now part of the floor pressing.
• Battery solenoid cable held to the floor by one continuous piece of metal.
• Four rectangular brackets welded to the underside of the floor to accept lifting shoes.
• Small holes stamped in front and rear floorpans, and fitted with rubber grommets. Pics 18 & 19
• Two stamped holes in rear tunnel for handbrake cables.

Fifth type
Mini Cooper registration number KEL 236 used for BMC publicity photographs is actually an earlier bodyshell. This can be checked by looking at the nearside outer sill. This vehicle has two blanking plugs fitted which suggests that it was foam filled, and there are no sill flutes evident.
• 997cc Cooper onward.
• Remote control hole stamped out of central tunnel for gearchange mechanism. Pic 20
• The floor incorporates the inner sills, which also have captive nuts for seatbelt mounting.
• Two smaller front floorpans. This floorpan size was standardised up until the deep floorpan models.
• East-west box section has eight captive nuts to take seat mounting brackets.
• Floor starter mounting is part of the floor pressing.
• Blanking plate (part number 14A9943) fitted over magic wand gearlever aperture. Pics 21 & 22
• Battery solenoid cable held to the floor by one continuous piece of metal.
• Four rectangular brackets welded to the underside of the floor to accept lifting shoes.
• Small holes stamped in front and rear floorpans, and fitted with rubber grommets.
• Two stamped holes in the rear tunnel for handbrake cables.

Sixth type
• Floor for hydrolastic saloons with non-remote gearlever.
• The floor incorporates the inner

ANATOMY OF THE CLASSIC MINI

sills, which also have captive nuts for seatbelt mounting.
• Two smaller front floorpans. This floorpan size was standardised up until the deep floorpan models.
• East-west box section has eight captive nuts to take seat mounting brackets.
• Floor starter mounting part of floor pressing.
• Battery solenoid cable held to floor by one continuous piece of metal.
• Four rectangular brackets welded to underside of floor to accept lifting shoes.
• Small holes stamped in front and rear floorpans fitted with rubber grommets.
• Two stamped holes in rear tunnel for handbrake cables.

Seventh type
• Floor for hydrolastic saloons.
• Remote control hole stamped out of central tunnel for gearchange mechanism.
• The floor incorporates the inner sills, which also have captive nuts for seatbelt mounting.
• Two smaller front floorpans. This floorpan size was standardised up until the deep floorpan models.
• East-west box section has eight captive nuts to take seat mounting brackets.
• Floor starter mounting part of floor pressing.
• Blanking plate part number 14A9943 fitted over magic wand gearlever aperture.
• Battery solenoid cable held to floor by one continuous piece of metal.
• Four rectangular brackets welded to underside of floor to accept lifting shoes.
• Small holes stamped in front and rear floorpans fitted with rubber grommets.
• Two stamped holes for handbrake cables, rear tunnel.

Rod-change gearbox models
From October 1975 safety catches were fitted to the rear floorpans to lock down the front seats. This required drilling two holes in each rear floorpan. This applied to all floors until the end of production.

Eighth type
• Mk3.5 saloons 1973 onward.
• Front tunnel pressing in-between front floorpans modified to accept rod-change gearbox. Pic 23
• The floor incorporates the inner sills, which also have captive nuts for seatbelt mounting.
• Two smaller front floorpans. This floorpan size was standardised up until the deep floorpan models.
• East-west box section for mounting front seats modified to fit rod-change gearbox front tunnel. Pic 24
• Front seats are still attached by brackets bolted through to eight captive nuts.
• Battery solenoid cable held to floor by one continuous piece of metal.
• Four rectangular brackets welded to underside of floor to accept lifting shoes.
• Small holes stamped in front and rear floorpans fitted with rubber grommets.
• Two stamped holes for handbrake cables, rear tunnel.

Ninth type
• Mk4 1976 onward.
• Front tunnel pressing in-between front floorpans modified to accept rod-change gearbox.
• The floor incorporates the inner sills, which also have captive nuts for seatbelt mounting.
• Two smaller front floorpans, this floorpan size was standardised up until the deep floorpan models.
• East-west box section for mounting front seats modified to fit rod-change gearbox front tunnel.
• Front seats are still attached by brackets bolted through to eight captive nuts.
• Battery solenoid cable held to floor by one continuous piece of metal.
• Four rectangular brackets welded to underside of floor to accept lifting shoes.
• Small holes stamped in front and rear floorpans fitted with rubber grommets.
• One stamped hole for single handbrake cable, rear tunnel. Pic 25

Deep-well floor models
Tenth type
Pic 26 (offside front), pics 27 & 28 (nearside front)
• First of the deep-well floors.
• Front tunnel pressing in-between front floorpans modified to accept rod-change gearbox.
• The floor incorporates the inner sills, which also have captive nuts for seatbelt mounting.
• Two small front floorpans, nearside pan split by central reinforcer.
• East-west box section for mounting front seats modified to fit rod-change gearbox front tunnel.
• Front seats still attached by brackets bolted through to eight captive nuts.
• Battery solenoid cable held to floor by one continuous piece of metal.
• Four rectangular brackets welded to underside of floor to accept lifting shoes.
• Small holes stamped in front and rear floorpans and fitted with rubber grommets.
• One stamped hole for single handbrake cable, rear tunnel.

Eleventh type
Pic 29, ECU (mounting platform)
• Also see Tenth type: Offside front, Nearside front
• Twin-point injection deep-well floor.
• Front tunnel pressing in-between front floorpans modified to accept rod-change gearbox.
• The floor incorporates the inner sills, which also have captive nuts for seatbelt mounting.
• Two small front floorpans, nearside pan split by central reinforcer.
• East-west box section for mounting front seats modified to fit rod-change gearbox front tunnel.
• Front seats are still attached by brackets bolted through to eight captive nuts.
• Battery solenoid cable held to floor by

BODYWORK

one continuous piece of metal.
- Four rectangular brackets welded to underside of floor to accept lifting shoes.
- Small holes stamped in front and rear floorpans, and fitted with rubber grommets.
- One stamped hole for single handbrake cable, rear tunnel.
- Offside rear floorpan has ECU mounting platform welded to floor.

English cabriolet inner sill strengthener
- Can't actually see the steelwork, but can make out the profile. Pic 30

Bodyshell lifting shoes
- These slot into brackets fitted to separate outer sill bodyshells. Pics 31-34 (Courtesy of Gaydon Heritage Motor Museum)

Jacking brackets
- Jacking bracket for separate outer sill floor models. Pic 35
- English cabriolet. These brackets are bolted to the underside of the floor. Pics 36 & 37

East-west box section (steelwork to which front seats are attached)
- First type box section, seat brackets (four) spot-welded to box section. Box section extends beyond upper sill step towards outer sill. Fitted to first three types of floor. Pics 38-44
- Non-rod-change vehicles. Seats bolted to box section. Pic 45
- Rod-change vehicles. Mk3.5 onward. Pic 46
- 1996 onward. Two recesses to allow loom to fit (refer to pic 28)

Outer sills
- Non factory, specially made for 1959-1960 early cars. Pic 47 (pair)
- Four-flute. Pic 48 (lower: four-flute, nearside)

ANATOMY OF THE CLASSIC MINI

BODYWORK

- Six-flute. Pic 49 (pair).

Rear radius arm shroud
Pic 50
- There were a pair of these fitted to early cars.

Heel boards
Panel with four built-in captive nuts to which the rear subframe mounts. Cooper 'S' models were fitted with a fuel pump breather pipe. This required a hole in the heel board close to the fuel pump.
- 1959 to 1991 vehicles with dry suspension.
- 1964 onward hydrolastic for Mk1/2 Minis and Mk3 Cooper 'S.' 1969 onward 1275GT.
- 1990s onward vehicles with fuel return pipe. Pic 51

Toe boards
Panel to which steering rack is attached.
- 1959 only. Two captive nuts welded to toe board to accept fastening bolts for front subframe rear legs. Fitted only to floors with large front floorpans. Chassis numbers A-A2S7-101 to 17987 (Austin) and M-A2S4-101 to 22441 (Morris). See AOK front floorpans.
- 1959 to 1976. Mk1 to Mk3.5. No captive nuts, and uses nuts and bolts. Part number 14A6487 also includes Riley Elf and Wolseley Hornet. Pic 52
- 1976 onward. Mk4, 5, 6 and 7. Two reinforcing plates to take fasteners for modified front subframe. Pic 53 (This picture shows the cockpit side of the toeboard, which is correct, but the two reinforcing plates cannot be seen)
- 1990s fuel return pipe models. Pics 54-56

Separate inner sills 1959 to Oct 1961 (Saloon)
These panels were fitted to vehicles which had the floor and outer sills pressed as one panel.
These inner sills had carpet fasteners attached to them. They also had drain channels pressed into them. This would probably explain why these early vehicles used to fill up with water!
- 14A6519 Front nearside. This panel extends from the front inner wheelarch rearward to the east-west box seat mounting box section, with the top part of the panel carrying on above the box section to meet the rear inner sill panel. Refer to Pic 57
- 14A6518 Front offside. This panel extends from the front inner wheelarch rearward to the east-west box seat mounting box section, with the top part of the panel carrying on above the box section to meet the rear inner sill panel. Pic 57
- Rear nearside. This panel extends from the east-west seat mounting box section rearward to the companion bin. Refer to Pic 58
- Rear offside. This panel extends from the east-west seat mounting box section rearward to the companion bin. Pic 58

ANATOMY OF THE CLASSIC MINI

When the Mini was launched in 1959 there were no inner sills inside the rear companion bins. Pics 59 & 60
These two reinforced inner sills are images from Andy Messham's race car. These are injected with foam.
- Nearside inside companion bin (reinforced). Plus nearside horizontal closing panel. Pic 61
- Offside inside companion bin (reinforced). Plus offside horizontal closing panel. Pic 62

Boot floor and rear seat panel
Boot floors fitted with spare wheel retaining bracket, unless otherwise stated.
If rear seatbelts were fitted to a Mk1/2 bodyshell there will be a stiffener fitted between the boot floor and rear seat brace, which became standard on later models.
- AOK boot floor. Small rubber grommet instead of large alloy blanking plug, plus captive nuts to take subframe bolts. I have since worked out that this boot floor has been modified. It would originally have had a large alloy blanking plug. Pics 63 & 64
- 1959 to 1961 approx. Large hole stamped in spare wheel well, filled with alloy blanking plug plus captive nuts to take subframe bolts. Pics 65 & 66
- October 1961 onward (all models) two small holes stamped in spare wheel well, fitted with rubber grommets. Pic 67
- 1964 onward. Hydrolastic for Mk1 saloons, Mk2 saloons and Mk3 Cooper 'S.' Additional metal tags to support hydrolastic pipes. (The two rectangular reinforcing plates were not fitted straight away, they were introduced later because the rubber bump stops attached to the radius arms were punching through the floor. Source Scott Turner.) Pics 68-71
- Boot floor without spare wheel retaining bracket.
- English cars 1982 onward. Two additional stamped holes for foglight wiring loom, left- and right-hand drive, without spare wheel retaining bracket.
- 1991 onward. Modification to nearside rear seat pan and boot floor aperture to take fuel return line, without spare wheel retaining bracket. Pics 72-75

Rear companion bins
- Mk1/2. Pic 76
- Mk3. (Plain companion bin.)
- Mk3 Mini and Clubman Mk1 onward with inertia reel seat belts. Pics 77 & 78
- Mk4 onward with relocated inertia reel seat belts. Pic 79 (Courtesy Mini Spares, Potters Bar)
- Mk7 onward. (Nearside only.) Deep-well floor model. (Twin-point injection.) Pic 80 (Courtesy Mini Spares, Potters Bar)

Inner door hinge panels (with hinge stiffener brackets)
Early Mk1 bodyshells did not have an inner door hinge panel. (Single-skin outer apex panel only.) They did have inner hinge stiffener brackets. Pics 81-85
I was originally of the opinion that the second skin (inner) was added along with a scuttle closing panel. I have since discovered that the second skin (inner) was originally added on its own, and was later fitted with a scuttle closing panel attached to it.
- Austin Seven Van nearside inner wing, part number 14A6489 up to COM(B)5174. Single-skin outer apex panel.
- Austin Seven Van nearside inner wing, part number 14A8389 plus inner apex panel only part number 14A8347. Pics 86 & 87
- It is my personal opinion that this type of construction also applied to the early saloons.
Inner door hinge panel with scuttle closing panel.
- Mk1/2 Minis.
- Mk1/2 Austin Countryman and Morris Traveller.
- Mk1/2 Riley Elf and Wolseley Hornet. Pics 88 & 89

Early Mk1 weather shields
Pics 90 & 91 (Courtesy Scott Turner)
Attached to inner wheelarch by three screws and nuts. You can see the fixing holes in pics 83 & 84.
- These shields, should you come across them, were retro fitted by the Austin and Morris dealers to try to prevent water ingress.

Separate outer door hinge panel (Apex panel)
- Mk1/2 Riley Elf/Wolesley Hornet. Pics 92 & 93
- Mk3 Mini onward, Clubman and Mk3 Riley Elf/Wolesley Hornet. Pic 94
- The panels shown here are for Mk1/2 models, they were purchased from M Machine in Darlington and are a very good repair panel. Pics 95 & 96

External bodyshell side Mini
Mini Mk1/2 saloon bodyshell sides were constructed as one complete panel, including B-post and side inner horizontal cant rail. The metalwork consisted of the rear quarter panel, the door hinge panel (apex panel), the door and the rear quarter window surround and the gutter above the door/rear quarter window. Lower quarter window stiffener.
Quarter panel cards slot into steel horizontal guide on lower quarter window stiffener, unless otherwise stated.
There were three different Mk1 B-posts.
- The first type was plain (no captive nut for seatbelt). Pic 99
- Second type had a captive nut mounted high in the B-post. Pic 97
- The third type was changed in 1964. The captive nut was moved to a lower position. Pic 98
From September 1964 courtesy light switches were fitted. This required the drilling of two holes in the inside door shuts.
- Mk1 (quarter panel card attached to lower quarter window stiffener with screws). Pics 100 & 101
- Mk1/2 saloons with external door hinges, more metal above quarter light window and door than Mk3 onward. Pics 102 & 103
- Mk3 Mini saloons 1969 onward with internal door hinges. Pics 104-106
- Canadian saloons with wind-up

BODYWORK

ANATOMY OF THE CLASSIC MINI

BODYWORK

windows and anti-burst doors. (Upper sill step drilled and captive nut fitted to take ferrule for locking door rod.) Pics 107 & 108

• Mk6 onward saloons. (Two drain channels in upper sill step.) Pics 109 & 110

• English cabriolet B-post stiffener. Pic 111

External bodyshell side Riley Elf and Wolseley Hornet

Mk1/2/3 Riley Elf and Wolseley Hornet have a horizontal seam running below the rear quarter windows. These sides are, therefore, constructed of multiple panels.

• Mk1/2 saloons with external door hinges (constructed without full door hinge panel). Pic 112

• Mk3 saloons (Internal door hinge models).

ANATOMY OF THE CLASSIC MINI

BODYWORK

Pic 143

Pic 144

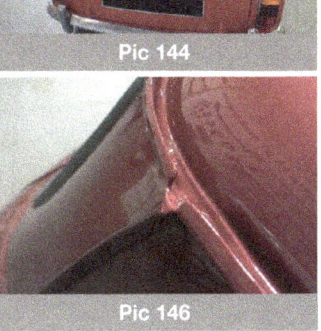
Pic 145 / Pic 146

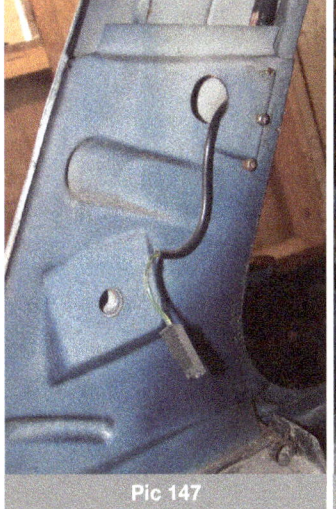
Pic 147

Pic 148

Doors
- 1959. Pic 113 (offside)
- 1959 without lock weather shields. 114 (offside), 115 (nearside), 116 (nearside)
- These two doors have riveted on lock weather shields. 117 (nearside), 118 (offside)
- Mk1/2 non-Cooper and Super. Pics 119-121 (120 & 121 Courtesy Mini Spares, Potters Bar)
- Cooper and Super Mk1/2. Pics 122 & 123
- Mk3 Riley Elf/Wolseley Hornet. Pics 124 & 125
- Mk3 Mini and Mini Clubman. Without captive nuts for door mirror. Pic 126
- Mk3 Mini and Clubman. With captive nuts for door mirror. Pics 127 & 128 (Courtesy Mini Spares, Potters Bar)
- Canadian Mini (door with anti-burst mechanism). Pic 129
- Mk3-shaped door without pressing for anti-burst mechanism. Pic 130
- Late windup window with angled internal door grab handle. Pic 131
- Late Mini door with built-in door bar. Pic 132
- English cabriolet door. Pic 133

Door hinges
- Brass fitted from 1959. (My October 1960 Austin Seven also has these.) Pic 134
- Cast iron replaces brass. Pic 135

- Aluminium, early Mk3 Riley Elf/Wolseley Hornet. Pic 136
- Cast iron, later Mk3 Riley Elf/Wolseley Hornet and all Minis from 1969 onward. Pics 137 & 138 (Courtesy Mini Spares, Potters Bar)

SALOON AND CABRIOLET REAR PANELS
Mainly for information. The saloon rear panel is manufactured complete with the upper inner horizontal cant rail, both boot lid stay brackets and rear gutter.

First type
Pics 139-142
- 1959 to approximately October 1960.
- No recess for rear windscreen rubber. (Small rear screen.)
- Small rear lamps.

Second type
- Recess for rear windscreen rubber. (Small rear screen.)
- Single fuel tank.
- Small rear lamps.

Third type
Pic 143
- Riley Elf and Wolesley Hornet. Mk1/2/3.
- Recess for rear windscreen rubber. (Small rear screen.)
- Single fuel tank.

Fourth type
- Cooper 'S' (Mk1).
- January 1960 onward.
- Recess for rear windscreen rubber. (Small rear screen.)
- Twin fuel tanks.
- Small rear lamps.

Fifth type
- Mk2 onward.
- Recess for rear windscreen rubber. (Larger rear screen.)
- Single fuel tank.
- Larger rear lamps.

Sixth type
Pic 144
- Cooper 'S' (Mk2/3).
- Recess for rear windscreen rubber. (Larger rear screen.)
- Twin fuel tanks.
- Larger rear lamps.

Seventh type
Pics 145 & 146
First saloon bodyshell to have plastic trim fitted all around roof gutter.
- 1980 onward.
- Metal removed from either end of gutter to create drainage holes.
- Recess for rear windscreen rubber. (Larger rear screen.)

ANATOMY OF THE CLASSIC MINI

- Single fuel tank.
- Larger rear lamps.

Eighth type
Cabriolet models.

C-post reinforcers
- Nearside (Mini 30 onward). Pic 147
- Offside (Mini 30 onward). Pic 148
- Nearside (twin-point bodyshells). Pic 149
- Offside (twin-point bodyshells).

Riley Elf and Wolesley Hornet rear windscreen panel
The Elf and Hornet does not really have a back panel as such. It is more like the upper half of a Mini saloon rear panel with modifications to the lower underside to attach to rear scuttle panel. Pic 150
- Small back window.

Front bulkheads
Unless otherwise stated, all front subframes were mounted with ten fixings.
    Early Mk1 vehicles were not fitted with a heater from the factory. The bulkhead had the facility to take the large air pipe from under the bonnet. Vehicles without heater were fitted with a blanking plate (part number 14A9992).
    The Elf and Hornet had a totally different bonnet hinge, the bulkhead brackets were spaced accordingly. Unless otherwise stated, all front bulkheads have heater brackets.
- Mk1 Mini with dry suspension and square-bodied wiper motor, with no heater brackets. (Note the four rivets – these are holding the heater brackets to the bulkhead. This car left the factory without a heater.) Pics 151 & 152
- Mk1 Mini with dry suspension and square-bodied wiper motor.
- Mk1 Riley Elf, Wolseley Hornet with dry suspension. With square-bodied wiper motor.
- September 1964 onward. Mk1/2 Mini with hydrolastic suspension and square-bodied wiper motor.
- September 1964 onward. Elf/Hornet with hydrolastic suspension. With square-bodied wiper motor.
- Late Mk2 Mini Cooper 'S' with hydrolastic suspension and round-bodied wiper motor up to March 1970.
- Mk3 Mini and Clubman with dry suspension, round-bodied wiper motor and relocated bonnet hinges. Pics 153-155
- Mk3 Mini Cooper 'S' with hydrolastic suspension, round-bodied wiper motor and relocated bonnet hinges.
- Mk3 Riley Elf, Wolseley Hornet with hydrolastic suspension. With round-bodied wiper motor. The pressing in the bulkhead for mounting the wiper motor is the same shape as previous bulkheads that take the square wiper motor. The only difference being the three holes are not punched out to fix the wiper motor in place. Instead a horseshoe clamp is used, fixed to the bulkhead with a pair of rivnuts and screws.
- Mk4 and Clubman with eight-fixing-point front subframe.
- 1988 onward vehicles fitted with horizontally mounted brake master cylinder and servo (brake compensating valve location moved) with eight-fixing-point front subframe.
- ERA turbo. East-west box section centre section removed and bulkhead box put in place to clear turbo. Pic 156 (Courtesy Mini Spares, Potters Bar)
- Single-point injected models with eight-fixing-point front subframe. Additional brackets affixed for relay assembles. Pics 157 & 158
- Multipoint injected models (twin-point) with eight-fixing-point front subframe. Identical to single-point models with the exception of no centrally-mounted speedometer hole. Pic 159 (Courtesy Mini Spares, Potters Bar)

Nearside front inner wings
This is for right-hand drive models only.

Bodyshells without separate outer sills
- Mk1 Mini with single-skin apex panel, square-bodied wiper motor for bodyshells without separate outer sills. Part number 14A6489. (Metal radiator cowling welded to inner wing.) No scuttle closing panel fitted.
- Mk1 Mini with double-skin apex panel, square-bodied wiper motor for bodyshells without separate outer sills. Part number 14A8389. (Metal radiator cowling welded to inner wing.) Pic 160 Also refer pic 173

Bodyshells with separate outer sills.
- Mk1/2 and Elf/Hornet with double-skin apex panel and square-bodied wiper motor. (Metal radiator cowling welded to inner wing.) Pic 161
- 1966 onward Mk3 Elf/Hornet. (Pressings for eyeball vents. Metal radiator cowling welded to inner wing.)
- Late Mk2 Mini Cooper 'S' with double-skin apex panel and round-bodied wiper motor. (Metal radiator cowling welded to inner wing.) Pic 162
- 1969 onward Mk3. (Metal radiator cowling welded to inner wing.) Refer to text for offside inner wings.
- 1969 onward Clubman, note rubber grommet hole. (Metal radiator cowling welded to inner wing.) Pic 163 (Courtesy Mini Spares, Potters Bar)
- Circa 1974 Mini (not Clubman). (No metal radiator cowling welded to inner wing.) This was changed about the same time as the cowling bolted to the radiator. Pic 164 (Courtesy Mini Spares, Potters Bar)
- Vertical stiffener. (12in wheel models.) Circa 1984 onward. Pic 165
- Vertical stiffener with trafficator (hole for loom). Please see offside front inner wings.
- Vertical stiffener 1991 onward with trafficator (hole for loom) and large circular hole for fan. Pics 166 & 167
- Vertical stiffener with trafficator (hole for loom) and holes for carbon canister pipes, injection models. Pic 168 (Courtesy Mini Spares, Potters Bar)
- 1996 onward. Solid inner wing. Pic 169 (Courtesy Mini Spares, Potters Bar)
- English cabriolet. Pic 170

BODYWORK

ANATOMY OF THE CLASSIC MINI

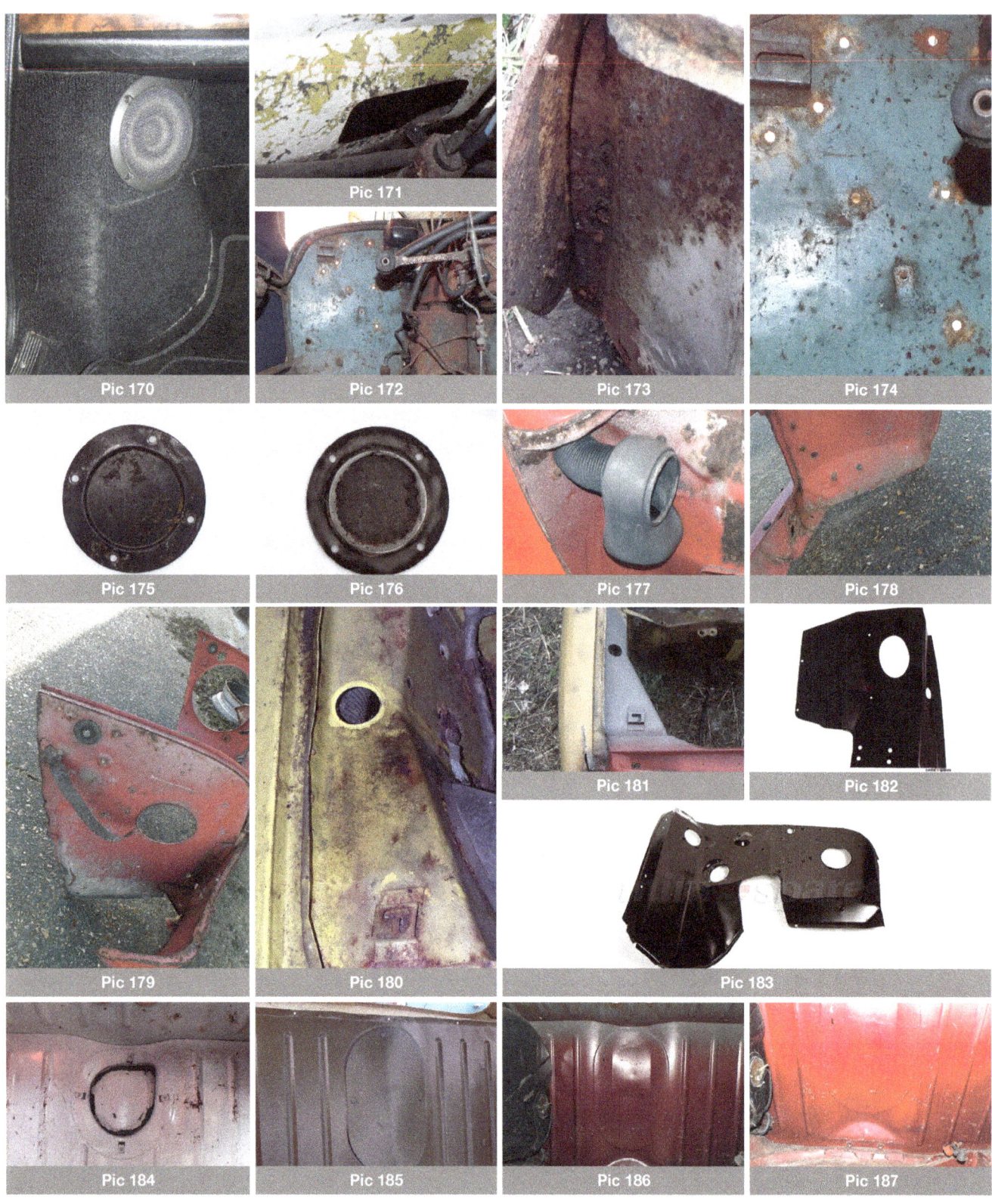

BODYWORK

Offside front inner wings
This is for right-hand drive models only. The left-hand drive models would have an additional pressing to take the round-bodied wiper motor.

Bodyshells without separate outer sills
• Early Mk1 Mini with single-skin apex panel. Rectangular access hole for offside metal brake pipe to flexible pipe, and square-bodied wiper motor for bodyshells without separate outer sills. No scuttle closing panel fitted. Pic 171 (Courtesy Scott Turner)
• Mk1 Mini with single-skin apex panel but without rectangular access hole. Pic 172
• Mk1 Mini with double-skin apex panel, square-bodied wiper motor for bodyshells without separate outer sills. Without rectangular access hole. Pic 173

Bodyshells with separate outer sills
• Mk1/2 and Elf/Hornet with double-skin apex panel, square-bodied wiper motor.
• Early 997 Cooper to take brake booster valve.
• Mk1/2 Cooper 'S.' (Drillings for servo mounting brackets.) Pic 174
• 1966 onward Mk3 Elf/Hornet. (Pressings for eyeball vents.)
• 1969 onward Mk3. (Redesigned bodyshell without exterior door hinges. No eyeball vents. Blanking plates fitted.) If eye ball vents are fitted the blanking plates are not required. Pics 175-179
• 1969 onward Mk3 Cooper 'S.' (Drillings for servo mounting brackets.)
• 1969 onward Clubman. Pics 180-182 (Courtesy Mini Spares, Potters Bar)
• Clubman 1275GT. (Drillings for servo mounting brackets.)
• Vertical stiffener. (12in wheel models.) Circa 1984 onward. Please see nearside front inner wings.
• Vertical stiffener with trafficator (hole for loom). Pic 183 (Courtesy Mini Spares, Potters Bar)
• English cabriolet. Please see nearside front inner wings.

Rear seat brace
• 1959 onward Mk1/2 (off-round aperture in centre). Pic 184
• January 1966 onward Cooper 'S' (off-round aperture in centre). Two brackets with four studs mounted on offside of panel to mount right-hand petrol tank. For image please refer to *Original Mini Cooper* by John Parnell. ISBN 187097932X Page 113.
• 1969 onward Mk3 and Mk1 Clubman (large vertical oval aperture in centre). Pic 185
• 1969 onward Mk3 Cooper 'S' (large vertical oval aperture in centre). Two brackets with four studs mounted on offside of panel to mount right-hand petrol tank.
• 1976 onward Mk4 and Mk2 Clubman (non-aperture type). Four holes stamped in lower panel for seatbelt-sized bolts. Two captive nuts can be seen attached to reinforcing bracket at bottom in middle. Pics 186 & 187
• English (non-Lamm) Cabriolet. Pics 188 & 189

FRONT WINDSCREEN PANELS
The gutter attached to the front windscreen panel did not have any form of water drainage when the cars left the factory in 1959.

Any form of water drainage other than the factory stamped eyelets will have been done manually. (Probably by the supplying dealer.)

If you purchased a base model car you would only get a driver-side sunvisor. The passenger side was fitted with a blanking plate. Pic 190

First type
Pics 191-194
• No recess for front windscreen rubber.
• Two windscreen wiper wheel box holes.
• Two washer jet holes.

Second type
• Recess for front windscreen rubber.

Pic 188

Pic 189

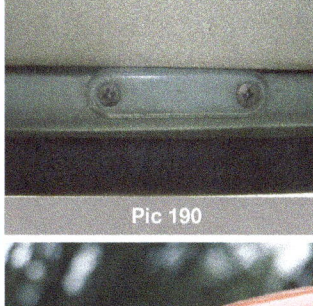
Pic 190

Pic 192

Pic 191

Pic 193

ANATOMY OF THE CLASSIC MINI

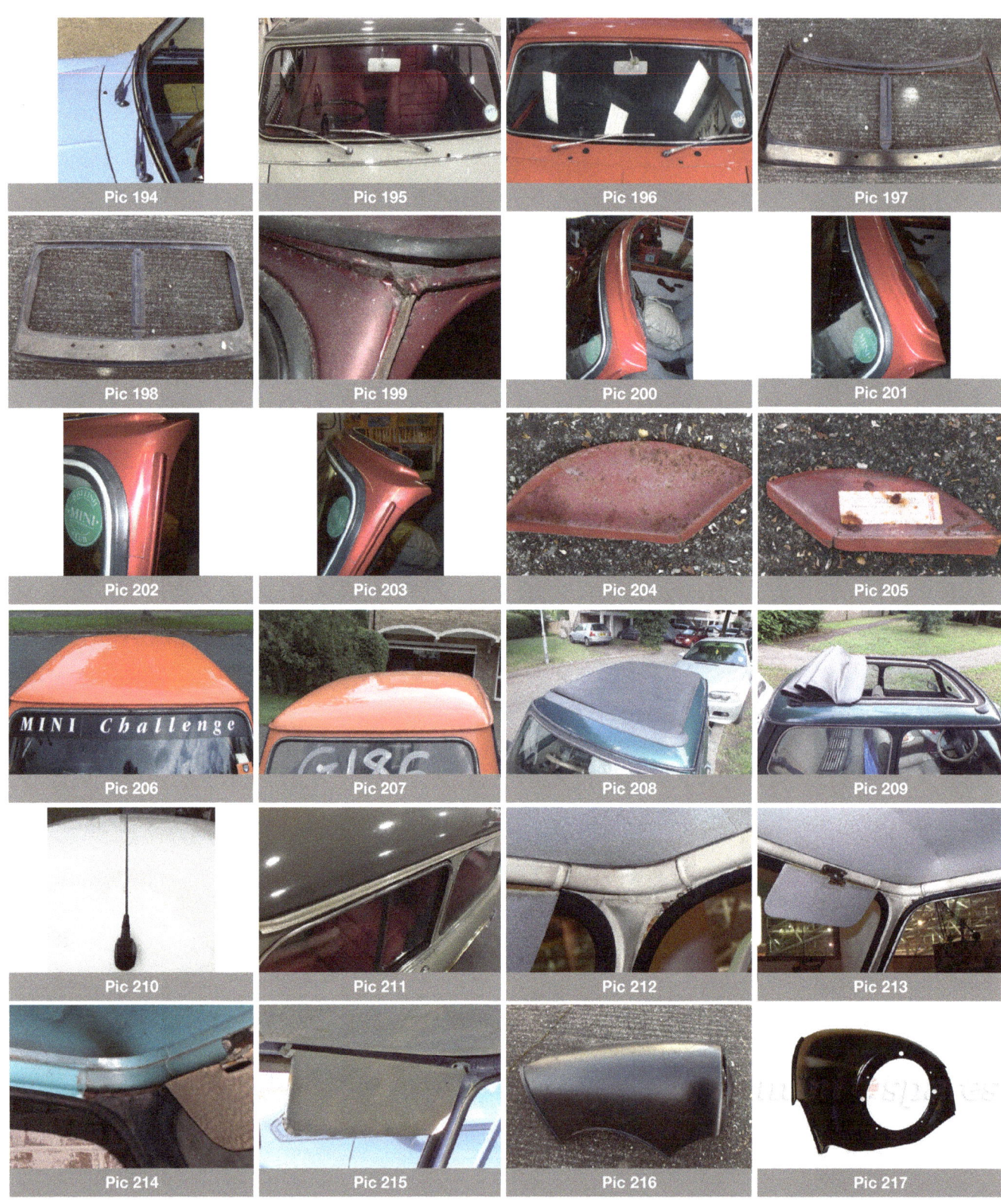

BODYWORK

- Two eyelets in gutter for drainage.
- Two windscreen wiper wheel box holes.
- Two washer jet holes.

Third type
Pic 195
- Riley Elf/Wolseley Hornet Mk1, 2 and 3.
- Recess for front windscreen rubber.
- Two eyelets in gutter for drainage.
- Two windscreen wiper wheel box holes.
- Repositioned washer jet holes to clear chrome scuttle panel trim.

Fourth type
Pics 196-198
- Recess for front windscreen rubber.
- Two eyelets in gutter for drainage.
- Four windscreen wiper wheel box holes.
- Two washer jet holes.

Fifth type
Pic 199
- Recess for front windscreen rubber.
- Metal removed from both ends of gutter to create drainage holes.
- Four windscreen wiper wheel box holes.
- Two washer jet holes.

English cabriolet
Pics 200-203
- Note split in A pillar.

FRONT SCUTTLE PANEL, CLOSING PANELS

Early Mk1 bodyshells with single-skin apex panel did not have front scuttle closing panels.

The panels were fitted to try to prevent water ingress.
- Nearside.
- Offside. Pics 204 & 205

Roof (Saloon)
- Plain. Part number 14A5503. Pics 206 & 207
- Cooper RSP with removable glass sunroof.
- Electric sunroof. Pics 208 (front) & 209 (offside)
- Aerial. Pic 210

Drip rails (shedders)
When the car was launched in 1959 it was not fitted with drip rails.

The part numbers that appear here have been taken from a 997 Cooper parts catalogue.

The drip rails were originally supplied, along with a packet of rivets, to the Austin and Morris main dealers.

- Right-hand drip rail part number 14A8462.
- Left-hand drip rail part number 14A8463. Pic 211
- Rivet part number 2K2610 (quantity 20).

Front upper inner cant rails and corner pieces
- 621A0K. Pics 212 & 213
- Mini and Riley Elf/Wolseley Hornet. Pic 214
- Circa 1965. Pic 215
- Mk2 onward

Front wings (offside) non-Clubman
All wings have holes for wing trafficators, unless otherwise stated.
- Standard round fronted wing also fits Elf and Hornet with round headlamp aperture (no hole for trafficator). Pic 216
- Mini 1100 Special fitted with 1100/1300 (AD016) front indicator.
- Round-fronted wing with round headlamp aperture. Pic 217 (Courtesy Mini Spares, Potters Bar)
- Late model round-fronted wing with off-round headlamp aperture. Pic 218 (Courtesy Mini Spares, Potters Bar)
- Sports pack model round-fronted wing with off-round headlamp aperture (cut to clear 13in wheel).
- Reinforcer fits behind apex panel, front wing and front panel. 1996 onward. Pic 219

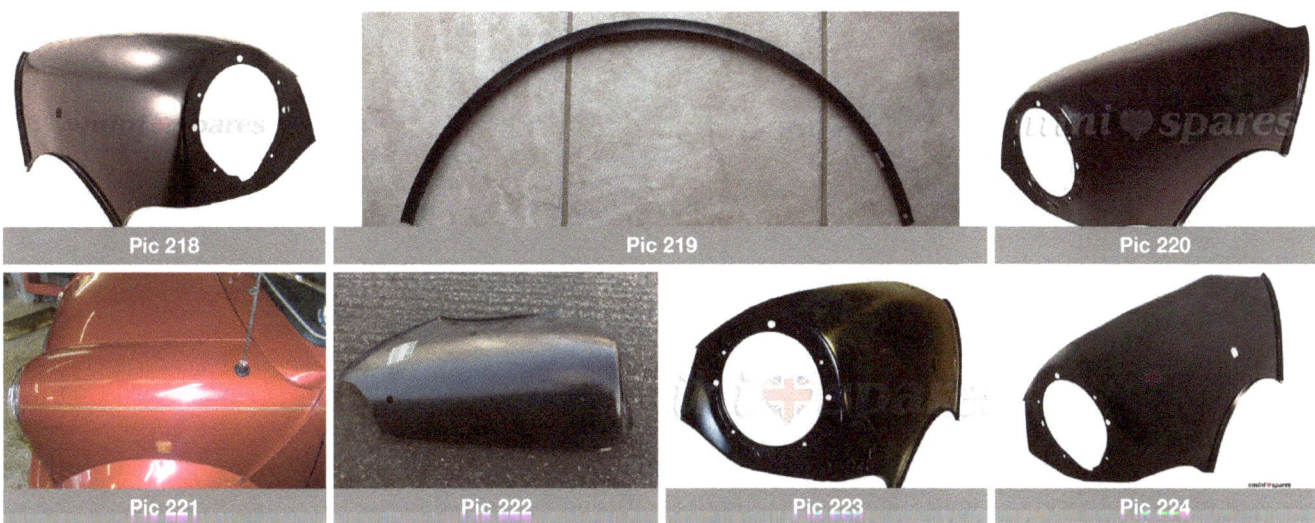

Pic 218　　Pic 219　　Pic 220
Pic 221　　Pic 222　　Pic 223　　Pic 224

ANATOMY OF THE CLASSIC MINI

Pic 225
Pic 226
Pic 227
Pic 228
Pic 229
Pic 230
Pic 231
Pic 232
Pic 233
Pic 234
Pic 235
Pic 236
Pic 237
Pic 238
Pic 239
Pic 240
Pic 241
Pic 242
Pic 243
Pic 244
Pic 245

BODYWORK

Front wings (nearside) non-Clubman
All wings have holes for wing trafficators, unless otherwise stated.
- Standard round-fronted wing also fits Elf and Hornet with round headlamp aperture (no hole for trafficator). Pic 220 (Courtesy Mini Spares, Potters Bar)
- Mini 1100 special fitted with Morris 1100/1300 (ADO16) front indicator.
- Round-fronted wing with round headlamp aperture and hole for aerial. Pics 221 & 222
- Round-fronted wing and round headlamp aperture. Pic 223 (Courtesy Mini Spares, Potters Bar)
- Late model round-fronted wing with off-round headlamp aperture. Pic 224 (Courtesy Mini Spares, Potters Bar)
- Sports pack model round-fronted wing with off-round headlamp aperture (cut to clear 13in wheel).
- Reinforcer that fits behind apex panel, front wing and front panel. 1996 onward models. Pic 225

Front wings (offside) Clubman
- Standard Clubman front wing. Pic 226
- Mk1 Clubman estate with drillings for stainless steel trim.
- Wing trafficators fitted to continental models.

Front wings (nearside) Clubman
- Standard Clubman front wing. Refer to pic 226
- Mk1 Clubman estate with drillings for stainless steel trim.
- Wing trafficators fitted to continental models.

FRONT PANELS
- All the front panels listed here are mainly for information.
- All front panels have two bolt holes in front panel mounting brackets to locate to front subframe, unless otherwise stated.
- 1964 onward, all front panels had two cut-outs in front valance to aid front brake cooling.
- From 1976 onward all models were fitted with a rubber-mounted front subframe to cut down on cockpit noise.

First type
- Saloon 1958 only.
- Grille part of front panel.
- Four holes in front panel mounting brackets, two for bolts and two for subframe locating dowels.
- Full front valance.
- Test cars at Chalgrove had these fitted.
- Photo can be found on page 249 of *Mighty Minis* by Chris Harvey, ISBN 094660911X

Second type
Note. Two square pressings to take metal tags, to hold wiring loom. Pics 227 & 228
- 1959 only.
- Saloon Austin or Morris.
- Two holes in front panel mounting brackets.
- Mk1.
- Separate front grille, full front valance.

Third type
- Pics 229-231
- Saloon Austin or Morris.
- Two holes in front panel mounting.
- Circa 1960 to 1964.
- Mk1
- Separate front grille, full front valance.

Fourth type
- Part number ALA 5201
- October 1961 onward.
- Mk1/2 Riley Elf and Mk1/2 Wolseley Hornet.
- Full front valance.

Fifth type
Pics 232 & 233
- This is a pattern Mk1 front panel. It should not have the vent hole cut in it on the nearside behind the front grille.
- 1964 to 1967.
- Mk1.
- Separate front grille.
- First of the two cut-out front panels (as heading at beginning of front panel section).

Sixth type
Pic 234
- Part number ALA 5482
- 1964 onward.
- Mk2 Riley Elf and Mk2 Wolseley Hornet.
- First of the Elf/Hornet front panels with two cut-outs in front valance.

Seventh type
Pic 235
- January 1966 onward.
- Mk1 Cooper 'S' with oil cooler.
- Separate front grille.
- Upper front valance flattened out in the middle to mount cooler.
- Vertical stiffener moved and angled to avoid cooler.

Eighth type
- Part number ALA 6298
- October 1966 onward.
- Mk3 Riley Elf and Mk3 Wolseley Hornet with air intake vents.

Ninth type
- 1967 onward.
- Mk2 non-Cooper 'S.'
- Separate front grille.
- Front panel drilled to take Mk2 grille mounting screws.

Tenth type
- 1967 to 1970.
- Cooper 'S' Mk2.
- Modifications as Mk1 Cooper 'S' (as above).

Eleventh type
- 1969 to 1976.
- Mk3 non-Cooper 'S.'
- As Mk2 (as above) but with additional triangular hole stamped in nearside, below grille for eyeball vent air feed.

Twelfth type
Pic 236
- 1969 onward.
- Mini Clubman Mk1.

Thirteenth type
- 1970 to 1971.
- Mk3 Cooper 'S.'

ANATOMY OF THE CLASSIC MINI

Pic 246 Pic 247 Pic 248 Pic 249
Pic 250 Pic 251
Pic 252 Pic 253
Pic 254 Pic 255 Pic 256
Pic 257 Pic 258 Pic 259 Pic 260
Pic 261

BODYWORK

- Modifications as Mk1 Cooper 'S' (as above) but with additional triangular hole stamped in nearside, below grille for eyeball vent.

Fourteenth type
Pics 237 & 238
- This is a pattern front panel, it does not have the holes drilled in it to take the front grille screws.
- 1976 onward.
- Mk4 and Mk5.
- Same as Mk3 non-Cooper 'S' front panel, but with modified mountings between front subframe and front panel.

Fifteenth type
Pics 239-240 (refer also to pic 236)
- Part front panel shown.
- 1976 onward.
- Mini Clubman Mk2.
- Modified mountings between front subframe and front panel.

Sixteenth type
Pics 241 & 242

- 1986 to 1996.
- Front panel pressing modified to accept larger front indicators.

Seventeenth type
- Cooper RSP with oil cooler. Pics 243 & 244 (Courtesy of Lawton Tang, Mini Spares, Potters Bar)

Eighteenth type
- Part number ASJ 36002.
- Single-point injection.
- Front panel with two spot lamp mounting holes.

Nineteenth type
- Mini Cabriolet front panel. Pics 245-248

Twentieth type
Pics 249-256 (These four photos were taken from behind the lower front valance.
- Part number ASJ 360070.
- 1996 onward.
- Twin-point injection cars with 12in wheels.

Twenty-first type
- Twin-point injection cars with 13in wheels.
- Same front panel as 1996 onward, but with metal removed to clear 13in wheels.

BONNETS
- Early Mk1 (bonnet prop bracket attached to offside front underside crossbrace above bonnet lip). For photograph please refer to *The Mini Story* by Laurence Pomeroy (1964). Published by Temple Press Books Limited. First photo featured in the book.
- 14A6482 (non-drilled) 1959 to 1967 all Mk1 models. (Different drillings needed for 'Austin' and 'Morris' badges.) Pics 257 & 258
- 1961 onward Riley Elf and Wolseley Hornet. Pics 259 & 260
- 1967 to 1970 all Mk2 models. (Extended front lip to take front grille top trim. Different drillings for 'Austin' and 'Morris' badges.) Pic 261

ANATOMY OF THE CLASSIC MINI

BODYWORK

- 1969 onward. Oddball bonnet (non-Clubman) to take modified bonnet hinges. The underside crossbraces are Riley Elf and Wolseley Hornet. Pic 262
- 1969 onward. (Bonnet hinges moved to same configuration as Mini Clubman. Extended front lip to take front grille top trim.) Pics 263-266
- 1969 onward. Mini Clubman. Pic 267
- 'F' registration onward. Mini 1000. (Recess in bonnet bracing on right-hand side to clear horizontal brake master cylinder.) Pic 268
- 1989 onward. ERA Turbo Mini. (Circular holes cut into bonnet and fitted with fibreglass reverse scoop to aid with cooling.) Pics 269-271
- 1996 onward. Twin-point injection.

Bonnet hinges
- Mk1 onward. Pics 272 & 273
- Mk1/2/3 Riley Elf and Wolseley Hornet. Pic 274
- Mk3 (Odd ball). See pic 262

Boot hinges
- 1959 to 2000 Mini saloon. Pic 275
- Mk1 Riley Elf and Wolseley Hornet.
- Mk2/3 Riley Elf and Wolseley Hornet. With helper spring. Pic 276

Boot lids
Pics 277-279
- The green bootlid has holes for clips to hold aperture seal. The red bootlid has none.
- Mk1 to December 1966. Pics 280 & 281
- Riley Elf and Wolseley Hornet. Pics 282 & 283
- Mk1/2. December 1966 onward. (Solid inner skin.) Pics 284 & 285
- Mk2. (Looks like a Mk3, but is actually a late Mk2.) Pics 286-289
- Early Mk3. (Solid inner skin.) Pics 290 & 291
- 1969 to 1988. Mk3 onward. Pic 292
- 1988 onward. Rubber seal fitted to bodyshell as opposed to boot lid. (No holes in boot lid for seal clips.) Pics 293-296

Rear valance
The first and second types of rear valance are externally identical. The first type of rear valance came with additional pieces of metal attached to the inside.
- 1959 onward. Rear valance (large closing panel type).
- Riley Elf Wolsey Hornet rear valance Mk1/2/3.
- Non-captive nut type rear valance (non foglamp). I believe this valance was first used when the Mini went over to hydrolastic suspension. Pic 297
- Rear valance with captive nuts for left and right-hand drive foglamp. Pic 298

Rear valance closing panels
- Nearside dry suspension, large. Refer to pic 299
- Offside dry suspension, large. Pic 299
- September 1964 onward. Nearside hydrolastic suspension, small. Pic 300
- September 1964 onward. Offside side hydrolastic suspension, small. Refer to pic 300

ANATOMY OF THE CLASSIC MINI

Pic 310 Pic 311 Pic 312 Pic 313
Pic 314 Pic 315 Pic 316 Pic 317
Pic 318 Pic 319

Closing panels in front of rear wheelarches
- Nearside.
- Offside.
- These panels never changed, they attach to the top of the heel board. Pic 301

Rear wheelarches (offside)
- Cooper and Cooper 'S.' Part number 14A6496.
- Standard rear wheelarch. Part number 14A7234. Pics 302 & 303
- Cooper and Cooper 'S.' Part number 14A9558.
- USA Cooper and Cooper 'S' Mk1. Part number 24A2226.
- Rear wheelarch with rear seatbelt anchoring bracket. Please see rear wheelarches (Nearside).
- Rear wheelarch with rear seatbelt anchoring bracket and washer bottle mounting bracket. Pic 304

Rear wheelarches (nearside)
- Cooper and Cooper 'S.' Part number 14A6497.
- Standard rear wheelarch. Part number 14A7235.
- Cooper and Cooper 'S.' Part number 14A9559.
- USA Cooper and Cooper 'S' Mk1. Part number 24A2227.
- Rear wheelarch with rear seatbelt anchoring bracket. Pic 305

Rear parcel shelf
- First type. Pic 306
- Elf/Hornet Mk2 and 3 type.
- English (non Lamm) Cabriolet type. Pics 307-309
- Late model type with cut-outs for two speakers. Pic 310 (Courtesy Mini Spares, Potters Bar)

Top dash rail
- 1959 type. (More than one version of this, hot air flutes angled.) Pics 311 & 312
- Post 1959 type with standardised hot air flutes. 14A6675. Pic 313 (Courtesy Mini Spares, Potters Bar)
- 1969 onward, Clubman type. (Four holes to take top dash fixings.) Pic 314
- Mk3 and later Clubman type. (Two holes to take top dash fixings.) Pic 315

Lower dash rail & front parcel shelf
- Mk2 lower rail switch panel aperture larger than Mk1. Fitted from 1967-2000.
- Mk1/2. Pic 316
- Mk3 and Clubman to 1999. Pic 317
- Same as above but additional holes added to affix radio bracket (hangs below dash on nearside. For example, the Mini 30). Pics 318 & 319

Chapter 2
Braking

The parts listed in this chapter are the mechanical components. The hydraulic components are listed in a later chapter.

BACKPLATES

All backplates are handed (ie left- or right-hand).

Single leading-shoe front drum brake backplate (1)

Pic 1
- 1959 onward.
- Single wheel cylinder fitted to backplate.
- Two mechanical brake shoe adjusters.

Single leading-shoe front drum brake backplate (2)

Similar to the first type, but without two pressings to locate wheel cylinder.
- I believe this backplate does not have the two pressings to align the wheel cylinder.
- Single wheel cylinder fitted to backplate.
- Two mechanical brake shoe adjusters.

Twin leading-shoe front drum brake backplate (Mk1 only)

- September 1964 onward.
- 112906RH (17H8145).
- 112907LH (17H8159).
- Two wheel cylinders fitted to backplate.
- Two mechanical brake shoe adjusters.

Twin leading-shoe front drum brake backplate (Mk2 to 1984)

Pics 2 & 3
- Circa 1967 onward.
- 4561-732RH (37H2013).
- 4561-733LH (37H2014).
- Two wheel cylinders fitted to backplate.
- Two mechanical brake shoe adjusters.

Rear drum brake backplates

Whilst I have found *three* pairs of part numbers, I have photos of *four* different backplates.

Pics 4-7 (all rear backplates)
- 17H8075 (right-hand) 17H8076 (left-hand) to fit wheel cylinders GWC1101 and GWC1129.
- 21A209 (right-hand) 21A210 (left-hand).
- 21A1058 (right-hand) 21A1060 (left-hand).
- Backplates 21A209 and 21A210 take rear wheel cylinder 17H7614, 17H7767 and 17H781 (refer to the chapter on hydraulics for these cylinder numbers)

FRONT BRAKE DRUMS
Front brake drum (1)

Pics 8 & 9
- 1959 onward (originated from the 1956 Austin A35 and 1958 Austin A40 Mk1).
- Nine-hole brake drum.
- Two holes were for fastening screws.

Front brake drum (2)

Pic 10
- Seven-hole brake drum.
- Two holes were for fastening screws.

REAR BRAKE DRUMS
Rear brake drum (1)

See pics 8 & 9

ANATOMY OF THE CLASSIC MINI

BRAKING

- 1959 onward (originated from the 1956 Austin A35 and 1958 Austin A40 Mk1).
- Nine-hole brake drum.
- Two holes were for fastening screws.

Rear brake drum (2)
Pic 11 (right).
- Seven-hole brake drum.
- Two holes were for fastening screws.

Rear brake drum (3)
See pic 11 (middle)
- Seven-hole brake drum.
- Small built-in spacer.
- Fitted to Mini Cooper with wider tyres.

Rear brake drum (4)
See pic 11 (left)
- Seven-hole brake drum.
- 1in built-in spacer.
- Fitted to Mini Cooper 'S.'
- Fitted to 10in wheeled 1275GT Mini Clubman.
- Fitted to all 12in wheeled Minis from 1984 onward.

BRAKE SHOES
Shoe material was originally riveted to steelwork. Over time this method was dropped, and the shoe material was bonded to the steelwork.

Front brake shoe (1)
Pic 12
- 1959 onward.
- All shoes were originally 1.25in width.

Front brake shoe (2)
Pic 13
- 1.5in width.
- These were first fitted to the Riley Elf Mk1 and Wolseley Hornet Mk1.

Rear brake shoe
See pic 12
- 1959 onward.
- 1.25in width.

BRAKE DISCS
All brake discs are solid, unless otherwise stated.

The 1275cc GT Mini Clubman had the Denovo safety tyre available from August 1974. This wheel and tyre combination became standard fit from August 1977 onward. The 1275cc GT was fitted with the 8.4in front disc brakes in 1974. If the Denovo safety tyre and wheel combination were not fitted, a 12in wheel and tyre were in its place.

Front brake disc (1)
Pic 14
- 1961 onward.
- Fitted to the 997cc and 998cc Mini Cooper (0.250in thick).
- 7in diameter.

Front brake disc (2)
Pic 15
- 1963 onward.
- Fitted to the 1071cc, 1275cc, 970cc Mini Cooper 'S' (0.375in thick).
- Fitted to the 10in wheeled 1275GT Mini Clubman up to 1974.
- 7.5in diameter.
- Different design to 7in Mini Cooper disc.

Front brake disc (3)
Pics 16 & 17
- Fitted to the 310mm Denovo-shod 1275GT Mini Clubman.
- Fitted to all 12in wheeled Minis from 1984 onward.
- 8.4in diameter.

Front brake disc (4)
Pics 18 & 19
- 1989 onward.
- Fitted to the 1275cc ERA turbo Mini.
- 8.4in diameter.
- Ventilated discs.

FRONT BRAKE PADS
Front brake pad (1)
Pic 20
- 1961 onward.
- Fitted to 997cc Mini Cooper.
- 7in disc.

Front brake pad (2)
Pic 21
- 1963 onward 997cc Mini Cooper.
- 1964 onward 998cc Mini Cooper.
- 7in disc.

Front brake pad (3)
Pics 22 & 23
- March 1963 onward.
- Fitted to 1071cc, 1275cc, 970cc Mini Cooper 'S.'
- Fitted to 1275cc GT Mini Clubman with 10in wheels.
- 7.5in disc.

Front brake pad (4)
Pic 24
- Fitted to the 310mm Denovo-shod 1275GT Mini Clubman.
- Fitted to all 12in wheeled Minis from 1984 onward, plus 13in-wheeled vehicles.
- 8.4in disc.

Front brake pad (5)
Pic 25
- 1989 onward.
- Fitted to the 1275cc ERA turbo Mini.
- Vented disc.

FRONT DISC BACKPLATES
Each backplate is made up of two halves, those being top and bottom. All backplates are handed (ie left- or right-hand).

Front disc backplate (1)
- 1961 onward.
- Fitted to 997cc, 998cc Mini Cooper.
- 7in disc.

Front disc backplate (2)
Pics 26 & 27
- March 1963 onward.
- Fitted to 1071cc, 1275cc, 970cc Mini Cooper 'S.'
- Fitted to 1275cc GT Mini Clubman with 10in wheels.
- 7.5in disc.

Front disc backplate (3)
Pics 28 & 29

ANATOMY OF THE CLASSIC MINI

Pic 25 | Pic 26 | Pic 27 | Pic 28 | Pic 29 | Pic 30 | Pic 31 | Pic 32 | Pic 33 | Pic 34 | Pic 35 | Pic 36

- Fitted to the 310mm Denovo-shod 1275GT Mini Clubman.
- Fitted to all 12in-wheeled Minis from 1984 onward, plus 13in-wheeled vehicles.
- 8.4in disc.

HAND BRAKE CABLES
- 1959 cables for non-quadrant type radius arms (2A5853 x2).
- Cables for quadrant type radius arms (21A186 x2).
- Cables for hydrolastic type (GVC1021 x2).

HANDBRAKE LEVERS
- Twin-cable, chrome button. Pic 30
- Twin-cable, non-chrome button. Pic 31
- 1976 onward, single-cable. Pic 32 (Courtesy Mini Spares, Potters Bar)
- Single-cable late. Pic 33

HANDBRAKE QUADRANTS
- Second type of fabricated rear radius arm (three versions), fitted with phosphor bronze bush. Part numbers 21A182 and 2A388 fitted with phosphor-bronze bush. 21A797 was fitted with an oilite bush. Pic 34
- Cast iron rear radius arm (dry suspension). Pic 35
- Cast iron rear radius arm (hydrolastic). Pic 36 (Courtesy Mini Spares, Potters Bar)

Chapter 3
Breathing

For timing chain covers with breathers see Camshafts, cam followers, etc.

Tappet chest covers and rocker covers were painted green between 1959 and 1969.

1969 onward everything was painted black.

FRONT TAPPET CHEST COVERS (848CC, 997CC, 1098CC, 998CC, 1071CC, 1275CC 'S' AND 970CC)

- 1A2199 (848cc) first type.
- 12H155.
- 12H948 Pics 1 & 2
- 12H156 (997cc).
- 12G152, 12G280, 12A1171, 12A1382 (1098cc) Pic 3
- 997cc second type.
- 12A1382 (998cc).
- 12A1212 (Rubber gasket type) (1098cc and 998cc). Was part number 12G577. Pics 4-7

- Oddball front tappet chest cover breather. This item has been modified for racing. It started out as a cork gasket type with breather tank. I think it has come off of an inline 1098cc engine. Pics 8 & 9
- Front plate breather for Innocenti 1275cc Photos taken at Chris Allitt's (Allitt Motorsport). Pic 10

BREATHER PIPE FROM TAPPET CHEST EXTENSION PIECES

Tappet chest covers part numbers 1A2199, 12H155 and 12H948 did not have extension pieces.
- 997cc.
- 1098cc. Pic 11

BELLHOUSING BREATHERS
Pre A+

- 1275cc Morris front-wheel drive range, (AD016) etc. (Short) metal. Please refer to *The story of the BMC 1100* page 52. ISBN 978-1-84549-539-8. Riley kestrel 1300 photograph.
- 1275cc Morris front-wheel drive range, (AD016) etc. (Short) plastic. (Part number 12G1938 was 12G1562.) Pics 12 & 13
- 1275cc (AD016) (Tall) metal. Automatic with positive crankcase ventilation. (Part number 12G1113 became 12G1440.) Pic 14
- 1275cc (AD016) (Tall) metal. (Part number 12G2619.) This breather is identified by O-rings pressed into breather tank for image of breather tank please refer to front tappet chest breathers above.

A+

All A+ breathers were painted black.
- 1275cc October 1980 onward. Mini Metro. A+ bellhousing breathers had taller pipes and shorter breather tanks. Pic 15 (This item has been chromed)
- 1275cc October 1980 onward. Mini Metro. (Automatic).
- Part number LLC10047. 1275cc 1990 onward and SPI. (To clear horizontally-mounted brake master cylinder and servo.) Pic 16 (Courtesy Mini Spares, Potters Bar)
- Part number LLC10051. 1275cc Automatic.

ROCKER COVERS

Rocker covers came with Austin, A+,

ANATOMY OF THE CLASSIC MINI

BREATHING

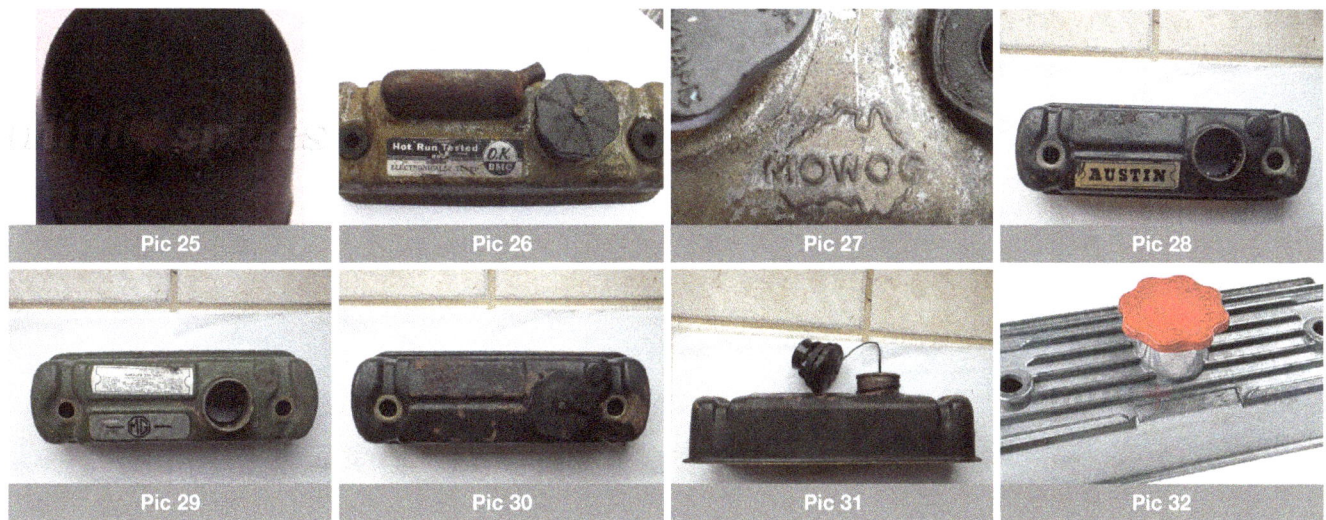

Pic 25 | Pic 26 | Pic 27 | Pic 28
Pic 29 | Pic 30 | Pic 31 | Pic 32

Leyland, MG, Mini Cooper, Morris, Princess, Riley, Wolseley badges.

These badges were originally riveted to the rocker cover, and were later stuck on. The A+, Leyland and Mini Cooper badges were only available as stick-on.

All rocker covers are made of steel, unless otherwise stated.

Rocker covers with chrome filler cap.

- 848cc saloon Mini and Austin Seven Van part number 2A902.
- 848cc saloon Mini part number 2A903. Pics 17-19
- 997cc Cooper part number 12A269. Breather pipe angled away from standard position.

Rocker covers with plastic oil filler cap

All rocker covers in this section use the filler cap with part number 12A402. Part number AEG172, AEG512, 12A477, 12A1196, 12A1197, 12A1530, 12G121, 12G579, 12G604, 12G712, 12G714, 12G823, 12G1530, 12G1583.

- 997 Cooper (plastic filler plug). Breather pipe angled away from standard position. Pic 20
- 848cc saloon Mini, Elf and Hornet. 1098cc front-wheel drive Morris 1100 (ADO16) FWD, etc. Part number 12G121 became 12A1196. Pics 21-24
- 1098cc front-wheel drive Morris 1100 (ADO16) FWD etc. 1098cc A40 Mk2. Part number 12A477 became 12A1196.
- 1098cc front-wheel drive Morris 1100 (ADO16) FWD etc. 1098cc A40 Mk2. 998cc Mini. 1275cc front-wheel drive Morris 1300 (ADO16) FWD etc. Part number 12A1196.
- 1098cc 8G156/157/160/161 rationalized engines part number AEG172 with AEA789/AEG789 blanking plug. Vertical breather pipe same as 1951 Austin A30. (Looks like a CAM4126 water pump bypass blanking plug.) Pic 25 (Courtesy Mini Spares, Potters Bar)

Australian rocker cover

Not sure what engine size this has come off of. Pics 26 & 27

Closed circuit breather rocker covers with plastic oil filler cap

Listed mainly for information.

All rocker covers in this section use the filler cap with part number 13H2296. Pics 28 & 29

- 1098cc/998cc/1275cc front-wheel drive part number 12A1197.
- 1098cc front-wheel drive Morris 1100 (ADO16) front-wheel drive, etc. Part number 12G579.
- 1098cc front-wheel drive Morris 1100 (ADO16) front-wheel drive, etc. Part number 12G604.
- 1098cc front-wheel drive Morris 1100 (ADO16) front-wheel drive, etc. Part number 12G712.
- 1098cc front-wheel drive Morris 1100 (ADO16) front-wheel drive, etc. Part number 12G1530.
- Chrome rocker cover for 1098cc front-wheel drive (ADO16). Vanden Plas part number 12G714.
- Chrome rocker cover for 1098cc front-wheel drive (ADO16). Vanden Plas part number 12G823.
- Chrome rocker cover for 1098cc/1275cc front-wheel drive (ADO16). Vanden Plas part number 12G1583.
- 1275cc front-wheel drive Morris 1300 (ADO16) front-wheel drive, etc. Part number AEG512. Code 199 has twin carburettors, dynamo, carburettor crankcase ventilation and four-synchro close-ratio gearbox.
- 12A1530 painted black 1969 to 1980. Pics 30 & 31
- Aluminium alloy rocker cover for MG Metro, Metro Turbo and Metro Vanden Plas part number CAM6822. Pic 32 (Courtesy Mini Spares, Potters Bar)

ANATOMY OF THE CLASSIC MINI

Pic 33 | Pic 34 | Pic 35 | Pic 36
Pic 37 | Pic 38 | Pic 39 | Pic 40
Pic 41 | Pic 42 | Pic 43 | Pic 44

- 1275cc Austin Maestro and Montego. Pic 33
- 1984 onward Mini part number LDR10074. (Shorter filler neck.) Pics 34 & 35

Cooper 'S' and Austin Morris 1300GT

Two extra cut-outs to clear stud number ten and one bolt.
- 1071 'S' to fit pancake filter type air cleaners (with eleven cylinder head fasteners).
- 1071 'S' with metal air box for twin SUs (modified position for breather pipe).
- Green (with eleven cylinder head fasteners) non-breather type. Cooper 'S' and Austin Morris 1300GT.

Rocker cover fasteners

- Standard fixing bolt. Pic 36
- Chrome for aluminium rocker covers. Pic 37
- Carburettor 1275cc Cooper. Pic 38

Oil filler caps (plugs)

- Chrome with Bowden cable (8G612). Pic 39
- Plastic with strap (breather type) (GFE6003). Pics 40 & 41 (Courtesy Mini Spares, Potters Bar)
- Plastic without strap (breather type) (13H2296).
- Plastic breather cap (non-breather type rocker cover) (12A402->GFE6022). Pic 42

- MG Metro with strap.
- MG Metro without strap (GFE6007). Pic 43 (Courtesy Mini Spares, Potters Bar)

Rocker cover colours (steel rocker covers)

- Green 1951 onward.
- Ministry of Defence blue. Pic 44
- Chrome (Austin Princess Vanden Plas 1100/1300 (AD016), FWD).
- Orange (BMC Mini tractor).
- Black 1969 onward.
- Almond Green 1996 Cooper 35 limited edition.
- Bright Green 1998 Paul Smith limited edition.

Chapter 4
Brightwork

Also see Glass and Lighting.

ALLOY FACIA
- Special edition John Cooper (1999).
- Special edition Mini 40 (1999).
- Special edition Cooper 'S' Works (1999) turned alloy dash.

ALLOY DOOR FURNITURE
- Special edition Cooper 'S' Works (1999).
- I believe that these can still be purchased.

ALLOY FOOT PEDALS
For accelerator pedal refer to Fuel system.
- Special edition Cooper 'S' Works (1999). Pic 1
- These attach to the brake and clutch pedals.

ASH TRAYS
Believe it or not, they are actually different.
- 1959 ash tray. Pic 2
- Central upper dash rail-mounted ash tray also used as rear companion bin ash trays. Pic 3
- Cooper and Super central upper dash rail-mounted ash tray. Pics 4 & 5 (Courtesy Mini Spares, Potters Bar)
- Central exhaust tunnel-mounted ash tray. Pic 6

BEZEL FOR CENTRE SPEEDOMETER
- Mk1. Pic 7 (Courtesy Brian Hore)
- Mk2/3 and 4. (Curved.) Pic 8

OVAL BEZEL FOR MINI COOPER AND SUPER
Pic 9
- Three-clock dash.

BONNET EMBELLISHER (RILEY ELF/WOLSELEY HORNET)
- Chrome strip that runs up the centre of bonnet. Part number ALA4811. Pic 10

BOOT HANDLES
- Mk1/2 (Saloon). Part number 14A6582. Pic 11
- Mk1/2/3 Riley Elf/Wolseley Hornet. Part number ALA4813. Pic 12
- Mk3 onward (Saloon). Part number JRC2844 chrome. Pic 13
- Part numbers JRC2843 Black, JRC8182 Nimbus Grey. Pic 14
- 1992 onward. Part numbers CXB101260MMM chrome, CXB101260PMD Black. Pic 15

BUMPERS
All front and rear bumpers are attached to vehicle with three fixings, unless otherwise stated.
- 1959, five-fixing type (more wrap around). Please refer to Mighty Minis by Chris Harvey page 249 ISBN 094660911X
- Five-fixing chrome bumper. Non-corner bar type. Part number 14A6779.
- Five-fixing chrome bumper. Corner bar type. Part number 14A9871. Pic 16
- Five-fixing chrome bumper. Corner bar type with blanking plug. Source Kevin Palmer. Pics 17 & 18
- Chrome non-corner bar type. Pic 19 & 20
- Chrome corner bar type. Pic 21
- Stainless type. Pics 22 & 23
- Clubman front, chrome. Part number CZH600. Pics 24 & 25

ANATOMY OF THE CLASSIC MINI

BRIGHTWORK

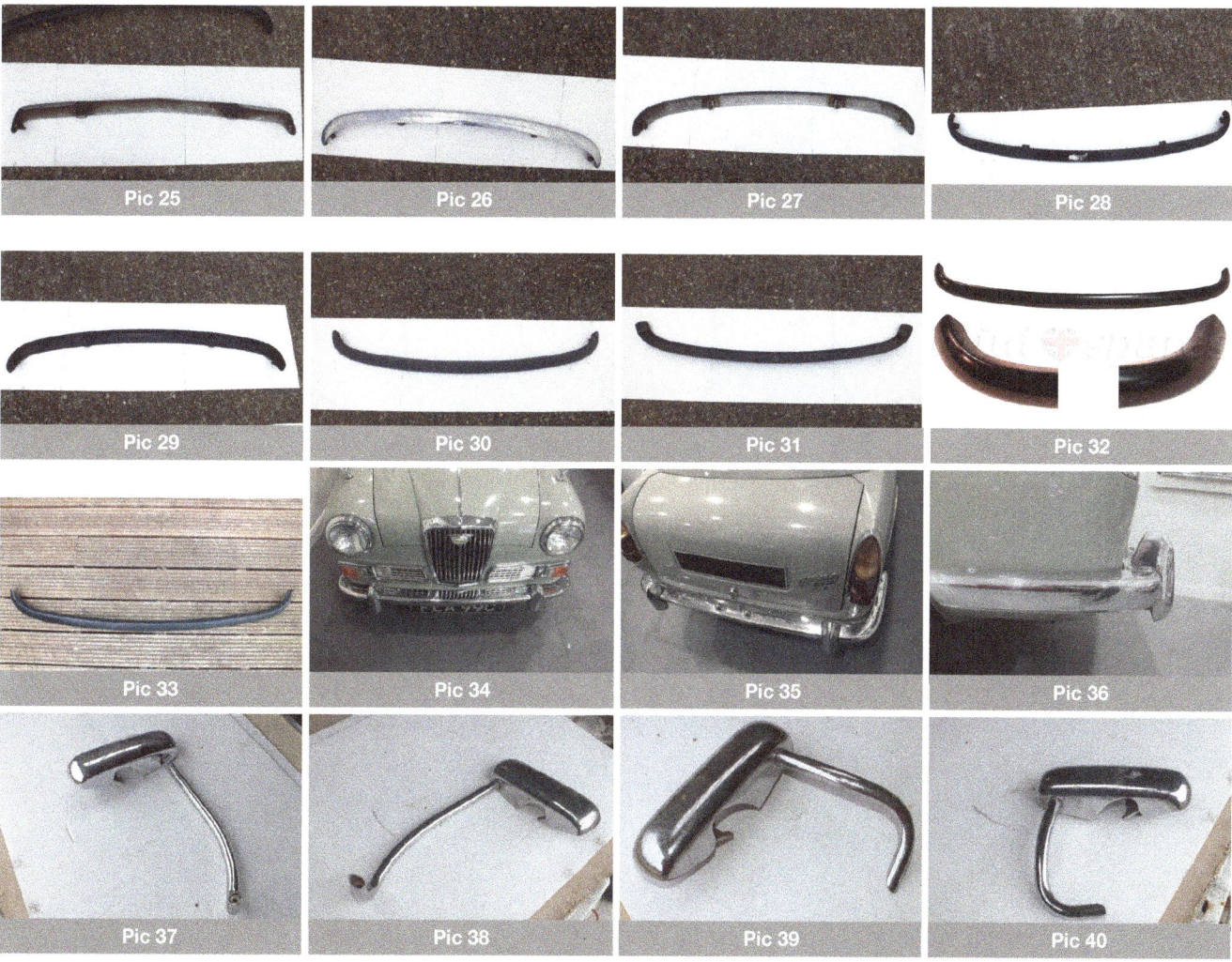

- Clubman rear, chrome. Part number CZH605. Pics 26 & 27
- Clubman rear in Nimbus grey. Part number JRC8296.
- Clubman rear gloss black. Part number EAM9219. Pics 28 & 29
- Non-Clubman in Nimbus grey. Part number JRC8268. Pics 30 & 31
- Non-Clubman gloss black. Part number CZH4341. Pic 32 (Courtesy Mini Spares, Potters Bar) & pic 33
- Non-Clubman stainless steel with rolled safety ends twin-point models part number DPB10166
- Mk1 Riley Elf/Wolseley Hornet front bumper, chrome. Corner bar type. Part number ALA4740.
- Mk1 Riley Elf/Wolseley Hornet rear bumper, chrome. Corner bar type. Part number ALA4741.
- Mk2 Riley Elf/Wolseley Hornet front bumper, chrome. Non-corner bar type. Pic 34
- Mk2 Riley Elf/Wolseley Hornet rear bumper, chrome. Non-corner bar type. Pics 35 & 36

BUMPER CORNER BARS
Mini

- Front. Part numbers 14A9877 right-hand, 14A9878 left-hand. Pics 37 & 38
- Rear. Part numbers 14A9919 right-hand, 14A9920 left-hand. Pics 39 & 40

Mk1 Riley Elf and Wolseley Hornet only
- Front. Part number ALA5090 (two per vehicle).
- Rear. Part number ALA5091 (two per vehicle).
- Listed in BMC parts catalogue AKD3071.

BUMPER OVER-RIDERS/UNDER-RIDERS
- Mk1 over-riders non-corner bar type. Pics 41 & 42
- Mk1 over-riders corner bar type. Part

ANATOMY OF THE CLASSIC MINI

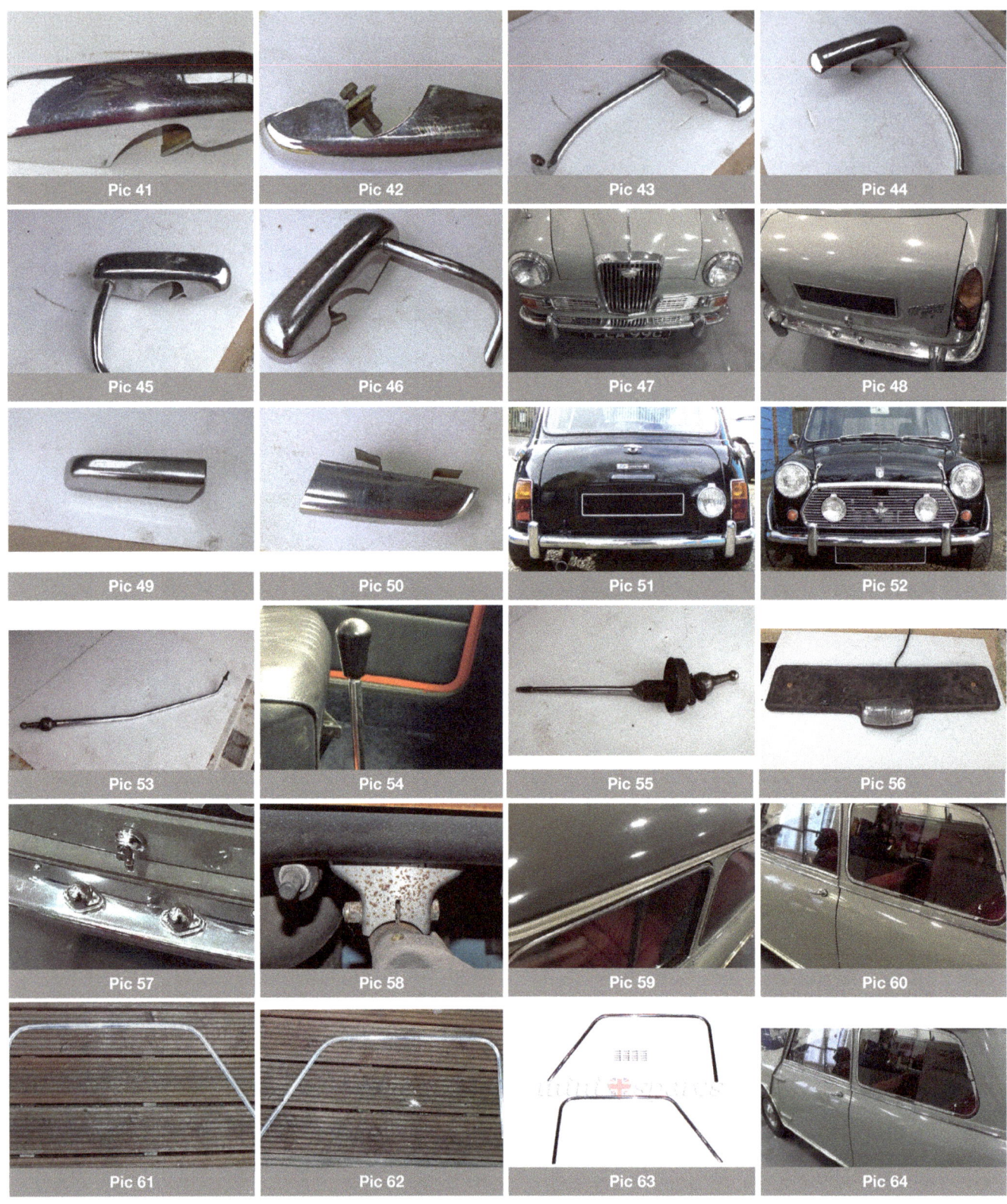

BRIGHTWORK

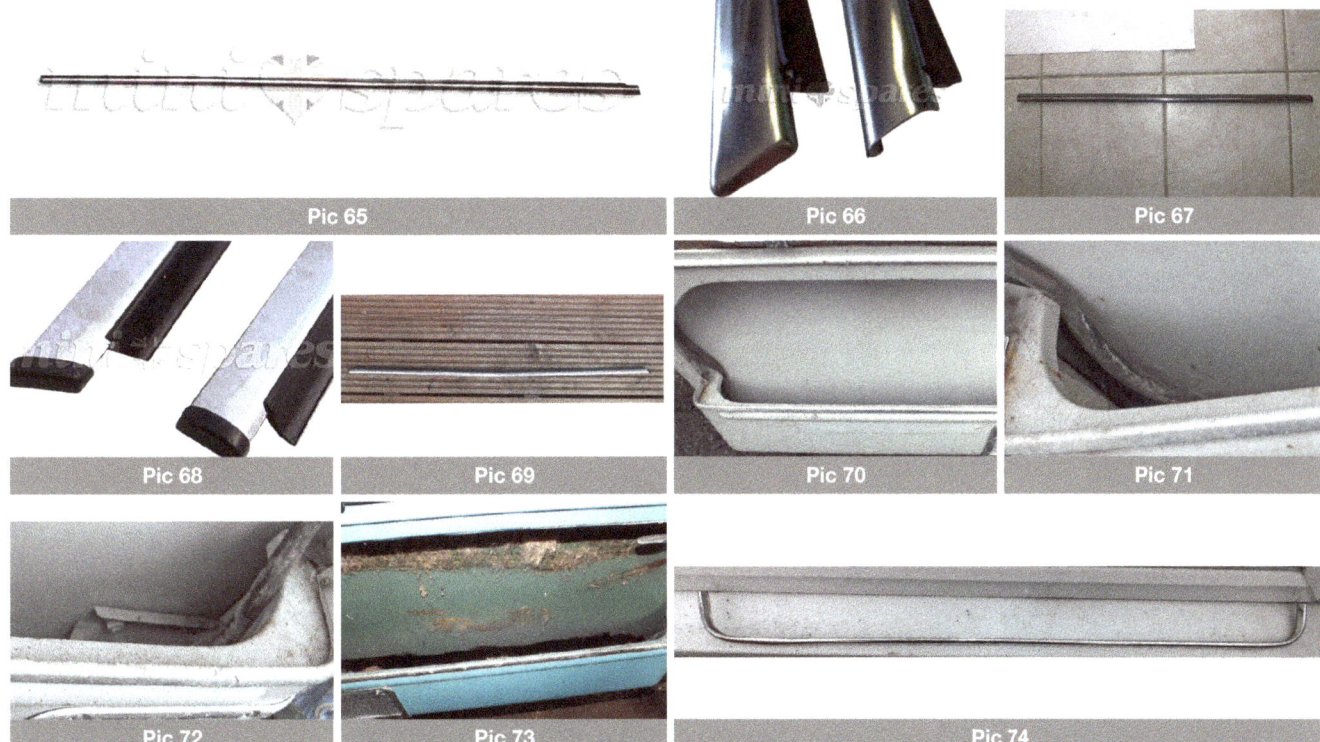

Pic 65 | Pic 66 | Pic 67
Pic 68 | Pic 69 | Pic 70 | Pic 71
Pic 72 | Pic 73 | Pic 74

numbers 14A9923 right-hand, 14A9924 left-hand. Pics 43-46
- Mk2 and 3 over-riders (Same as Mk1 non-corner bar type).
- Mk1 Riley Elf/Wolseley Hornet front and rear over-riders. Corner bar type.
- Mk2 Riley Elf/Wolseley Hornet front and rear over-riders. Part number ALA5087 (Four per vehicle). Pics 47 & 48
- Clubman under-riders (Front only). UK. Part number CZH1762. Pics 49 & 50
- Clubman rear over-riders (non-UK). Pics 51 & 52 Rear bumper used on front. (Courtesy P Giffen)

CHROME EXHAUST EXTENSION
- Mini Ritz 1985 onward. Mini Red Hot/ Jet black.
- Mini Neon.

CHROME GEARLEVERS
- Austin and Morris 850 Super and Riley Elf/Wolseley Hornet. Part numbers 22A312, 22A313. Pic 53
- Cooper/Cooper 'S'/Mk2/3 Riley Elf/ Wolseley Hornet. Part number 22G1190. Pics 54 & 55
- 1990's Cooper. Part number 22A1932.

CHROME NUMBERPLATE LIGHTS
- Mk1 Mini. Pic 56
- Riley Elf/Wolseley Hornet (All). Pic 57

CHROME WINDOW WINDER
- Mk3 Wolseley Hornet.
- These can be fitted to Minis. They have to be fitted along with the window regulator.

COLUMN SUPPORT BRACKET
- Cooper and Super. Part number 21A322 chrome. Pic 58

COOPER AND SUPER EXTERNAL DOOR GLASS SURROUND PLUS RILEY ELF/ WOLSELEY HORNET
- Mk1/2. Part numbers 14A9773 right-hand, 14A9774 left-hand. Pics 59-62
- Mk3 Elf/Hornet only. Pic 63 (Courtesy Mini Spares, Potters Bar)

COOPER AND SUPER EXTERNAL HORIZONTAL DOOR MOULDING PLUS RILEY ELF/WOLSELEY HORNET PLUS MK3 MINI ONWARD
- Mk1/2. Part numbers 24A341 right-hand, 24A342 left-hand. Pics 64 & 65 (Courtesy Mini Spares, Potters Bar)
- Mk3/Riley Elf/Wolseley Hornet. Part numbers CZH1666 right-hand, CZH1667 left-hand. Pics 66 (Courtesy Mini Spares, Potters Bar) & 67
- 1981 onward, Mini. Part numbers PAM1014 right-hand, PAM1015 left-

ANATOMY OF THE CLASSIC MINI

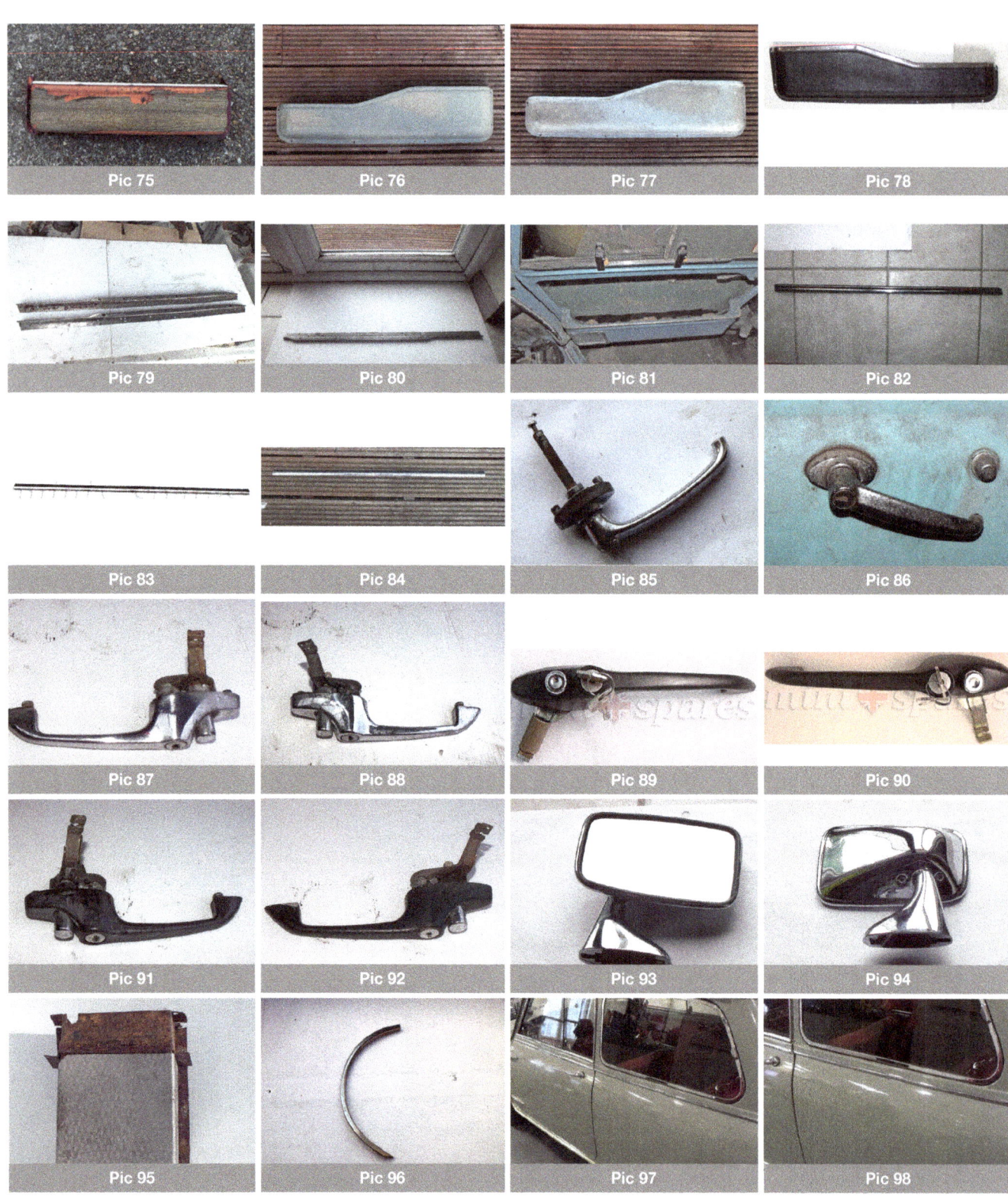

BRIGHTWORK

hand. Pics 68 (Courtesy Mini Spares, Potters Bar) & 69

DOOR CAPPINGS
- Special edition Cooper 'S' Works (1999).

DOOR POCKETS
- Mk1 Mini (early) held to door by two screws. Part number 14A6879 (two per vehicle). Pics 70-72
- Mk1/2 Mini held to door by clips. Part number 24A1169 (two per vehicle). Pics 73-75
- Mk3 Riley Elf/Wolseley Hornet. These door pockets are made of plastic. They came in different colours. Pics 76-78

INTERNAL HORIZONTAL TRIMS
- Mk1 very early. For photograph refer to *Mighty Minis* by Chris Harvey. ISBN 094660911X page 70.
- Mk1 early (multiple comfort settings). Part numbers 14A6769 right-hand, 14A6770 left-hand. Pic 79
- May 1963 onward Mk1/2. Part numbers 24A1303 right-hand, 24A1304 left-hand. Pics 80 & 81
- Mk3 early. Part numbers ALA5772 right-hand, ALA5773 left-hand (taller, more chrome). Pic 82
- Mk3 late onward. Part number JPC8153 (two per vehicle). Pics 83 (Courtesy Mini Spares, Potters Bar) & 84

EXTERNAL DOOR HANDLES
- Mk1. Part numbers 14A6828 right-hand, 14A6829 left-hand. Pic 85
- Modified Mk1, includes Mk2. Pic 86
- Mk3 onward, chrome. Pics 87 & 88
- Nimbus grey Mini Twenty-five, 1984 (will fit all models from Mk3 onward). Pics 89 & 90 (Courtesy Mini Spares, Potters Bar)
- Gloss black (will fit all models from Mk3 onward). Pics 91 & 92

DOOR MIRRORS
- 1976 1000cc Special Edition nearside and offside chrome door mirrors fitted.
- 1969 onward 1275GT Clubman. Drivers side only. Pics 93 & 94
- 1976 onward 1275GT Clubman nearside and offside chrome door mirrors fitted.

EAST-WEST BOX SECTION EMBELLISHERS
Pic 95
Austin Seven vehicles only.
- Two per car.

FINISHER FOR CENTRE SPEEDOMETER
These fit to cardboard trim either side of the speedo. Pic 96
- Chrome PVC.
- All Mk1 onward vehicles with centre speedometer only.
- Part number 14A8008 (two per car).

FINISHER FOR DOOR (EXTERNAL)
- Mk1/2 Riley Elf/Wolseley Hornet door finisher. Part numbers ALA4742 right-hand, ALA4743 left-hand. Pic 97
- Mk3 Riley Elf/Wolseley Hornet.

FINISHER FOR REAR QUARTER PANEL (EXTERNAL)
- Mk1/2 Riley Elf/Wolseley Hornet rear quarter panel. Part numbers ALA4744 right-hand, ALA4745 left-hand. Pic 98
- Mk3 Riley Elf/Wolseley Hornet.

FINISHER FOR WINDSHIELD (EXTERNAL)
Pic 99
- Front windshield panel finisher.
- Part number ALA4746.
- Mk1/2/3 Riley Elf/Wolseley Hornet.

FUEL FILLER CAPS (INFORMATION ONLY)
- Primed (In primer, paintable). Part numbers 2A2164, 2A2165.
- Chrome. Mini. Part number 8G702.
- Chrome without lock. Riley Elf/Wolseley Hornet and 997cc Mini Cooper. Part number 21A94.

FRONT DOOR KICK PLATES
- Black plastic. Pic 100
- Bright aluminium. Part number 14A7176 right-hand. Part number 14A7177 left-hand. Pic 101

FRONT DOOR KICK PLATE SURROUNDS
Pic 102
- Bright surround for black plastic kick plate.

FRONT GRILLES
The two prototype Minis that were used for testing had an integral front grille. This front panel with integral front grille later became standard fit on the commercial Minis, such as the Mini Van and the Mini Pickup.

Mk1 front grilles
- Saloon with integral front grille. For picture refer to Bodywork chapter, front panels.
- Austin (Wavy) grille. Part number 14A7299. Pic 103
- Morris grille (painted) base model. Pic 104
- Morris grille (chromed). Pic 105
- Austin Super grille. As Austin Wavy grille but had additional vertical trims. Pic 106
- Morris Super grille. As Morris chromed grille but had additional vertical trims. For photographs of Morris Super grille upright embellishers please refer to *Amazing Mini* by Peter Filby. ISBN 0856140600 pages 27 and 39. Pic 107 (lower horizontal trim shown)
- Austin Cooper and 'S' grille. Part number 24A198. Pic 108
- Morris Cooper and 'S' grille. Part number 14A2158. Pic 109
- Riley Elf grille. Pic 110
- Wolseley Hornet grille. Pic 111
- Mk1 'Works' front grille. (Made from cut down Farina-bodied Austin A55 Cambridge Mk2 and A60 type grilles.) Pic 112

Mk2 onward grille surround mouldings
English items aluminium, Innocenti

ANATOMY OF THE CLASSIC MINI

Pic 99, Pic 100, Pic 101, Pic 102, Pic 103, Pic 104, Pic 105, Pic 106, Pic 107, Pic 108, Pic 109, Pic 110, Pic 111, Pic 112, Pic 113, Pic 114, Pic 115, Pic 116, Pic 117, Pic 118, Pic 119, Pic 120, Pic 121, Pic 122

BRIGHTWORK

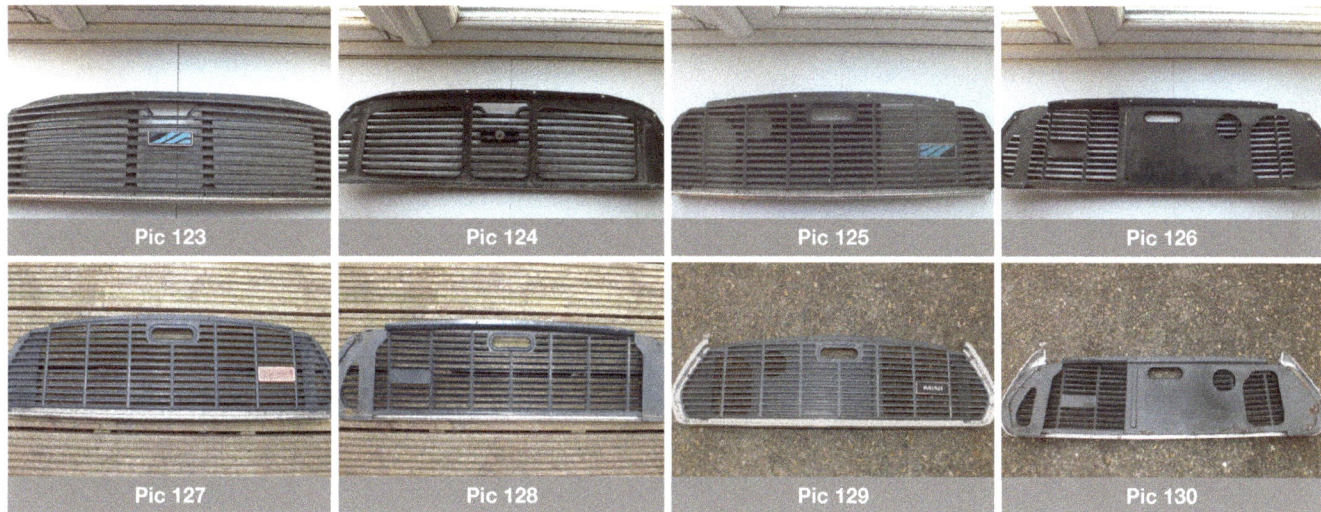

Pic 123 | Pic 124 | Pic 125 | Pic 126
Pic 127 | Pic 128 | Pic 129 | Pic 130

items Italian stainless steel. Pic 113
- Part numbers ALA6508 (right-hand), ALA6509 (left-hand).
- 1967 to 2000.

Mk2 front grilles
- Austin Mk2 grille. Totally restyled front grille which required additional trim to bonnet front edge, with nearside and offside grille cappings. Pic 114 (Courtesy Mini Spares, Potters Bar)
- Morris Mk2 grille. This is the only Mk2 grille that has never been reproduced. Pic 115
- Cooper 'S' Mk2 grille. (Seven slats). Pic 116 (Courtesy Mini Spares, Potters Bar)

Mk3 and Mini Clubman front grilles
- Mk3 standard Mini and 'S' front grille, same as Austin Mk2 front grille. Pic 117
- Standard Clubman grille. Pic 118 (Part number CZH762 became CZH4372)
- 1275 GT Clubman grille. Pic 119 (Part number CZH 1200)

Mk4 1976 onward
- Matt black grille June 1977 onward. Pics 120 & 121
- Mini Clubman grille. Pic 122
- Plain black grille with badge mounted in the centre. Pics 123 & 124
- UK spec 1100 special 1979 onward.

- Plain black grille with badge mounted on nearside of grille, April 1982 onward. Pics 125 & 126

Mk5 1984 onward
- Nimbus grey front grille July 1984 onward Mini 25 special edition, Mini Ritz 1985 onward.
- Plain black with 'Austin' badge located on nearside of front grille, UK cars 1985 to 1987. Pics 125 & 126
- Plain black grille with jet black logo on front grille, January 1988 onward. See Red Hot for image of grille.
- Plain black grille with Red Hot logo on front grille, January 1988 onward. Pics 127 & 128
- Nimbus grey Mini Designer 1988 onward with 'Mini' badge located on nearside of front grille. Pics 129 & 130

Mk6 1989 onward
- Plain black grille with 'Mini' badge located on nearside of front grille.
- ERA Turbo grille. (Two types.) Pic 131 (Production type shown).
- Plain white grille. These became available October 1992 onward, fitted to The Italian Job special edition. (Part number DHB 10146NMV.) Pics 132 & 133
- Cooper type grille vehicle fitted with internal bonnet release cable. Internal bonnet release October 1991 onward.

Pic 134 (Courtesy Mini Spares, Potters Bar)

Mk7 1996 onward cars fitted with twin-point injection engines
- Mini Seven special edition grille (wavy type) fitted with internal release cable, 1996 onward. Part number 8B12508). Pic 135 (Courtesy Mini Spares, Potters Bar)
- Paul Smith limited edition grille fitted with a green British Isles badge, 1998 onward. Pic 136

Front inner sill trims
Pic 137
- Austin Seven vehicles only.
- Aluminium front inner sill trim.
- Trims only fitted to front inner sills (never fitted to the rear).

FRONT PANEL GRILLES
- Riley Elf. Pics 138 & 139
- Wolseley Hornet. Part numbers ALA4808 right-hand, ALA4809 left-hand. Pics 140-143
- Mk3 Riley Elf/Wolseley Hornet. These vehicles were fitted with eyeball vents.

FRONT PARCEL SHELF FINISHER
- Mk1/2 Mini.
- Mk1/2 Riley Elf/Wolseley Hornet.

ANATOMY OF THE CLASSIC MINI

BRIGHTWORK

Pic 155

Pic 156

Pic 157

Pic 158

Pic 159

Pic 160

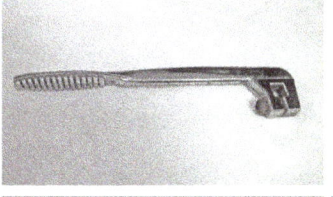
Pic 161

Pic 162

- Chrome PVC. Part number 14A8009.

FRONT WINDSCREEN INFILL
Non-base models. Pic 144
- Chrome PVC. Part number 14A8606.

GRILLE MOUSTACHE PLUS EXTENSIONS
- Grille moustache part number 14A7781. Pic 145
- Left-hand extension part number 14A7783. Pic 146 (Courtesy Mini Spares, Potters Bar)
- Right-hand extension part number 14A7782. Pic 147 (Courtesy Mini Spares, Potters Bar)

HANDBRAKE LEVER
- Twin cable. Chrome button. Pic 148

HEADLAMP BEZELS
- Brass rivet type, chrome. Refer to brass rivets for headlamp bezels.
- Plain chrome type. Pic 149
- Cibié type (non-Clubman). Part number 13H7588.
- Mini Clubman headlamp surrounds/bezels, one each for the nearside and offside – very similar looking, but different.
- Grey (painted).
- Part number DHF100060 for quad optic unit. Pic 150 (Courtesy Mini Spares, Potters Bar)

- If you have a Radford custom Mini, these bezels come off of a Riley 1500. Pic 151

BRASS RIVETS FOR HEADLAMP BEZELS
- Brass rivet. Pic 152

HORN PUSH SURROUND
Pics 153 & 154
- Mk1 Austin and Morris.

HUBCAPS
- Small hubcap, chrome for 10in wheels. Part numbers 2A8069 aluminium alloy, 2A8070 chromium plate, 21A72 chrome iron.
- Large hubcap for 10in wheels (rectangular vent holes). Does not quite cover the whole wheel rim. Part number 21A156. Pic 155
- Large hubcap for 10in wheels (half-moon vent holes). Part number 21A462. Pic 156
- Small hubcap, stainless for 10in wheels. Pic 157 (Courtesy Mini Spares, Potters Bar)
- Small hubcap, stainless for Clubman with 10in wheels. Part number 88G555. Pic 158

INDICATOR BEZEL
- 1959 onward. Part number 7H5182. Pic 159 (Courtesy Mini Spares, Potters Bar)
- Larger late front indicator. Part number 575457A. Pic 160 (Courtesy Mini Spares, Potters Bar)

INTERNAL DOOR HANDLES
- Mk1/2 Mini and Mk1/2 Riley Elf/Wolseley Hornet. Pic 161
- Part number 14A9048. (Two per car.)

INTERNAL DOOR LOCK
- Early Mk1 (large chrome latch). Pic 162
- Mk1/2 (small chrome latch). Pic 163

INTERNAL WINDOW LATCHES
- Very early type. Refer to *Mighty Minis* by Chris Harvey. ISBN 094660911X p70.
- 1959 type. Single fixing screw. Part numbers 14A7060, 14A7061, 14A7062 and 14A7063. Pic 164
- Post 1959 type. Location screw plus circular locating lug. Part numbers 14A7812, 14A7813, 14A7814 and 14A7815. Pic 165

KICKING STRIP FOR DOOR SILL (INNER)
- Mk1/2 Mini, Riley Elf/Wolseley Hornet. Aluminium. Part number 14A7270 (two per vehicle). Pic 166
- Mk3 Cooper S. Plastic (rare). (Courtesy Scott Turner)

ANATOMY OF THE CLASSIC MINI

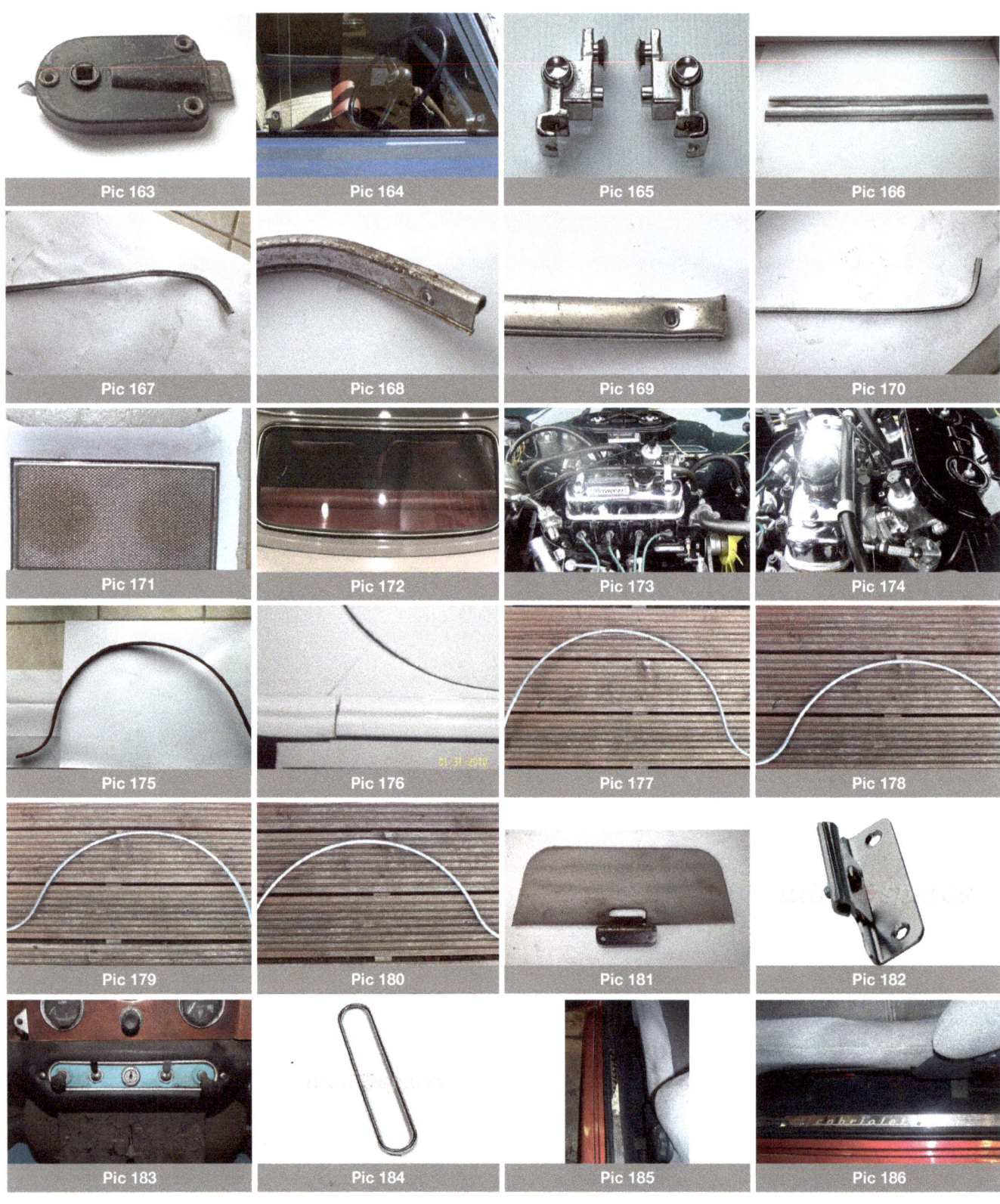

Pic 163 | Pic 164 | Pic 165 | Pic 166
Pic 167 | Pic 168 | Pic 169 | Pic 170
Pic 171 | Pic 172 | Pic 173 | Pic 174
Pic 175 | Pic 176 | Pic 177 | Pic 178
Pic 179 | Pic 180 | Pic 181 | Pic 182
Pic 183 | Pic 184 | Pic 185 | Pic 186

BRIGHTWORK

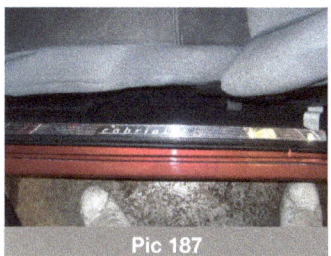
Pic 187

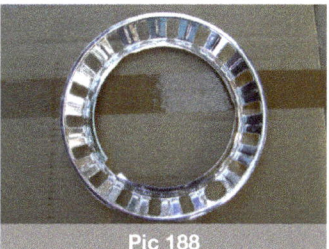
Pic 188

Pic 189

Pic 190

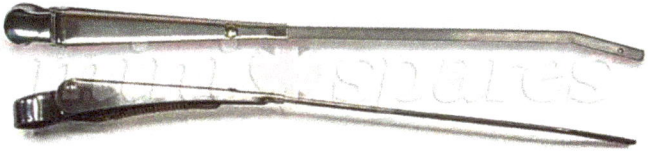
Pic 191

REAR COMPANION BIN TRIMS
• 1959 to May 1962 (approx). Mk1 early, attached to companion bins by two screws. Right-hand part number 14A6880, left-hand part number 14A6881. Pics 167-169
• Mk1/2, attached by clips.
• Mk3 onward, attached by clips. Pic 170

REAR SPEAKER GRILLE
Pic 171
• Mini.
• Riley Elf/Wolseley Hornet.
• This particular grille came from a 1962 Morris Mini Minor Super.

REAR WINDSCREEN INFILL
Non-base models. Pic 172
• Chrome/PVC. Part number 14A8607.

ROCKER COVER (CHROME)
Pics 173 & 174
• Non-breather pipe type.
• Princess Vanden Plas. (AD016)

SIX-PIECE TRIM KIT (PAINTED)
Pic 175 (offside front) & pic 176 (nearside front/nearside outer sill strip)
• Saloon models.
• Full front valance vehicles only.

SIX-PIECE TRIM KIT (STAINLESS)
Pics 177-180
• Saloon models.
• Full front valance vehicles only.

SUNVISOR
Base models had driver's sunvisor only.
Pics 181 & 182 (Courtesy Mini Spares, Potters Bar)
• 1959 to October 1964. (Chrome centre hinge part number 14E3381).

SWITCH CARRIER BEZEL
• Mk1 Mini/Riley Elf/Wolseley Hornet. Part number 14A7172. Pic 183
• Mk2 and 3 Mini/Riley Elf/Wolseley Hornet. Part number ALA6640. Pic 184 (Courtesy Mini Spares, Potters Bar)

UPPER SILL STEP TRIM
• English Cabriolet. Pics 185-187

WHEEL EMBELLISHERS (CLUBMAN)
• Rectangular ventilation holes. Part number 12A2233. Pic 188
• Round ventilation holes. Part number 21A2742. Pic 189

WIPER ARMS
• Mk1/2. Part numbers: 13H470 right-hand; 13H471 left-hand. Pic 190
• Late Mk2 and Mk3. Pic 191 (Courtesy Mini Spares, Potters Bar)

Chapter 5
Camshafts, cam followers, etc

CAMSHAFT THRUST PLATES
- Original type with phosphor bronze backing. Pic 1
- Second type with white metal backing. Pic 2
- Third type distributor-less ignition. (No soft metal backing.) Pic 3 (Photograph by kind permission of Mini Spares, Potters Bar.)

CAM BEARINGS
- Single cam bearing. Part number 2A52. Pic 4
- Three cam bearings (small bore engines). Part number 28G133 became AEC3046. Pic 5 (Courtesy Mini Spares, Potters Bar)
- Three cam bearings (large bore engines). Part number AEC3063. Pic 6
- Three cam bearings (small bore pre A+ automatic engines). Pic 7
- Three cam bearings (large bore automatic engines). Part number AEC3046.

CAMSHAFTS
Pic 8
- The purpose of this photograph is to demonstrate what can happen when a pin drive camshaft gets very worn out. (The pin falls out.)
- Pic 9 This is a picture of the actual 'Spider' for the spider drive camshafts.
- Pin drive (with plain centre bearing journal). This is a camshaft from an 803cc engine, 1951 onward. Pics 10 & 11
- Pin drive (with grooved centre bearing journal). Pic 12 (Courtesy Mini Spares, Potters Bar)
- Spider drive automatic. Pre A+. Pic 13
- Spider drive manual. Pic 14
- A+ drive manual. Pic 15

CAM FOLLOWERS
These items used to be available in oversize outside diameter, such as +0.010in.
Pic 16
Left: Standard without oil drain hole.
Right: Standard with oil drain hole.
- Standard without oil drain hole.
- Standard with oil drain hole.
- +0.010in part number 2A0013 10.
- +0.020in part number 2A0013 20.

REAR TAPPET CHEST COVERS
Cork gasket type
Pics 17-21
- 12H152 (948cc/848cc/997cc/1098cc).
- 12H941 (948cc/848cc/1098cc).
- 2A770 (848cc).
- 12A1170 (1098cc).

Rubber gasket type
- 12A1386 (1098cc/998cc). Pics 22 & 23
- This tappet chest cover can be used on either the front or rear tappet chest. The two flat pressings can be bored into and a breather fitted. (I think this cover goes back to the development of the four-wheel-drive rally cross Mini, which had two tappet chest breathers on it.) Pics 24 & 25

Tappet chest gaskets
Pic 26
Left: Early cork thin type. Middle:

CAMSHAFTS, CAM FOLLOWERS, ETC

ANATOMY OF THE CLASSIC MINI

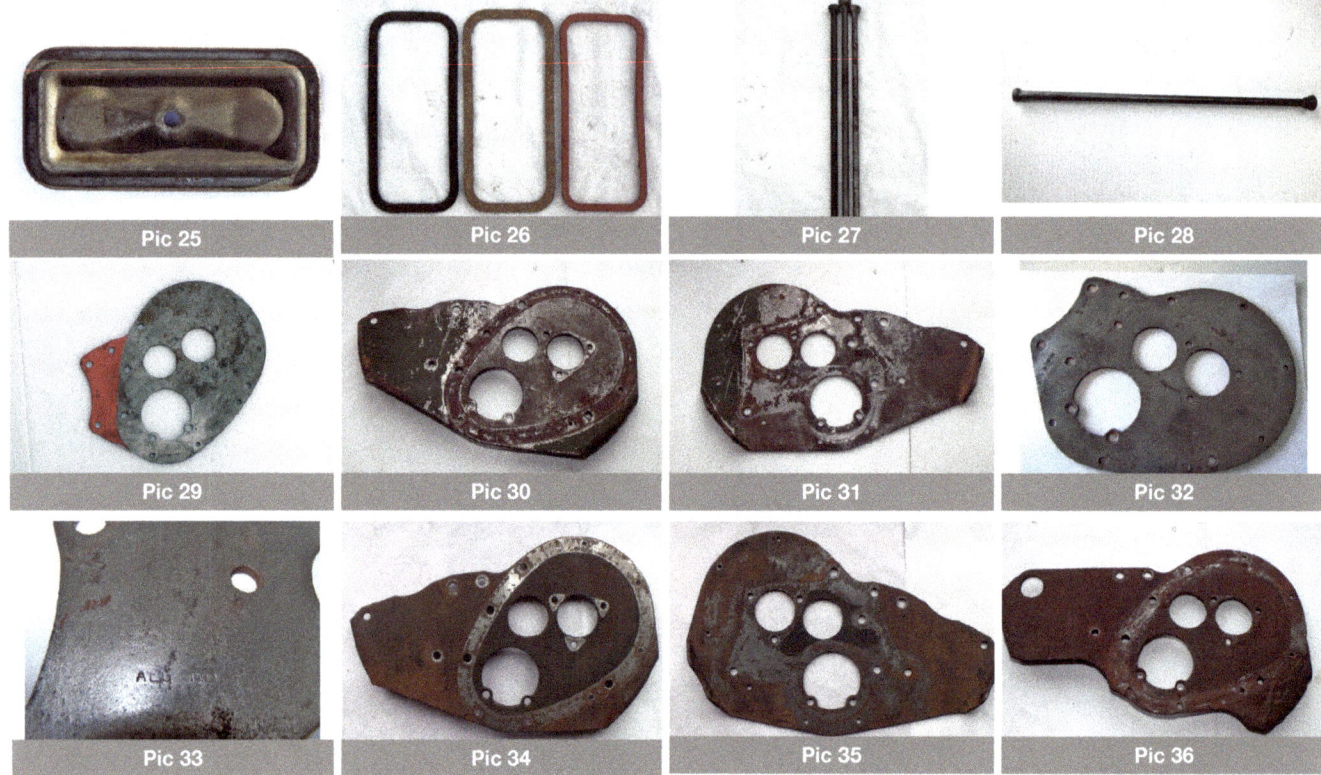

Pic 25 | Pic 26 | Pic 27 | Pic 28
Pic 29 | Pic 30 | Pic 31 | Pic 32
Pic 33 | Pic 34 | Pic 35 | Pic 36

Standard cork thick type. Right: Rubber type.

- Early cork thin type.
- Standard cork thick type.
- Rubber type.

PUSHRODS
Pre A+ (thickness of pushrod 237 thou)
Pic 27
Middle: 1275cc engines, longer pushrod.

- All engines sizes except 1275cc.
- 1275cc engines only (longer pushrod).

A+ (thickness of pushrod 235 thou)
Pic 28

- All engines sizes except 1275cc.
- 1275cc engines only (longer pushrod).

ENGINE FRONT PLATES/TIMING GEAR/TIMING COVERS
Engine front plates

All engine front plates are for engines with manual gearboxes, unless otherwise stated.

1959 onward
Pic 29

- Transverse engines and 1098cc Marina Van engines.
- Simplex chain.
- Accepts two bolts. (Screw into front main bearing cap.)
- Mini/Riley Elf/Wolseley Hornet 848cc/997cc/1098cc/998cc.

March 1962 onward
Pics 30 & 31

- Transverse engines.
- Simplex chain.
- Accepts two bolts. (Screw into front main bearing cap.)
- Morris 1100 FWD (ADO16) range, etc.

March 1963 onward
Pics 32 & 33

Image shown here is AEG161 Cooper 'S' front plate.

- Transverse and inline engines.
- Duplex timing chain.
- Accepts two countersunk allen screws. (Screw into front main bearing cap.)
- 1071cc/1275cc/970cc Cooper 'S.'
- 1275GT Clubman pre A+ (non-tension).
- Also Morris Marina 1275cc (non-tension).

1965 onward

Looks similar to 1275cc (ADO16) automatic.
Transverse engines.

- Simplex chain.
- Accepts two bolts. (Screw into front main bearing cap.)
- Automatic only.
- Morris 1100 FWD (ADO16) range, etc.

CAMSHAFTS, CAM FOLLOWERS, ETC

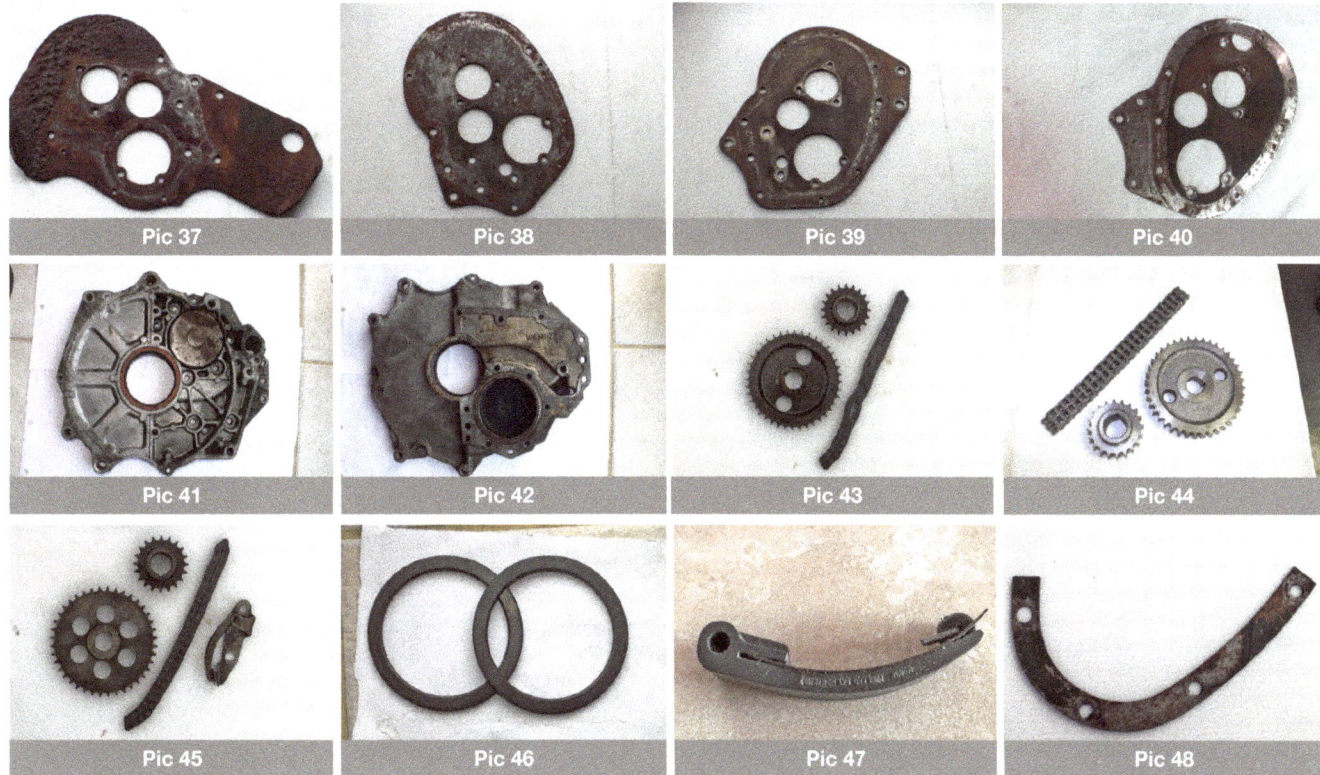

Pic 37 | Pic 38 | Pic 39 | Pic 40
Pic 41 | Pic 42 | Pic 43 | Pic 44
Pic 45 | Pic 46 | Pic 47 | Pic 48

1966 onward (manual)
Pics 34 & 35
- Transverse engines.
- Duplex timing chain.
- Accepts two countersunk allen screws. (Screw into front main bearing cap.)
- Morris 1300 FWD (ADO16) range, etc.

1967 onward (automatic)
Pics 36 & 37
- Transverse engines.
- Duplex timing chain.
- Accepts two countersunk allen screws. (Screw into front main bearing cap.)
- Automatic only.
- Morris 1300 FWD (ADO16) range, etc.

Simplex timing chain with tensioner
Pic 38
- Engine front plate for simplex timing chain with tensioner.
- Transverse and inline Morris Marina/ Ital 1275cc engines.
- All A+ engines except Maestro/Montego.
- Allegro 1098cc/1275cc/998cc, Mini and Metro.
- Accepts two bolts. (Screw into front main bearing cap.)

Maestro/Montego
Pic 39
- Engine front plate for 1275cc Maestro/Montego.
- Accepts two bolts. (Screw into front main bearing cap.)

1275cc Innocenti Mini
Pic 40
- Transverse engines.
- Duplex timing chain.
- Breather hole.
- Accepts two countersunk allen screws. (Screw into front main bearing cap.)
- Yes, this image is of a copy! Very kindly supplied by Brian Hore. (AKA the heater man.)

ENGINE BACKPLATES
Pics 41 & 42
- Aluminium backplate, 1983 onward. Austin Maestro and Montego.

TIMING GEAR
- 1951 onward, simplex timing chain and sprockets. Pic 43
- March 1963 onward, duplex timing chain and sprockets. Pic 44
- Circa 1974 onward, simplex timing chain with tensioner. 850 did not get this until 1979. Pic 45

TIMING GEAR TENSIONERS
- Tensioners fitted to simplex camshaft sprocket. Pic 46
- External tensioner (simplex) runs on outside of chain. Pic 47

TIMING COVERS
- Stiffener for timing cover 12A666, 8AM not available onward. For service purposes only. Pic 48

57

ANATOMY OF THE CLASSIC MINI

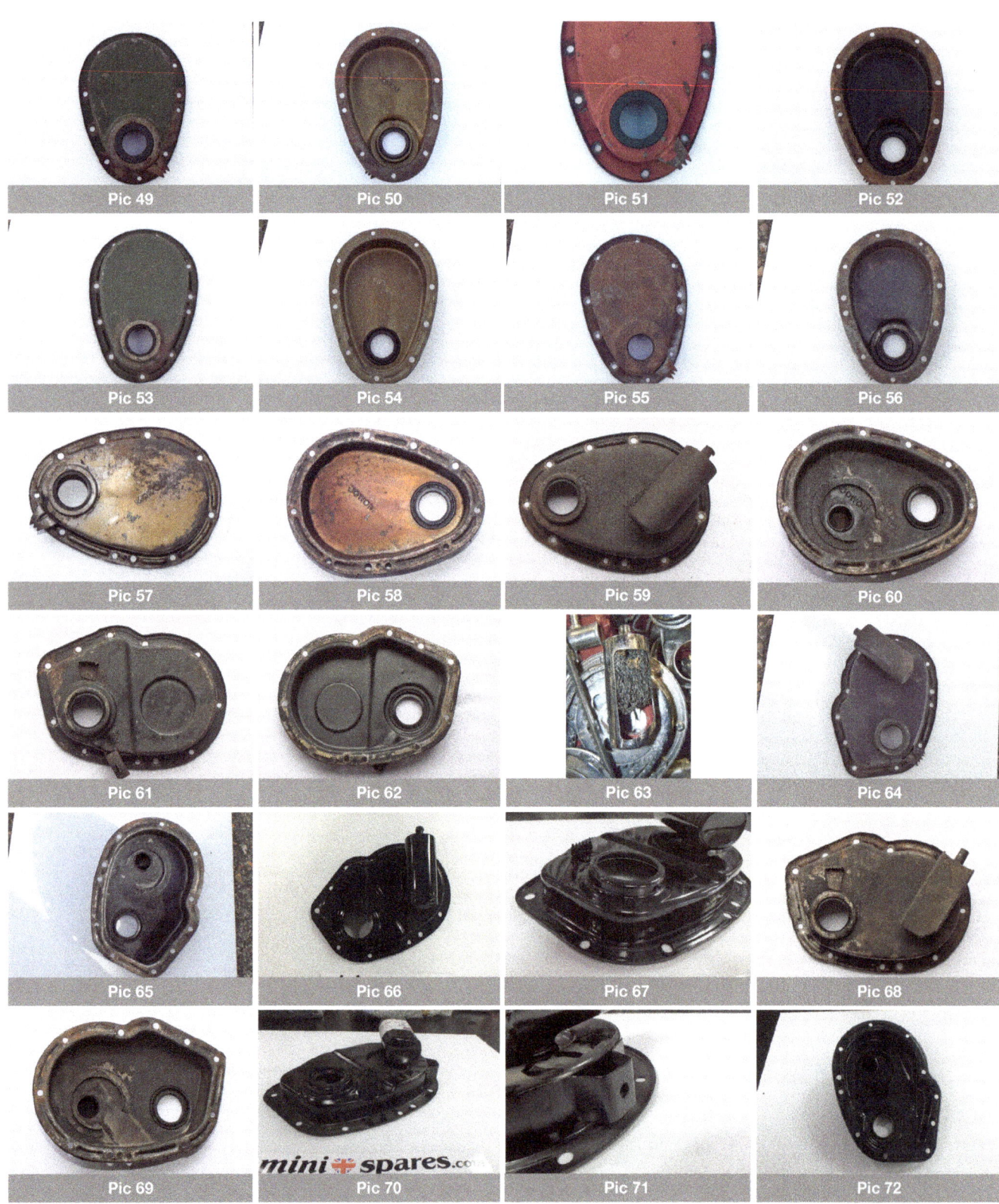

CAMSHAFTS, CAM FOLLOWERS, ETC

Pic 73

- Breather type: 12G2507, CAM4868, LJR10168 and LJR103470.
- Non-breather type: 2A937, 12A723, 12G789, 12G791, 12A1418, CAM4640 and CAM4904.
- 2A937 Oil seal type. Oil seal fits in from front of timing cover. Pics 49 & 50
- 12A723 Oil seal type. Oil seal fits in from front of timing cover with stiffener attached. Morris 1100 FWD (ADO16) 1098cc. Pics 51 & 52
- 12G789 Morris 1100 FWD (ADO16), etc less timing pointer. Pics 53 & 54
- 12G791 Morris 1100 FWD (ADO16), etc. Oil seal type. Oil seal fits in from back of timing cover. Pics 55 & 56
- 12A1418 became 12G2506. 1098cc, 998cc, 1275cc non 'S.' Not sure if this part should have a timing pointer as shown in the image (part of it has been bent through 90 degrees). Pics 57 & 58
- 1275cc with duplex timing chain. (Part number 12G2507.) Breather type. Pics 59 & 60
- Simplex timing chain with tensioner, breather type. (Part number 12G2623.)
- CAM4640 Non-breather type. Pics 61 & 62
- CAM4868 Non-fuel-injection, round breather. Simplex timing chain with tensioner. Pics 63-67
- CAM4904 Non-breather type, 850cc. Simplex timing chain with tensioner. A+.
- LJR10168 1991 onward. Single-point injection models with flattened type breather. Pics 68 & 69
- LJR103470 1996 onward. Twin-point injection models with flattened type breather. TDC stamped into cover. Pics 70-72

NON-STANDARD TIMING COVER

Pic 73
- Non-breather type.
- Note position of timing pointer.

Chapter 6
Cooling system

ADAPTER (BYPASS HOSE)
- Part number 12A2075. (Long.) Pic 1

AIR VENT NOZZLES
- Metal type. Pics 2 & 3
- Plastic type. Stapled together. Pic 4
- Plastic type. Pic 5 (Courtesy Mini Spares, Potters Bar) Pic 6

AUXILIARY RADIATOR
- ERA turbo.

BLANKING PLATE
Pic 7 (Courtesy Mini Spares, Potters Bar)
- 1951 onward.
- Austin A30s and Morris Minors were originally supplied without heaters, so a blanking plate was fitted from the factory.
- This blanking plate reappears on later models.

CORE PLUGS
- 803cc/948cc small bore/848cc/997cc/1098cc/998cc. Part number 2K8169. Pic 8 (Courtesy Mini Spares, Potters Bar)
- 948cc big bore/1071cc Cooper 'S'/1275cc Cooper 'S'/970cc Cooper 'S.' Pic 9 (Courtesy Mini Spares, Potters Bar)
- 1275cc inline/1275cc Non 'S' transverse and all A+ engines. Pic 10 (Courtesy Mini Spares, Potters Bar)

HEADER TANKS
- Part number PCF10060 (Cooper 1300).
- Part number PCF10097 (1992 onward). Pic 11
- Part number PCF101240 (Twin-point inject models.) Pic 12 (Courtesy Mini Spares, Potters Bar)

HEATERS
Heaters became standard fit on 848cc Minis in April 1974.
All heaters are of metal construction, unless otherwise stated.
- Fugstirrer. First type of blower motor fitted under bonnet. Accessory part. Pics 13-16
- Recirculatory type. Pics 17-19
- Fresh air heater. Vertical heater controls. Pic 20
- Late Mk2, fibreglass casing. Vertical heater controls. Pic 21
- Clubman, fibreglass casing. Horizontal heater controls. Pic 22
- 1985-1991 heater JEC10109.
- Late heater. The heater tap for this type of heater is fitted under the bonnet and suspended between four coolant pipes, part number JEC10112 (1991-1996). Pics 23-25
- Twin-point heater 1996 onward. Part number JEC101790.

Heater cables
- Bakelite type. Part number 14A9988. Pic 26
- Plastic type. Part number 24A2738 became CHM373. Pic 27 (Courtesy Mini Spares, Potters Bar)
- For suspended heater valve. Part number JFF10003. Pic 28 (Courtesy Mini Spares, Potters Bar)
- Single-point injection. Part number JFF10051. Pic 29 (Courtesy Mini Spares, Potters Bar)

COOLING SYSTEM

ANATOMY OF THE CLASSIC MINI

COOLING SYSTEM

- Twin-point injection. Part number JFF100910. Pics 30 & 31

Heater rheostat
- Part number 57H5260.

HEATER TAPS
First type
- 90-degree tap. For photograph please refer to *Mighty Minis* by Chris Harvey page ten ISBN 094660911X.

Second type
Pic 32
- Looks like Austin A40 Mk1 type.
- Square trunk.

Third type
Pic 33
- Brass (vertical with lever). Part number 12A479.

Fourth type
Pic 34
- Aluminium (horizontal).
- Square trunk.
- Angled.

Fifth type
Pic 35
- Aluminium (horizontal). Morris 1100 FWD range (AD016), etc.
- Round trunk.
- Angled.

Sixth type
Pic 36
- Aluminium (straight type).
- Round trunk.

Seventh type
Pic 37 (Courtesy Mini Spares, Potters Bar)
- 0.625in bore, 1990 onward. Part number JJB10011.

Eighth type
Pic 38 (Courtesy Mini Spares, Potters Bar)
- Twin-point models, 1996 onward. Part number JJB100260.

Special
Pic 39

- Brass (wheel type).
- Fitted to second version of 12A185 cylinder head.
- Mini Cooper fitted with formula Junior 1071cc type engine.

Heater tap spacers
Pic 40 Thin
Pic 41 Thick
- Made of aluminium, fits under heater tap, and requires longer studs. Morris 1100 FWD range (AD016), etc.

RADIATORS
Listed mainly for information. When the car was launched in 1959 the radiators were internally constructed to take 13 gills per inch of fluid.

First type
For photograph please refer to *Amazing Mini* by Peter Filby. ISBN 0856140600, page 27.
- 1959 onward.
- Common radiator.
- Square-tank type.
- Top hose at front of radiator.
- Coventry radiators badge attached.
- Part number ARA80. (848cc Saloon.)

Second type
- Less common radiator.
- Square-tank type.
- Morris radiators badge attached.

Third type
- 848cc saloon.
- 848cc Austin Seven Van.
- Part number ARA102.

Fourth type
- 848cc saloon.
- 848cc Riley Elf and Wolseley Hornet.
- 997cc Mini Cooper.
- Part number ARA1573.

Fifth type
Pics 42 & 43
- 1962 onward.
- Morris 1100 FWD range (AD016), etc.
- Part number ARA1627.

Sixth type
- 1962 onward.
- Morris 1100 FWD range (AD016), etc.
- For hot climate conditions.
- Part number ARA2052.

Seventh type
- Cooper 'S' radiator (taller neck).

Eighth type
Pic 44 (Courtesy Mini Spares, Potters Bar)
- Square-tank type.
- November 1964 onward.
- Part number ARP2000.
- Top hose moved back.

Ninth type
- January 1965 onward.
- 16 gills per inch.
- 3 core.
- Part number ARA2064
- 998 Cooper

Tenth type
Pics 45-48
- May 1965 onward.
- Rounded-header tank type.
- Top hose moved back.

Eleventh type
- 1989 ERA turbo Mini radiator.
- Part number ERA 1159.

Twelfth type
Looks similar to thirteenth type.
- Single-point injection models.
- Part number PCC10339B.

Thirteenth type
Pics 49 & 50 (Courtesy Mini Spares, Potters Bar)
- 4th May 1992 onward.
- 1275cc (12AG03 engines).
- Part number PCC10358B.

Fourteenth type
Pics 51-54
- Twin-point injection models.
- Front-mounted radiator.
- Part number GRD974.

Oddball radiator
Pic 55

63

ANATOMY OF THE CLASSIC MINI

COOLING SYSTEM

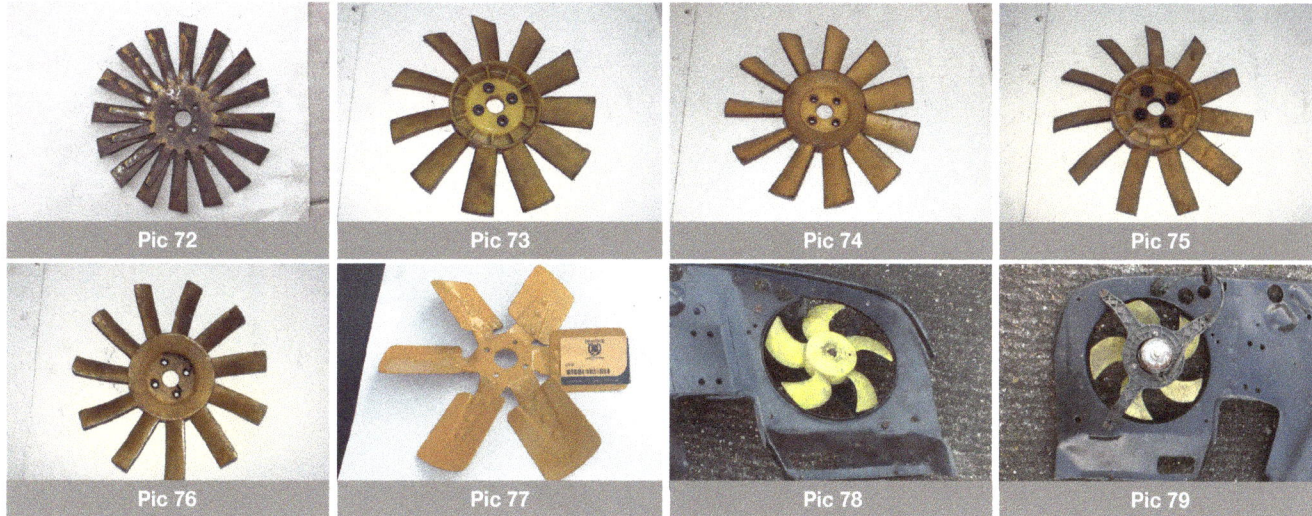

Pic 72　Pic 73　Pic 74　Pic 75
Pic 76　Pic 77　Pic 78　Pic 79

- I think the metal bracket attached to the centre of the top header tank was for a radiator fan transmitter.

RADIATOR BOTTOM BRACKETS

These photographs refer to the third and fourth types listed below. I do not know which is which. Pics 56-58

First type
Pic 59
- 848cc/998cc. Part number 22A29.

Second type
Pic 60 (Courtesy Mini Spares, Potters Bar)
- Mini Coopers 997cc/998cc. Part number 12A293.

Third type
- Part number 12G2458.

Fourth type
- Part number 12G3641.

Fifth type
Pic 61
- All models 1974 onward. Part number 12A2153.
- Plus tubular spacer. Part number ARP1073.

RADIATOR COWLINGS
One-piece cowlings
First type
- 1959 onward.
- Bolt securing lower part of cowling passes through a rubber bush.

Second type
Pics 62-64
- 1974 onward.
- No lower mounting bush.
- Secured by horizontal bolt.

Third type
Pics 65-67
- No lower mounting bush.
- Secured by horizontal bolt.

Two-piece cowlings
First type
- Top half. Part number ARA2768. Pic 68
- Bottom half. 848cc/998cc. Part number ARA2769. (Upper item: ARA2769 Lower item: ARA2770). Pic 69

Second type
- Top half. Part number ARA2768. See first type for image.
- Bottom half. 1961 onward Coopers and Cooper 'S.' Part number ARA2770. See Pic 69

Third type
See radiator for Morris 1100/1300 FWD (ADO16).
- 1962 onward Morris 1100/1300 (ADO16) FWD range, etc.

RADIATOR FANS (MECHANICAL)
- Two-blade in yellow. Part number 2A997. Pic 70
- Two-blade in red. Morris, part number 2A997.
- Four-blade fan two times part number 2A997. Pic 71
- Sixteen-blade metal in yellow. Also painted Morris Red. Part number 12A404. Pic 72
- Eleven-blade plastic fan in yellow, 1.5in blades. Part number 12G2129. (848cc Oct/Nov 1967 onward.) Pics 73 & 74
- Eleven-blade plastic fan in yellow, 1in blades. Part number 12G1305. Pics 75 & 76
- Export fan made of metal in yellow, six blades. Part number 2A998. Pic 77

RADIATOR FANS (ELECTRIC)
- Cooper 'SE' part number PGF10038.
- Cooper 1300cc part number YMV10046.
- 1992 onward open fan and motor assembly, part number PGG10058. Pics 78 & 79

ANATOMY OF THE CLASSIC MINI

COOLING SYSTEM

Pic 104

Pic 105

Pic 106

Pic 107

RADIATOR TOP BRACKETS
First type
Pics 80 & 81
- 1959 onward three-fixing type.

Second type
Pic 82
- Four fixing type up to 1974 848cc/998cc. Part number 12A201.

Third type
- Cooper 'S' type 1071cc/970cc. Part number 12G323.

Fourth type
- Cooper 'S' type 1275cc. Part number 12G617.

Fifth type
- 1969 onward 998cc Mini Clubman. Part number CAM4620.

Sixth type
Pic 83
- 1969 onward 1275 GT Mini Clubman. Part number 12G2453.

Seventh type
- 1275 GT Clubman with one-piece radiator cowling. Part number CAM4621. Use 12G2453.

Eighth type
Pic 84
- 1980 onward 848cc/998cc. Part number CAM4619.

Ninth type
- ERA turbo Mini three fixing type. Part number ERA1186.

Tenth type
Pic 85
- Three-fixing type. New 1300 Coopers. Part number PCU10135.

'T' PIECES
Pic 86
- 90s Mini.
- Metric bore size.

THERMOSTAT HOUSINGS
Thermostat housings are made of aluminium, unless otherwise stated.
- 848cc Mini. Part number 2A25. Pic 87
- 848cc Mini. Early bulbous. Pic 88
- 848cc Mini. Part number 12G103 (Bulbous). Pic 89
- 848cc Mini with temperature gauge. Part number 12A408. Pic 90
- Second type, blank where temperature transmitter should be fitted. Part number 12A408. Pic 91

Thermostat housings for Austin America (AD016) with EPAI cylinder head made of cast iron. Plus EPAI Mini.
- Austin Allegro Pre A+. Pics 92-94
- 1980 onward. A+ Allegro, Mini Metro and ERA turbo Mini. Part number CAM6117. Pic 95 (Courtesy Mini Spares, Potters Bar)
- 1983 onward. 1275cc Maestro/Montego. Part number TAM1151.
- 1990 onward. Carburettor models. HIF38. Part number PEQ10010. Pic 96 (Courtesy Mini Spares, Potters Bar)
- Cooper 1275cc fitted with HIF44 carburettor. Part number PEQ10019. Pic 97 (Courtesy Mini Spares, Potters Bar)
- Late single-point and automatic. Part number PEQ100690. Pic 98 (Courtesy Mini Spares, Potters Bar)
- Twin-point models. Part number PEQ100650. Pic 99
- Special, made of brass, fitted to Mini cooper with Formula Junior engine. (12A185 big valve head with eleven fixings.) Pic 100

THERMOSTAT HOUSINGS SANDWICH PLATES
- Originally fitted to the Austin Allegro/Metro. Pic 101 (Courtesy Mini Spares, Potters Bar)
- Cooper with carburettor. Part number PEM10036. Pic 102 (Courtesy Mini Spares, Potters Bar)
- 1992 TO 1996. Pic 103
- Part number PEG100030. Multi-point injection. Pic 104 (Courtesy Mini Spares, Potters Bar)

WATER PUMPS
Unless otherwise stated all water pumps have:
- Generator mounting lug.
- Bypass hose facility.
- Main body made of aluminium.

First type
Pics 105 & 106
Part numbers 2A774, 12G120, 12A1332 and 12G1284.
- 1959 onward.
- Cast iron body.
- Small impeller.
- Removable screw for lubrication.

Second type
Pics 107-109
Water pump shown does not have a

ANATOMY OF THE CLASSIC MINI

removable screw for lubrication, this is a later water pump.
Part number 12G1771.
- Cast iron body.
- Large impeller.
- Removable screw for lubrication.

Third type
Pic 110
- Cast iron body.
- Large impeller.
- Non bypass hose type.

Fourth type
Pic 111 (Courtesy Mini Spares, Potters Bar)
- Mini
- Made of aluminium.
- Small impeller.

Fifth type
Pic 112 (Courtesy Mini Spares, Potters Bar)
- Mini.
- Made of aluminium.
- Large impeller

Sixth type
Pic 113 (Courtesy Mini Spares, Potters Bar)
- Austin Allegro.
- Non-bypass hose type.
- Small impeller.

Seventh type
Pic 114 (Courtesy Mini Spares, Potters Bar)
- Austin Allegro/Metro.
- Non-bypass hose type.
- Large impeller.

Eighth type
I am not sure what the difference is between this pump and the pump listed for March 1989 onward (Maestro 1275cc). This is how they are listed, they look externally the same.
- 1983 onward. (Maestro 1275cc)
- 1275cc Montego.
- No lug to hang alternator as on earlier models.
- Large impeller.

Ninth type
Pic 115
- March 1989 onward. (Maestro 1275cc)
- 1275cc twin-point Minis.
- No lug to hang alternator as on earlier models.
- Large impeller.

WATER PUMP SPACERS
First type
Later vehicles, such as 1275cc carburettor Sprite, use two of the steel spacers, one each side of the plastic fan. This requires longer bolts. Pic 116
- Thin

Second type
Pic 117
- Thick (made from aluminium).

WATER PUMP PULLEYS
From 1969 most engine components were painted black. (It was cheaper than Green or Yellow paint.)

First type
Pic 118
- Made of pressed steel.
- Painted yellow from factory.
- First type of transverse water pump pulley.

Second type
Pics 119 & 120
- Made of cast iron.
- Painted yellow from factory.
- Mini Cooper 'S.'

Third type
Pic 121 (Courtesy Mini Spares, Potters Bar)
- Made of pressed steel.
- Painted black from factory.

Fourth type
Pic 122
- Made of pressed steel.
- Not painted.

Fifth type
Pic 123
- Made of pressed steel.
- Not painted.
- To fit twin-point injection cars.

COOLING SYSTEM

Pic 108
Pic 109
Pic 110
Pic 111
Pic 112
Pic 113
Pic 114
Pic 115
Pic 116
Pic 117
Pic 118
Pic 119
Pic 120
Pic 121
Pic 122
Pic 123

Chapter 7
Crankshafts & connecting rods

CRANKSHAFT ROTATION
Fact! All of the engines fitted to the classic Mini from 1959 to 2000; the Mini Moke; Austin Ant; the Austin Morris (AD016) range from 1962 to 1974; the Austin Allegro 1098cc, 1275cc, 998cc; and the Austin Mini Metro from 1980 to 1989 are all fitted to vehicles the wrong way round. The prototype 'Orange boxes' and the Austin Maestro and Montego 1275cc were fitted correctly.

All crankshafts are believed to be made of EN16T non-nitriding steel, unless otherwise stated.

CRANKSHAFTS 1959 ONWARD
Transverse pre A+ crankshafts
Oil-fed primary gear.
The Austin Seven and Morris Mini Minor were originally going to be fitted with the 948cc engine.

The one-off 'Zagato' Mini was fitted with a 948cc engine.

948cc small bore
- 1.75in main bearings.
- 1.625in big end bearings.
- Probably 1.375in crankshaft tail.
- Probably drilling in crankshaft for lubrication of primary gear.
- 76.2mm stroke.
- For picture see *Mighty Minis* by Chris Harvey, page 10. (ISBN 0 946609 11 X)

848cc 1959 onward Austin Seven & Morris Mini-Minor
Pics 1 & 2
22A62/3 crankshaft.
22A295 primary gear thrust washer.
22A79 primary gear.
No backing ring fitted.
2A3597 'C' washer.
22A53 flywheel. (This flywheel was fitted with a paper gasket, part number 22A130, between the bolt-in centre and flywheel.)
This flywheel could be fitted with any one of three oil seals.
- 13H106 (8A-U-H101 and 8MB-U-H101 to 8A-U-H16489 and 8MB-U-H14472).
- 13H435 (8A-U-H16489 and 8MB-U-14472 to 8A-U-H118461).
- 22A214 (8AM-U-118462 to Deva bush).
- Casting numbers 22A62 and 22A63.
- 1.75in main bearings.
- Main bearing width 1.187in (30.16mm).
- 1.625in big end bearings.
- 1.375in crankshaft tail.
- Drilling in crankshaft for lubrication of primary gear.
- 68.26mm stroke.

997cc 1961 onward Austin & Morris Cooper
Pic 3
12A298 crankshaft.
22A321 primary gear thrust washer.
22A344 primary gear.
22A334 washer DU thrust.
22A320 backing ring.
22A322 'C' washer.
22A327 flywheel. (This flywheel was fitted with a paper gasket part number 22A130, between the bolt-in centre and flywheel.)
This flywheel was fitted with oil seal 22A325. (Finished COM(E)160.)

CRANKSHAFTS & CONNECTING RODS

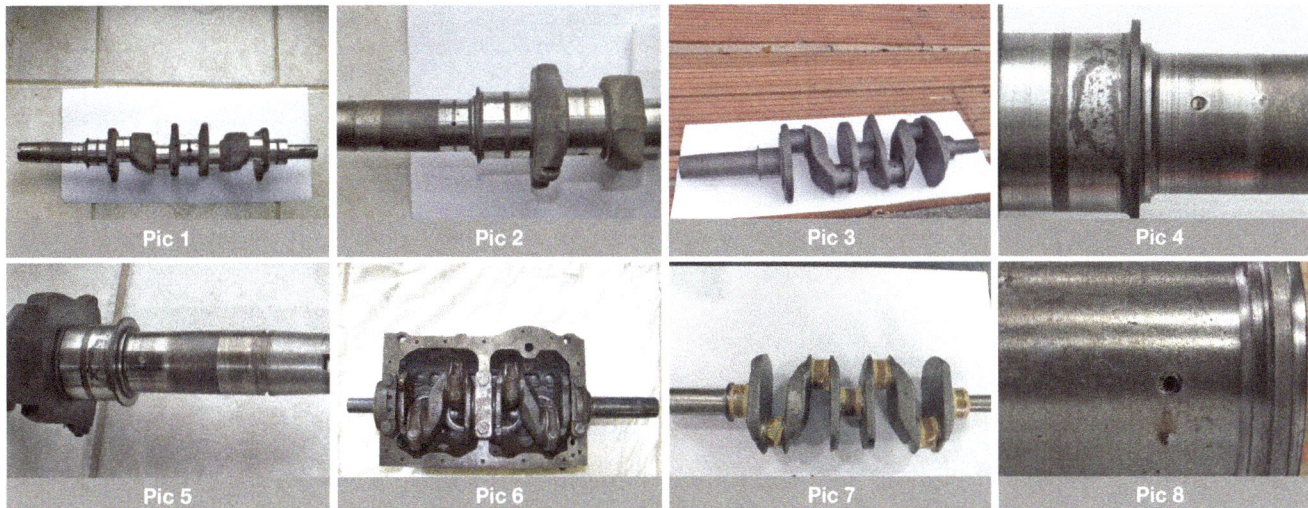

Crankshaft part number 12A298 was replaced by part number 12A375. See text for crankshaft part number 12A375.
- Part number 12A298. (Engine codes 9F101 to 9F160.)
- 1.75in main bearings.
- Main bearing width 1.0625in (26.99mm).
- 1.625in big end bearings.
- Cross-drilled big end journals.
- Drilling in crankshaft for lubrication of primary gear.
- 81.28mm stroke.

1098cc (ADO16)

I cannot actually find an oil seal listed for the back of a 1098cc flywheel. Research has led me to believe that they did have them.

Please refer to first type of 1098cc crankshaft.

The crankshaft did have an oil hole, but it was blocked off with a brass plug.

Transverse pre A+ crankshafts

Non oil-fed primary gear.

Modified 22A62/3 848cc Austin Seven & Morris Mini-Minor

Pics 4 & 5

22A62/3 crankshaft.
22A123 brass plug (to block off oil feed hole to primary gear). Brass plug fitted from factory.
22A295 primary gear thrust washer.
22A520 primary gear.
22A449 backing ring.
2A3597 'C' washer.
22A129 flywheel (this flywheel was not fitted with an oil seal or gasket).
- Casting numbers 22A62 and 22A63.
- 1.75in main bearings.
- 1.625in big end bearings.
- 1.375in crankshaft tail.
- Drilling in crankshaft for lubrication of primary gear (blocked off).
- 68.26mm stroke.

848cc Austin Seven & Morris Mini-Minor

22A298 crankshaft ('Deva bush' crankshaft). (Deva bush to 8AM-U-551624 and 8AM-FAU-H542754).
22A295 primary gear thrust washer.
22A520 primary gear.
22A449 backing ring.
2A3597 'C' washer.
22A443 flywheel. (Deva to 8AM-U-H551624 / 8AM-FAU-H542754).

- Casting number 22A298
- 1.75in main bearings.
- Main bearing width 1.187in (30.16mm).
- 1.625in big end bearings.
- 1.375in crankshaft tail.
- 68.26mm stroke.

848cc Austin Seven & Morris Mini-Minor

Pic 6

12A670 crankshaft.
22A322 primary gear thrust washer.
22A551 primary gear.
12G169 backing ring.
22A319 'C' washer.
12A669 flywheel. (8AM-U-H551625 onward / 8AM-FAU-H592755 onward.)
- Casting number 12A670.
- 1.75in main bearings.
- Main bearing width 1.187in (30.16mm).
- 1.625in big end bearings.
- 1.5in crankshaft tail.
- 68.26mm stroke.

997cc Austin & Morris Cooper

Pics 7-9
- 12A375 crankshaft.
- 22A321 primary gear thrust washer.
- 22A123 brass plug (to block off oil feed hole to primary gear).
- 12A380 primary gear.
- 12A384 washer DU thrust.
- 12A383 backing ring.
- 12A382 'C' washer.
- 12A377 flywheel. (COM(E)161 onward.)

- If you're replacing the earlier 997cc Cooper crankshaft, part number

ANATOMY OF THE CLASSIC MINI

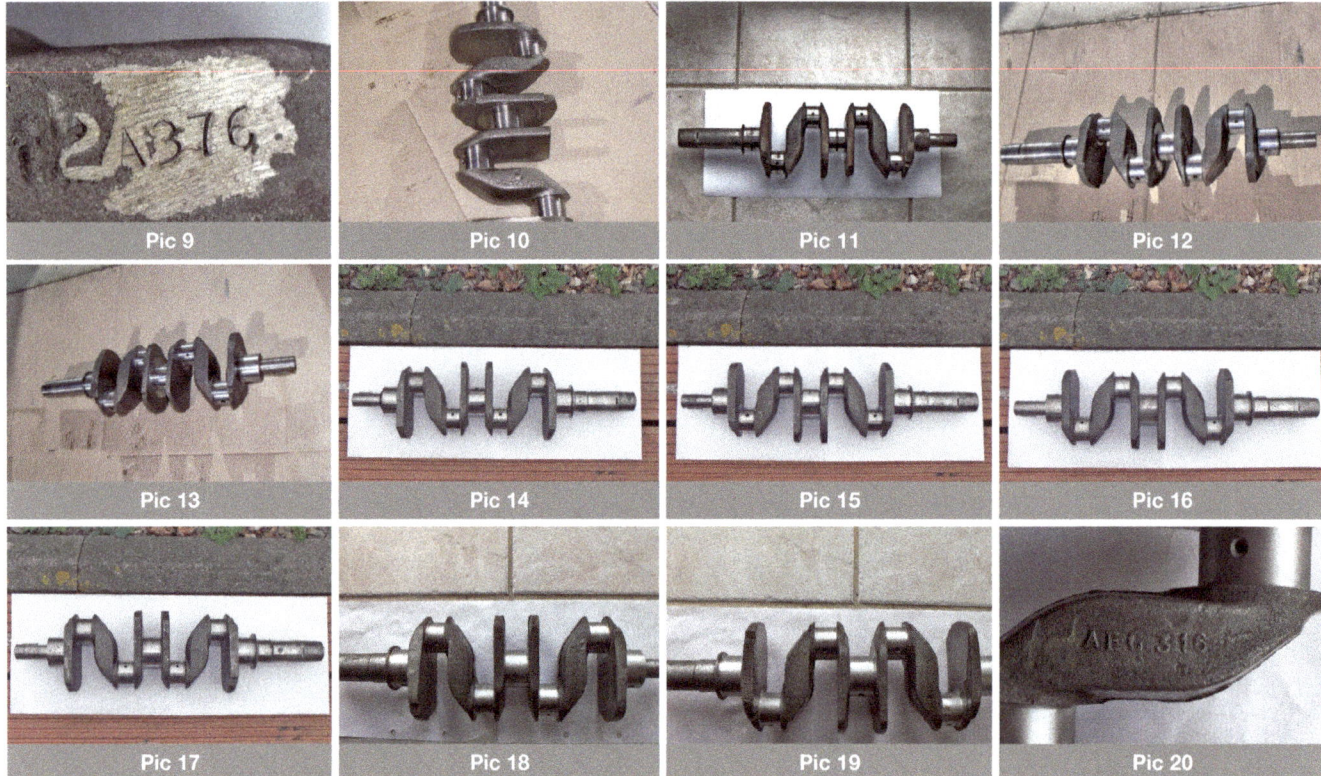

Pic 9 Pic 10 Pic 11 Pic 12
Pic 13 Pic 14 Pic 15 Pic 16
Pic 17 Pic 18 Pic 19 Pic 20

12A298, with crankshaft part number 12A375 (see Pic 9), you have to leave the primary gear lubrication hole unblocked.
• When using crankshaft part number 12A375 for engine code 9F161 onward, you have to block the primary gear lubrication hole with a brass plug (part number 22A123).
• Part number 12A375. (Engine code 9F161 onward.)
• Plug for blocking off oil lubrication hole (part number 22A123).
• 1.75in main bearings.
• Main bearing shell width 1.0625in (26.99mm).
• 1.625in big end bearings.
• Drilling in crankshaft for lubrication of primary gear.
• 81.28mm stroke.

997cc Austin & Morris Cooper

Simon Naylor had one of these for sale at the Mini Cooper Register show at Beaulieu in 2015.
12A375 with no oil hole drilled.

1098CC (AD016) 1962 ONWARD

• David A Scarbro advises that early 1098cc crankshafts had cross-drilled big end journals.
• 12G94 crankshaft (10GR/TA/101 to H5706).
• 22A123 brass plug (To block off oil feed hole to primary gear) (10GR/TA/101 to H5706).
• 22A321 primary gear thrust washer.
• 12A380 primary gear (10GR/TA/101 to H5706).
• 12A384 washer DU thrust (10GR/TA/101 to H5706).
• 12A383 backing ring (10GR/TA/101 to H5706).
• 12A382 'C' washer.
• 12G96 flywheel.
• Part number 12G94. (Use with primary gear 12A380 and flywheel 12G96.)

• 1.75in main bearings.
• 1.625in big end bearings.
• 1.5in crankshaft tail.
• Drilling in crankshaft for lubrication of primary gear.
• 83.72mm stroke.

Modified 12G94 1098cc Morris 1100 FWD range (AD016), etc

I believe that a modified crankshaft is one that was supplied by BMC already fitted with a brass plug.
• 12G94 crankshaft.

1098cc Morris 1100 FWD range (AD016), etc

Pics 10 & 11
• 88G204 crankshaft.
• 22A321 primary gear thrust washer.
• 22G106 primary gear ('Deva bush.')
• 22A551 primary gear.
• 22A1058 became 22A1493 primary gear.

CRANKSHAFTS & CONNECTING RODS

- 12G169 backing ring (for use with 22G106 and 22A551 primary gears).
- 22A319 'C' washer.
- 12A669 flywheel (six spring type).
- 12G424 flywheel (diaphragm type).
- Part number 88G204 was 12G82 and 12G244.
- 1.75in main bearings.
- 1.625in big end bearings.
- 1.5in crankshaft tail.
- 83.72mm stroke.

998cc Riley Elf & Wolseley Hornet 1962 onward

- 12A595 cast into crank.
- 1.75in main bearings.
- Main bearing shell width 1.0625in (26.99mm).
- 1.625in big end bearings.
- 1.5in crankshaft tail.
- 76.2mm stroke.

998cc
Pics 12 & 13

- 12A1451 cast into crank.
- 1.75in main bearings.
- Main bearing shell width 1.0625in (26.99mm).
- 1.625in big end bearings.
- 1.5in crankshaft tail.
- 76.2mm stroke.

948cc big bore pre-March 1963

Also see engine block chapter (flat-faced engine blocks).
- 2in main bearings.
- 1.625in big end bearings.
- Front-wheel drive 'Buckboard.'
- This crankshaft reappears later in the 970cc Mini Cooper 'S.'

1071cc Austin & Morris Cooper 'S' 1963 onward (made from EN40B nitriding steel)
Pics 14 & 15

- 707-641 cast into crank.
- Very early 1071 crank.
- 2in main bearings.
- Main bearing shell width 1.000in (25.4mm).
- 1.625in big end bearings.
- 1.5in crankshaft tail.
- 68.26mm stroke.

1071cc Austin & Morris Cooper 'S' (made from EN40B nitriding steel)
Pics 16 & 17

- AEG171 cast into crank.
- 2in main bearings.
- Main bearing shell width 1.000in (25.4mm).
- 1.625in big end bearings.
- 1.5in crankshaft tail.
- 68.26mm stroke.

1275cc Austin & Morris Cooper 'S' 1964 onward (made from EN40B nitriding steel)
Pics 18-20

Casting numbers AEG315 and AEG316.
- 2in main bearings.
- Main bearing shell width 1.000in (25.4mm).
- 1.625in big end bearings.
- 1.5in crankshaft tail.
- 81.33mm stroke.

1275cc Austin & Morris Cooper 'S' (made from EN40B nitriding steel)

No image (for AEG480 casting number see early Mk3 Cooper 'S')
- Casting numbers AEG479 and AEG480.
- 2in main bearings.
- Main bearing shell width 1.000in (25.4mm).
- 1.625in big end bearings.
- Cross-drilled big end journals.
- 1.5in crankshaft tail.
- 81.33mm stroke.

1275cc Austin & Morris Cooper 'S' (made from EN40B nitriding steel) Early Mk3 Cooper 'S'
Pics 21 & 22

- Casting numbers AEG479 and AEG480.
- Just above the AEG480 casting number can be seen the number 623. This identifies this crankshaft as an early Mk3 Cooper 'S' crank.
- 2in main bearings.
- Main bearing shell width 1.000in (25.4mm).
- 1.625in big end bearings.
- Cross-drilled big end journals.
- 1.5in crankshaft tail.
- 81.33mm stroke.

1275cc Austin & Morris Cooper 'S' non EN40B (Mk3 Mini Cooper 'S')
Pics 23 & 24

- AEG623 cast into crank.
- 2in main bearings.
- Main bearing shell width 1.000in (25.4mm).
- 1.625in big end bearings.
- This particular crankshaft has cross-drilled big end journals.
- 1.5in crankshaft tail.
- 81.33mm stroke.
- Although similar to the 12G coded non-'S' crankshaft, this crankshaft has the 'S' width centre main bearing journal, and 'S' width big end journals.

970cc Austin & Morris Cooper 'S' 1964 onward (made from EN40B nitriding steel)
Pics 25 & 26

- AEG330 cast into crank.
- 2in main bearings.
- Main bearing shell width 1.000in (25.4mm).
- 1.625in big end bearings.
- 1.5in crankshaft tail.
- 61.91mm stroke.

1275cc Morris 1300 front-wheel drive (ADO16), etc (12G coded engines)

- Pics 27-29 Photographs show 12G1287 is the part number, 12G1288 is the number stamped on the crankshaft.
- When stock of 12G1287 is exhausted, parts book advises use part number 12G1393.
- 2in main bearings.
- 1.625in big end bearings (accepts Cooper S connecting rods).

ANATOMY OF THE CLASSIC MINI

Pic 21　Pic 22　Pic 23　Pic 24
Pic 25　Pic 26　Pic 27　Pic 28
Pic 29　Pic 30　Pic 31　Pic 32

- 81.28mm stroke.
- Cross-drilled big end journals.
- Not to be confused with the third type of 1275cc Cooper 'S' crankshaft.
- This crankshaft has the narrower 1275cc non-'S' centre main bearing journal.

Part number 12G1304 (AD016)

When stock of 12G1304 is exhausted, parts book advises use part number 12G1505.
- 12H engine code.

1275cc Morris 1300 front-wheel drive (AD016), etc (12G coded engines)

Pics 30 & 31
- Part number 12G1393.
- 2in main bearings.
- 1.625in big end bearings (accepts Cooper S connecting rods).
- 81.28mm stroke.
- Cross-drilled big end journals.
- Not to be confused with the third type of 1275cc Cooper 'S' crankshaft.
- This crankshaft has the narrower 1275cc non-'S' centre main bearing journal.

1275cc Morris 1300 front-wheel drive (AD106), etc

Pic 32
- Part number 12G1505.
- 12G1505 cast into crank.
- 2in main bearings.
- 1.75in big end bearings.
- 81.28mm stroke.

1275cc Morris 1300 front-wheel drive (AD016), etc

When stock of 12G1683 is exhausted, parts book advises use part number 12G1505.
- Part number 12G1683.
- Tuftrided crankshaft.
- Based on 12G1505 casting.
- 2in main bearings.
- 1.75in big end bearings.
- 81.28mm stroke.

1275cc Morris 1300 front-wheel drive (AD016), etc

Pics 33-35 This crankshaft was listed for vehicles with twin carburettors/Lucas C40 dynamo/carburettor crankcase ventilation and a close-ratio four-synchromesh gearbox.

This crankshaft has a grey finish to its webs, this would suggest that it is also tuftrided.
- 12G1817 cast into crank.
- 2in main bearings.
- 1.75in big end bearings.
- 81.28mm stroke.
- Non cross-drilled big ends.

1098cc South African large bore 1100

Crankshaft supplied by Dez Nielson, Johannesburg, South Africa. Pics 36 & 37
- 2in main bearings.

CRANKSHAFTS & CONNECTING RODS

- 1.75in big end bearings.
- 1.5in crankshaft tail.
- 69.85mm stroke.

TRANSVERSE A+ CRANKSHAFTS 1980 ONWARD

1275cc Allegro & Mini Metro/Metro Turbo/90s Mini

Pics 38-40
CAM6232 cast into crank.
- 2in main bearings.
- 1.75in big end bearings.
- Rolled fillet radii big end journal.
- 1.5in crankshaft tail.
- 81.28mm stroke.

1098cc Mini Clubman Estate

Most likely a 88G204, listed in the picture (page 72) of the 1098cc Morris 1100 FWD range (AD016), etc.
- 1.75in main bearings.

- 1.625in big end bearings.
- 1.5in crankshaft tail.
- 83.72mm stroke.

848cc Chilean Metro 1982

Most likely a 12A670 (pictured on page 71). (848cc Austin Seven and Morris Mini-Minor.)
- 1.75in main bearings.
- 1.625in big end bearings.
- 1.5in crankshaft tail.
- 68.26mm stroke.

1275cc Metro Turbo 1982 onward

There were two versions of this crankshaft: treated and non-treated. The former is referred to as the black crank (because the finish is black). These were originally for the MG Metro Turbo Challenge cars.
Pic 41
- CAM6581 cast into crank (rare).
- 2in main bearings.

- 1.75in big end bearings.
- Rolled fillet radii big end journal.
- 1.5in crankshaft tail.
- 81.28mm stroke.

1275cc Austin Maestro 1983 onward. Austin Montego 1984 onward

Pics 42 & 43 This engine was mounted transversely under the bonnet, but had an inline crankshaft fitted.
- 2in main bearings.
- 1.75in big end bearings.
- Rolled fillet radii big end journal.
- Six flywheel bolts.
- 81.28mm stroke.
- Deeper flywheel boss than Morris Ital item.

998cc Allegro. Mini 1985 onward

Pics 44-47
- 1.75in main bearings.
- 1.625in big end bearings.
- 1.5in crankshaft tail.
- 76.2mm stroke.

ANATOMY OF THE CLASSIC MINI

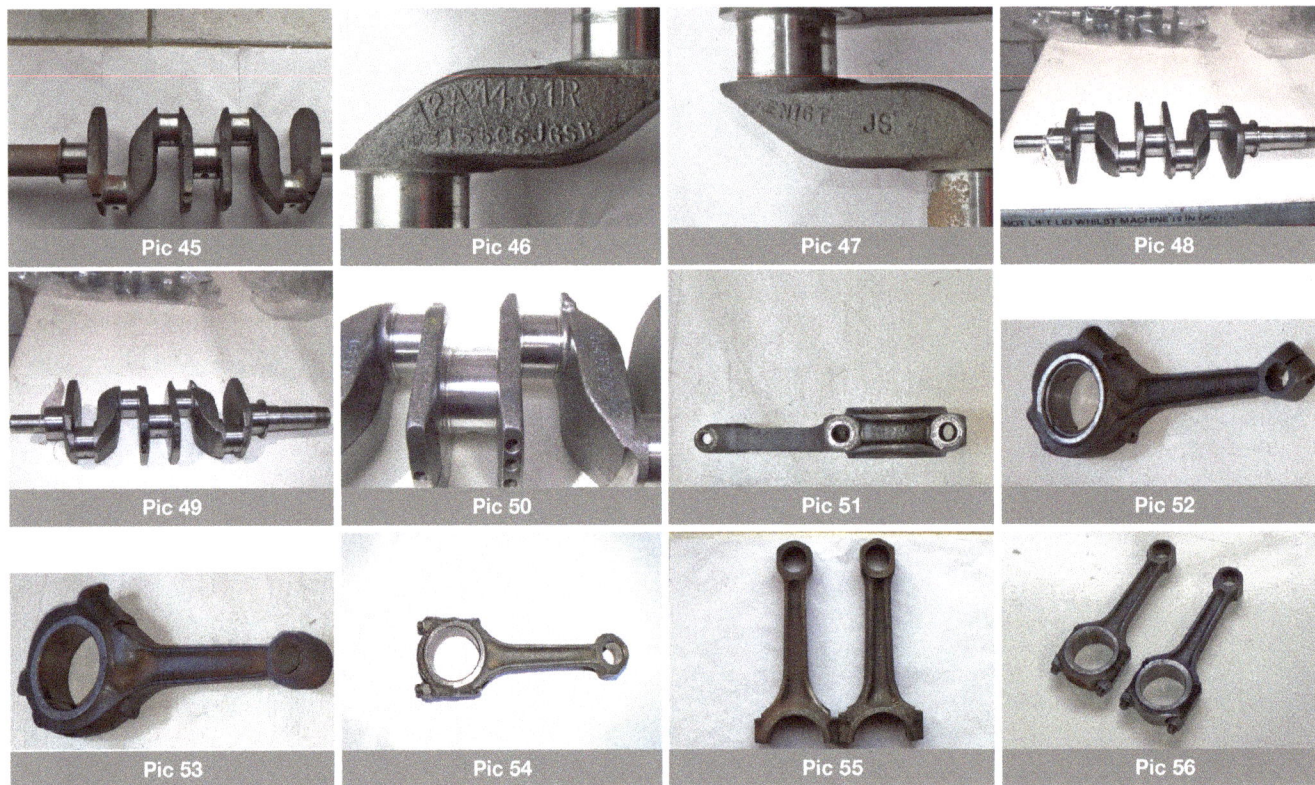

1275cc twin-point injection Mini 1996 onward

Pics 48-50
- CAM6232 cast into crank.
- 2in main bearings.
- 1.75in big end bearings.
- Rolled fillet radii big end journal.
- 1.5in crankshaft tail.
- 81.28mm stroke.
- Drillings in crankshaft webs for balance.

CONNECTING RODS 1959 ONWARD

Each set of four con rods are made up of two left-hand and two right-hand rods.

PRE A+ CONNECTING RODS 948cc/848cc 1959 onward /997cc 1961 onward

Pics 51 & 52
- Pinch bolt little end.
- Big end to fit 1.625in crankshaft journal.

948cc petrol large bore pre-March 1963

For image see 970cc AEG177 'S' rod in pic 56
- Interference fit gudgeon pin.
- Big end of rod to fit 1.625in crankshaft journal.
- AEG177 marking on rod.
- Appears later in the 970cc Cooper 'S.'
- Big end cap retained by 'S' studs and nuts.

1098cc 1962 onward

Pic 53
- Little end bush fitted to conrod in place of pinch bolt.
- Big end of rod to fit 1.625in crankshaft journal.

Cooper 'S' rod – demonstration purposes only

Pic 54 The purpose of this photograph is two fold.
- Little end still has its 'ears.' This is how the connecting rods came from the factory.
- The particular connecting rod has had another big end cap fitted to it. It probably has been re-align bored, but the thrust faces do not line up.

Cooper 'S' rod – demonstration purposes only

Pic 55 The purpose of this photograph is to demonstrate the difference between an AEG177 connecting rod and an AEG521 rod.
- The AEG177, be it 1071cc/1275cc/970cc, is the lighter of the Cooper 'S' connecting rods. (It has less material for the big end stud to pass through.)
- The AEG625 is virtually identical to the AEG521.
- Source Peter Giffen.

CRANKSHAFTS & CONNECTING RODS

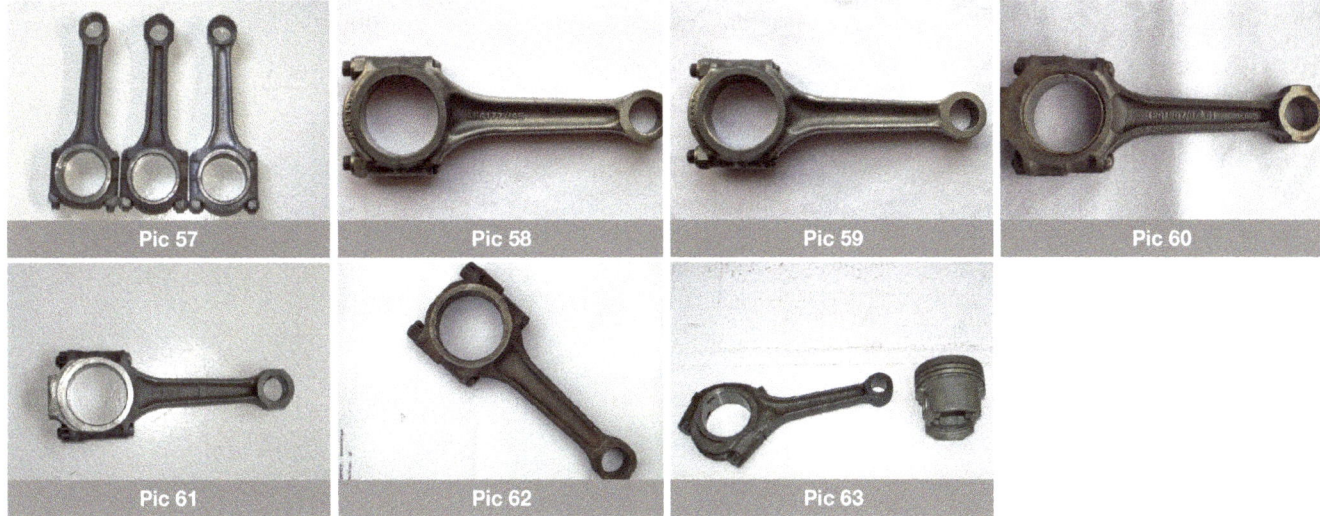

Pic 57   Pic 58   Pic 59   Pic 60

Pic 61   Pic 62   Pic 63

1071cc Cooper 'S' March 1963 onward/1275cc 1964 onward

Pic 56 (Left: 1071cc-1275cc. Right: 970cc)

1071cc-1275cc. Also shown in group picture under 1275cc Cooper 'S.'
- Interference fit gudgeon pin.
- Big end of rod to fit 1.625in crankshaft journal.
- AEG177 marking on rod.
- Whilst this rod has the same AEG177 marking as the 948cc petrol large bore, the centre-to-centre length is shorter at 5.75in.
- Big end cap retained by 'S' studs and nuts.

1275cc Cooper 'S'

Pic 57 (Left: AEG177 1071cc-1275cc. Middle: AEG521 Right: Sprite Midget)
- Interference fit gudgeon pin.
- Big end of rod to fit 1.625in crankshaft journal.
- AEG521 marking on rod.
- These rods have the same big end cap as previous 'S' rods but the rod itself is modified.
- Can also be found in 1275cc Sprite/Midget engines.
- Big end cap retained by 'S' studs and nuts.

Titanium Cooper 'S' connecting rod

Pics 58 & 59 Not fitted to production cars from the factory. Made of titanium. These look to be professionally made (probably by the factory) for racing.
- Interference fit gudgeon pin.
- Big end of rod to fit 1.625in crankshaft journal.
- AEG177/145 marking on rod.
- EN24V marking on the other side.
- AEG/145 A on big end cap.
- EN24V on other side of big end cap.

970cc Cooper 'S'

See picture 56 for 1071cc Cooper 'S' March 1963 onward/1275cc 1964 onward.
- Interference fit gudgeon pin.
- Big end of rod to fit 1.625in crankshaft journal.
- AEG177 marking on rod.
- Longer rod, gudgeon pin machining further away from big end.
- This rod was originally used in the 948cc Large bore petrol engine.
- Big end cap retained by 'S' studs and nuts.

1275cc Austin-Healey Sprite/MG Midget October 1966 onward

See picture 57 for 1275cc Cooper 'S.'
- Also can be found in Cooper 'S' engines.
- Interference fit gudgeon pin.
- Big end of rod to fit 1.625in crankshaft journal.
- AEG625 marking on rod.
- These rods have the same big end cap as previous 'S' rods but the rod itself is modified.
- Big end cap retained by 'S' studs and nuts.

1275cc non-Cooper 'S'/Non-Sprite & Midget 1967 onward

Pic 60
- Morris 1300 front-wheel drive (AD016) (etc)/1275 GT Mini/Morris Marina 1300.
- Interference fit gudgeon pin.
- Big end to fit 1.75in crankshaft journal.

Innocenti 1275cc

Pic 61
- Interference fit gudgeon pin.
- Big end of rod to fit 1.75in crankshaft journal.
- This rod is easily identified by a horizontal bar halfway up the rod.
- Big end cap retained by 1275cc non 'S' studs and nuts.

A+ CONNECTING RODS 1980 ONWARD 1275cc A+

Pic 62
1275cc A+ connecting rods are not

77

ANATOMY OF THE CLASSIC MINI

made up pf two pairs. One rod fits all.

- Interference fit gudgeon pin.
- Big end of rod to fit 1.75in crankshaft journal.
- Big end cap retained by 1275cc non 'S' studs and A+ 1275cc nuts.

998cc A+ 1986 to 1992
Pic 63

- Interference fit gudgeon pin.
- Big end of rod to fit 1.625in crankshaft journal.
- Big end cap retained by A+ bolts.

Chapter 8
Cylinder heads & rocker gear

For rocker covers see breathing chapter.

CYLINDER HEADS – PRE A+ 1959 TO 1980
• Numbers listed below can be found cast into cylinder heads below the rocker cover, unless otherwise stated.
• All cylinder heads retained to the block by nine studs unless otherwise stated.
• All cylinder heads have a bypass hose facility, unless otherwise stated.
• All cylinder heads have the facility for a temperature transmitter, unless otherwise stated.

2A629
Pics 1-3
• No facility for temperature transmitter.
• Painted green from factory.

2A629
Pics 4-7
• No facility for temperature transmitter.
• Two enlarged water galleries.
• Painted green from factory.

12A185
Pics 8-10
• 997cc Cooper.
• 997cc Cooper sized valves.
• Painted green from factory.

Bolt for Cooper 'S' and Austin Morris 1300 GT cylinder head
Pic 11

12A185
Pics 12 & 13
• This cylinder head originates from the Formula Junior engine.
• Prototype Cooper 'S.'
• Retained to the block by ten head studs and one bolt.
• Cooper 'S' sized valves.
• Painted green from factory.

12A185
• March 1963 onward.
• Cooper 'S.'
• Retained to the block by ten head studs and one bolt.
• Thermostat housing relocated.
• Cooper 'S' sized valves.
• Painted green from factory.

12G202
Pics 14-16
• Casting number between number two and number three rocker post bases.
• 997cc Cooper.
• 1098cc Morris front-wheel drive range (AD016), 1962 onward.
• Painted green from factory.

12G202
• 1098cc Mini Clubman, 1975 onward.
• 1098cc Morris front-wheel drive range (AD016), until 1974.
• Painted green from factory.

12G202
• 1973 onward.
• 1098cc Austin Allegro.
• No bypass hose facility.
• Painted black from factory.

12G202
Pics 17 & 18 Note: Three semi-circular castings protruding under rocker cover (front).
• Casting number between number two and number three rocker post bases.

ANATOMY OF THE CLASSIC MINI

CYLINDER HEADS & ROCKER GEAR

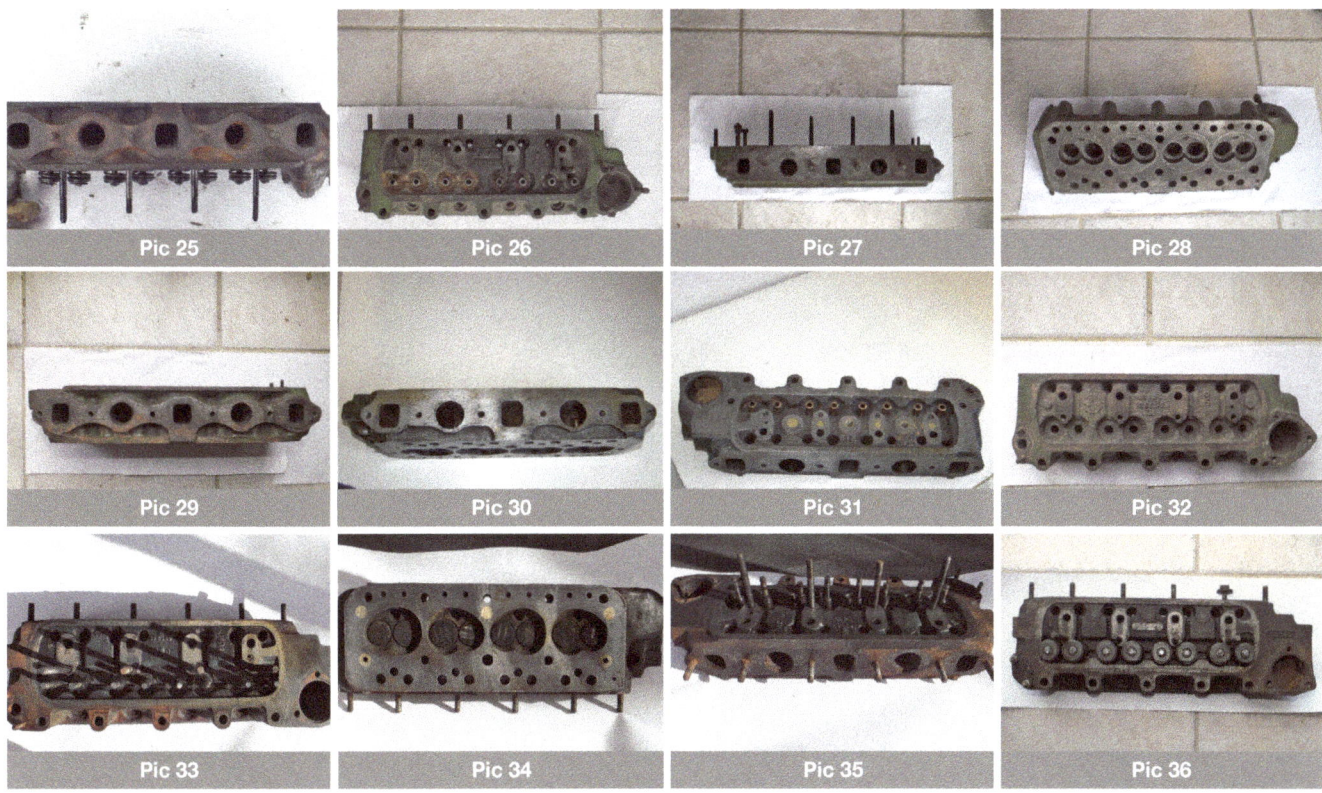

Pic 25 | Pic 26 | Pic 27 | Pic 28
Pic 29 | Pic 30 | Pic 31 | Pic 32
Pic 33 | Pic 34 | Pic 35 | Pic 36

- 1098cc Morris front-wheel drive range (AD016).
- Painted green from factory.

12G202
Pics 19 & 20
Note: Three semi-circular castings protruding under rocker cover (front).
- Late 1098cc A Series.
- Casting number between number four rocker post base and rocker cover gasket face.
- Painted black from factory.

12G206
Pics 21 & 22
- 1098cc Morris front-wheel drive range(AD016), with twin carburettors.
- 998cc Mini Cooper.
- Painted green from factory.

12A1456
Pics 23-25
- 848cc and 998cc (non Cooper).
- Painted green from factory.

12A1456 (J50808)
Pics 26-28
- This head used to be favoured by the 998cc (Class one) grass track racers.
- Painted green from factory.

AEG163
For other images of AEG163 please see next AEG163.
Pic 29
- Fully sculpted inlet and exhaust manifold face.
- Cooper 'S.'
- Retained to the block by ten head studs and one bolt.
- Cooper 'S' sized valves.
- Painted green from factory.

AEG163
Pics 30 & 31
This particular cylinder head has been drilled through three rocker post plinths. The purpose of this was to declag the cylinder head of casting sand and debris; these were not practically good heads. The three holes were then fitted with brass plugs. I believe that Downton used to do this type of work.
- Semi sculpted inlet and exhaust manifold face.
- Cooper 'S.'
- Retained to the block by ten head studs and one bolt.
- Cooper 'S' sized valves.
- Painted green from factory.

12G295
Pic 32
- 1098cc Austin-Healey Sprite, 1964 to 1966. (10cc engine code.)
- 1098cc MG Midget, 1964 to 1966. (10cc engine code.)
- 998cc Mini Cooper, 1964 onward.
- Painted green from factory.

12G940
Pics 33-35
- 1966 onward.
- 1275cc Austin-Healey Sprite.
- 1275cc MG Midget.

ANATOMY OF THE CLASSIC MINI

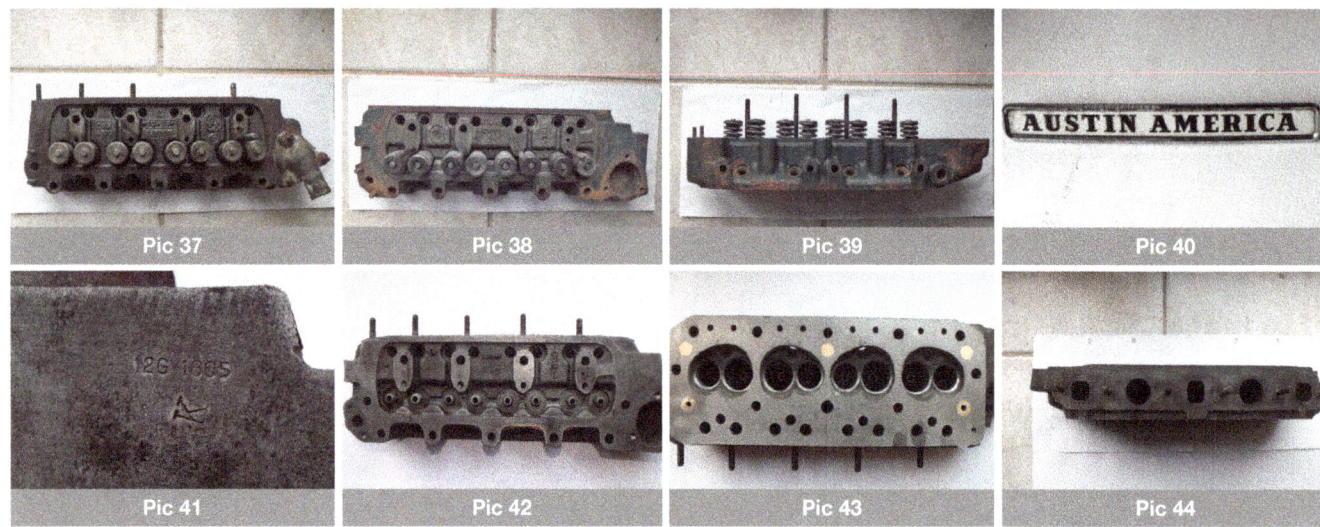

- 1275cc Morris 1300 ETC (ADO16).
- 1275cc Clubman GT.
- Painted green from factory.
- When fitted to post-1969 vehicles, heads were painted black from factory.

12G940
- 1973 onward.
- 1275cc Austin Allegro.
- No bypass hose facility.
- Painted black from factory.

12G940
Pic 36
- Austin Allegro.
- Late 12G940 cylinder head.
- Casting number behind thermostat housing.
- No bypass hose facility.
- Painted black from factory.

CAM4810 (J5181)
Pic 37
- Another 'J' head.
- Painted green from factory.

CAM4004
- 998cc Mini.
- Small bore anti-smog head.
- Painted black from factory.
- CAM4004 cast into head between number four rocker post and rocker cover gasket.
- Officially known as an exhaust port air-injection cylinder head.

12G1316
Pics 38-40
- Anti-smog head.
- 1275cc Austin-Healey Sprite.
- 1275cc MG Midget.
- 1275cc Austin America (ADO16).
- 1275cc Morris Marina.
- Painted black from factory.
- Officially known as an exhaust port air-injection cylinder head.

12G1805
Pics 41-44
- Mk3 Cooper 'S.'
- Austin/Morris 1300GT.
- Retained to the block by ten head studs and one bolt.
- Cooper 'S' sized valves.
- Painted green from factory.
- When fitted to Post 1969 vehicles heads were painted black from factory.

Cylinder Heads – A+ October 1980 to 2000
Leaded cylinder heads.

CAM4810
Please refer to unleaded cylinder heads images.
- 998cc Mini.
- Painted yellow from factory.

CAM4810
Please refer to unleaded cylinder heads images.
- 998cc Austin Allegro.
- 998cc Austin Mini Metro.
- No bypass hose facility.
- Painted yellow from factory.

12G202
Pics 45 & 46
- 1098cc Mini Clubman estate.
- Painted yellow from factory.
- 12G202 cast into head between end rocker post base and rocker cover gasket face.

12G940
- 1275cc GT Mini.
- 1275cc Morris Ital.
- Small inlet valve.
- Painted red from factory.

12G940
For similar head please refer to 12G940 leaded MG Metro.
- 1275cc Austin Allegro.
- 1275cc Austin Mini Metro.
- No bypass hose facility.
- Painted red from factory.

848cc Chilean Mini Metro Van (1982)
- Probably 12A1456 casting.

CYLINDER HEADS & ROCKER GEAR

- No bypass hose facility.
- Probably painted yellow from factory.

12G940
Pics 47 & 48
- 1275cc MG Metro.
- 1275cc Austin Maestro.
- 1275cc Austin Montego.
- Large inlet valve cylinder head.
- No bypass hose facility.
- Painted red from factory.

12G940
Pics 49-51
- 1275cc turbo Metro 1982 onward.
- Turbo heads had thicker exhaust valve stems (obvious to the eye).
- Have seen 'T' stamped on head casting around front stud hole.
- No bypass hose facility.
- Painted red from factory.

UNLEADED CYLINDER HEADS
CAM4810
Pics 52-55
- 998cc
- 'DN' and other markings behind thermostat housing.
- This head is the currently desired item by (Class one) grass track racers.
- Can be found with or without bypass hose facility.
- Painted yellow from factory.

CAM4810
- 998cc Austin Metro.
- No bypass hose facility.
- Painted yellow from factory.

12G940
Pics 56-58
This particular cylinder head is from a 1993 British Open Classic Mini automatic. The driver obviously does not understand what a temperature gauge is for! The black deposit on valve number three is melted oil filler plug (plastic).
- 1275cc Austin Mini Metro GS, 1989 onward. (Green Specification.)
- No bypass hose facility.
- Painted red from factory.

12G940
For image refer to leaded 12G940 MG Metro head.
- 1275cc MG Metro.
- 1275cc Austin Maestro.
- Large inlet valve cylinder head.
- No bypass hose facility.
- Painted red from factory.

12G940
For image refer to leaded 12G940 turbo Metro head.
- 1275cc turbo Metro.
- 1275cc ERA turbo Mini.
- No bypass hose facility.
- Turbo heads had thicker exhaust valve stems (obvious to the eye).
- Have seen 'T' stamped on head casting around front stud hole.
- Painted red from factory.

12G9408
Pics 59-61
- 1275cc carburettor.
- Painted red from factory.
- For example 1275cc carburettor Mini sprite.

12G9408
Almost identical to 12G9408 carburettor models.
- 1275cc single-point injection.
- No facility for temperature transmitter.
- No bypass hose facility.
- Painted red from factory.

TWIN-POINT INJECTION CYLINDER HEAD
Pics 62-65
- 1996 onward.
- 1275cc
- Unique head casting.
- No bypass hose facility.
- Painted black from factory.

FOREIGN CYLINDER HEAD
NMQ-BMC (South Africa) 12G940
Pics 66 & 67
- This particular head is based on the English 12G940 head casting.

ROCKER GEAR
Rocker posts
- Aluminium. Pic 68
- Cast iron. Looks exactly like the aluminium one but made of cast iron.
- Cast iron 1275cc for 12G940 head. Pic 69

Rocker shafts
- Oil feed hole to number one rocker post. (Early) Pic 70
- Oil feed hole to number two rocker post. Pic 71 (Courtesy Mini Spares, Potters Bar)

ALL PRE A+ ROCKERS ARE FITTED WITH REMOVABLE BUSHES
Pic 72 Left to right
803cc forged rocker.
Pressed steel small pad.
Forged Cooper 'S' for 12A185 head and AEG163 head.
Pressed steel wide pad for 1275cc non 'S' engines.
Forged wide pad for 1275cc 'S' engines with 12G940 based heads.
Sintered A+ rocker for all A+ engines.
Special: Rover Sport. These were originally for MG Metro Turbo Challenge cars.
Forged wide pad for 1275cc 'S' engines with 12G940 based heads, different part number from earlier type. (Part number 12G1221.)

803cc rocker (forged) small pad
Pics 73-75
- This rocker was the very first type of 'A' series rocker (a scaled down version of the 'B' series). Sometimes it has been confused with the 'S' item fitted to the 12A185 and AEG163 cylinder heads. It can be identified by the number in the forging and by the size of the adjuster nut. The nut accepts a $7/16$in spanner as opposed to the larger nut on the 'S' item.

848cc rocker (pressed steel) small pad
Pics 76 & 77
- The first type of pressed steel rocker.

ANATOMY OF THE CLASSIC MINI

CYLINDER HEADS & ROCKER GEAR

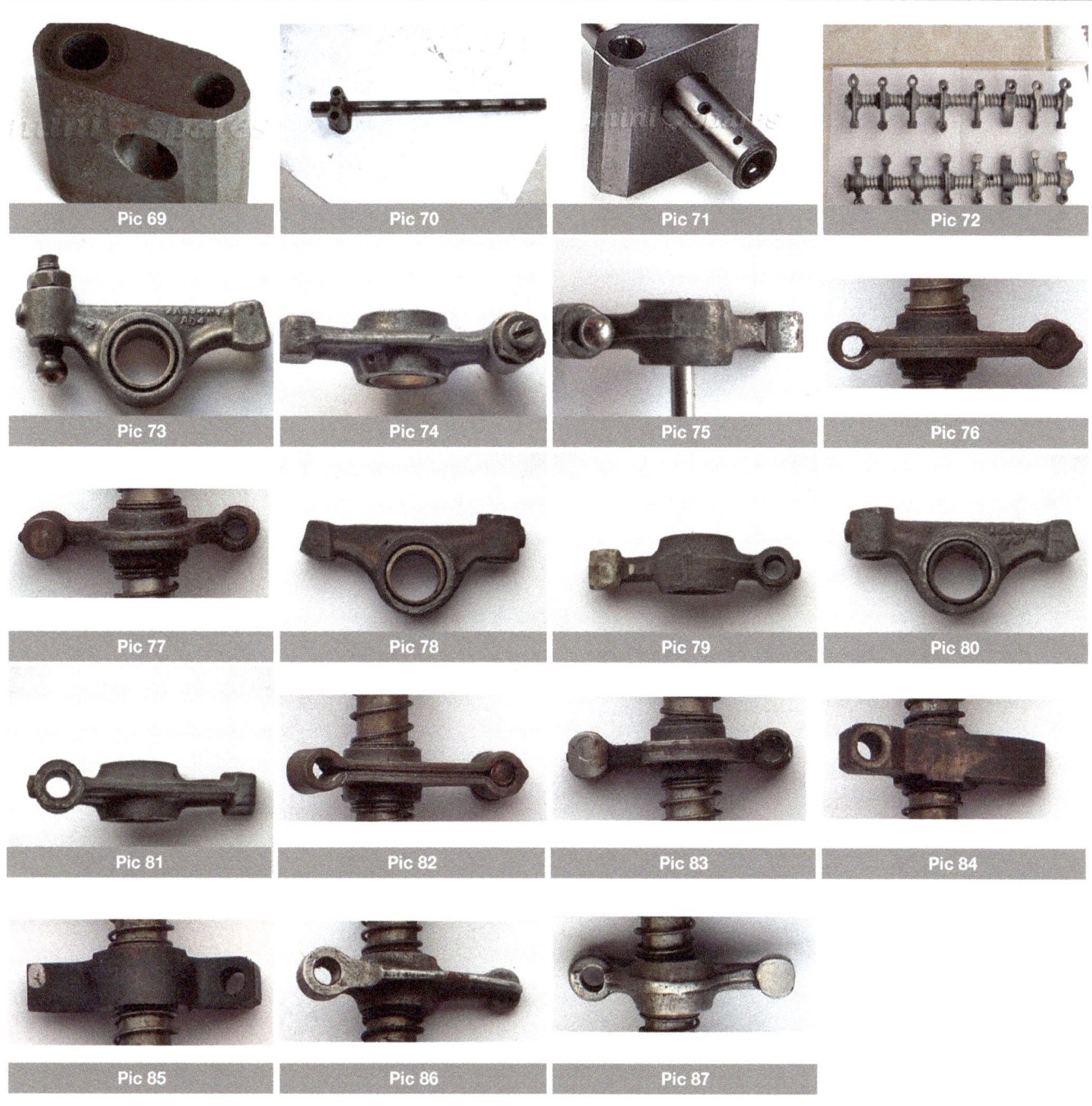

Pic 69 | Pic 70 | Pic 71 | Pic 72
Pic 73 | Pic 74 | Pic 75 | Pic 76
Pic 77 | Pic 78 | Pic 79 | Pic 80
Pic 81 | Pic 82 | Pic 83 | Pic 84
Pic 85 | Pic 86 | Pic 87

These have sometimes been confused with the 1275 pressed steel rocker.

Fitted to almost all the small bore engines up until 1979, for example, 848cc, 1098cc, 998cc and almost all 997cc Coopers.

Again, as per the 803cc type rocker, this uses a 7/16in sized adjusting nut.

1071'S' / 1275'S' / 970'S' (forged) Non 12G940 cylinder head
Pics 78-81

• Similar to the original small bore forged item, but used on all three sizes of 'S' fitted with the 12A185 and AEG163 cylinder heads. A larger adjusting nut to accept a 0.5in AF spanner. The pad that comes into contact with the valve is also a different profile from the small bore item.

ANATOMY OF THE CLASSIC MINI

1275 rocker (pressed steel) large pad
Pics 82 & 83
• Second type of pressed steel rocker. The most obvious difference being the shape of the contact pad. These first became available in 1966 on the Austin-Healey Sprite MkIV and MG Midget MkIII. Also fitted to the 12G1805 cylinder head.

1275'S' rocker (forged) large pad to fit 12G940 cylinder head.
Two different part numbers forged into these rockers (second part number 12G1221.)
• Third type of forged rocker. These have a wide pad because of the different spacing of the valves on the 12G940 head.

A+ rocker (sintered)
Pics 84 & 85
• This rocker will fit every 'A' series engine ever built. By producing one rocker for both small and large bore engines, production costs could be reduced.
• These rockers run directly on the rocker shaft, unlike the Pre A+ items which are fitted with a removable bush.

A+ rocker (forged) not fitted at factory
Pics 86 & 87
• This forged rocker was available through RoverSport and was produced for the Metro Challenge cars. Like the A+ sintered rocker, it runs directly on the rocker shaft, unlike the pre A+ items, which are fitted with a removable bush.

Chapter 9
Crankshaft pulleys & dampers

First type
I still do not know what the difference is between a 2A940 and 12A1380. This is the way that they were listed in the BMC parts books. Pics 1 & 2
- Pressed steel pulley.
- Part number 2A940.
- When dynamo is fitted.

Second type
- Pressed steel pulley.
- Part number 12A1380.
- When alternator is fitted.

Third type
I still do not know what the difference is between a 88G305 and 12G1055. This is the way that they were listed in the BMC parts books. Pics 3 & 4
- Crankshaft damper.
- Part number 88G305.
- Fitted to Morris 1100 front-wheel drive range (AD016) and 1275cc non-Cooper 'S.'
- When dynamo is fitted.

Fourth type
- Crankshaft damper.
- Part number 12G1055.
- Fitted to Morris 1100 front-wheel drive range (AD016) and 1275cc non-Cooper 'S.'
- When alternator is fitted.

Fifth type
Pics 5 & 6
- September 1961 onward.
- 997cc Cooper two-piece type damper.
- Pulley part number 12A366.
- Damper part number 12A367.

Sixth type
See pics 5 & 6
- 1962 onward.
- 1098cc (ADO16) two-piece type damper.
- Pulley part number 12A366.
- Damper part number 12A367.

Seventh type
Pics 7 & 8
- March 1963 onward.
- Cooper 'S' two-piece type damper.
- Pulley part number AEG454.
- Damper part number 12A367.

1980 ONWARD (ALL A+ VEHICLES)
Eighth type
Pics 9 & 10
- Pressed steel pulley.
- Timing plate fixed to back of pulley.

Ninth type
Pics 11-13
- Damper.
- Similar to type fitted to Morris 1100 (ADO16) front-wheel drive range (Second type).
- Timing plate fixed to back of pulley.
- TAM1241.

Tenth type
Pics 14-16
- Damper.
- Similar to type fitted to Morris 1100 (ADO16) front-wheel drive range (Second type).
- Timing plate fixed to back of pulley.
- Tam2011.

Eleventh type
Pic 17
- Damper.

ANATOMY OF THE CLASSIC MINI

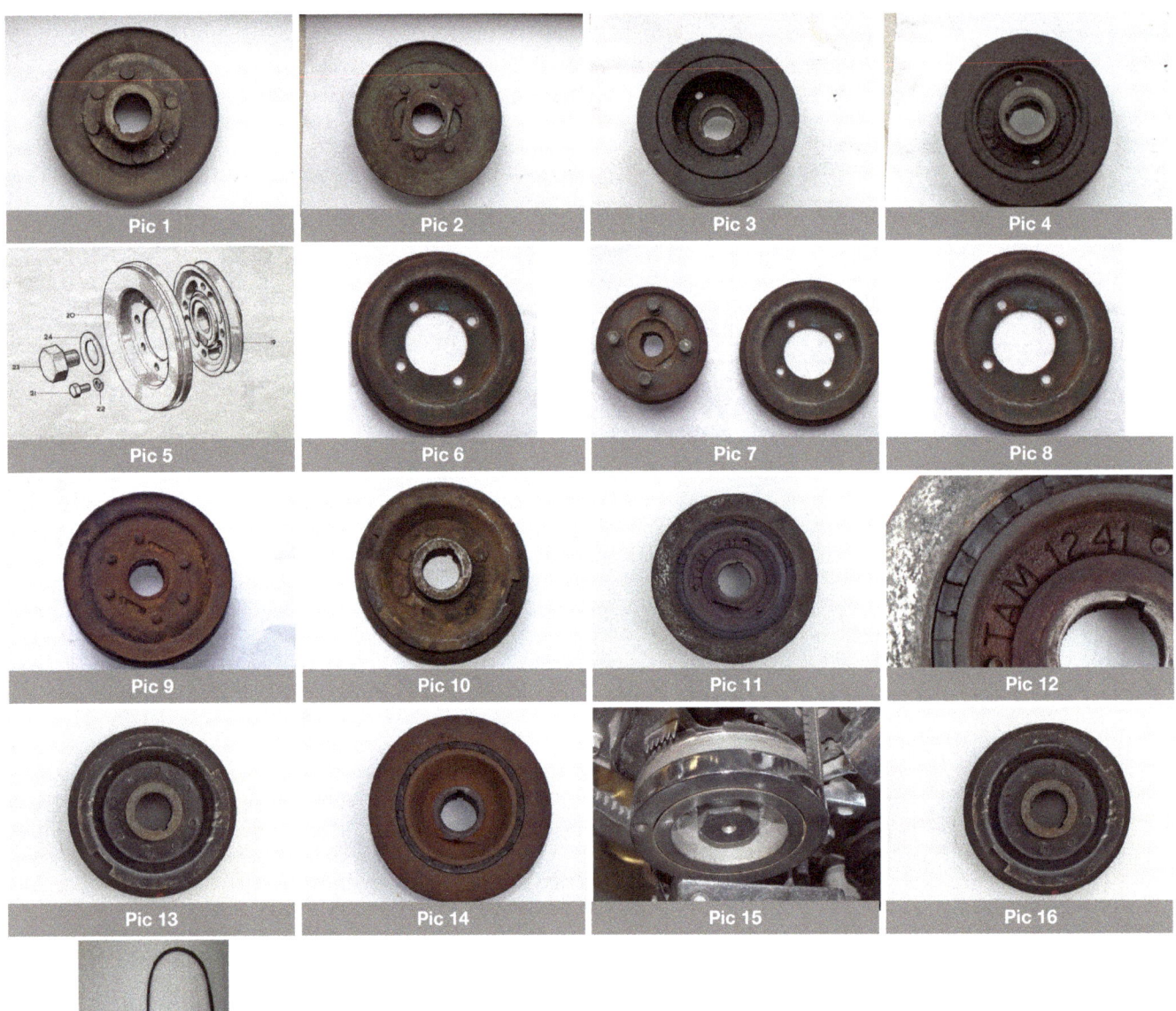

- Twin-point models only.
- Accepts multi vee-type belt.
- No timing plate fitted to back of damper.

Chapter 10
Distributors & drives

DISTRIBUTORS
Listed below are the different types of distributor.
- There are various versions of each type depending on engine size, compression ratio, type of fuel, etc.
- All distributors are of Lucas manufacture, unless otherwise stated.
- All distributors have vacuum units, unless otherwise stated.

Pre A+ distributors
First type
Pic 1 & 2
- 1959 onward.
- Vacuum pipe screws to vacuum unit.
- Fitted with first type of vacuum unit.

Second type
- Vacuum pipe pushes onto vacuum unit. Pic 3

Third type
This is a 40819 'S' distributor. I believe the Mk3 'S' had a different number on it. Pic 4
- Cooper 'S' Mk1/2.
- Vacuum-less distributor.

Fourth type
- Fitted to the Morris Marina.
- Externally the same as Cooper 'S' Marks one, two and three.
- Fitted with different mechanical advance mechanism.
- Vacuum-less distributor.

Fifth type
- Redesigned distributor. See sixth type for shorter clips.
- Vacuum pipe pushes onto vacuum unit.
- Shorter distributor cap retaining clips.

Sixth type
Pic 5
- Redesigned distributor.
- Shorter distributor cap retaining clips.
- Morris Marina 1970 to 1971.
- Vacuum-less distributor.

Seventh type
- Ducellier type distributor.
- Fitted to Mini 998cc, January 1979 onward.
- Fitted to 1275GT Clubman, January 1979 to August 1980.
- Fitted to Allegro, January 1974 to July 1983.

Distributor housings (pre A+)
- Housing without rubber O-ring. Part number 2A612. Pic 6
- Housing with rubber O-ring. Part number 12A1136. Pic 7
- O-ring part number 13H2792.

A+ distributors
The retaining clamp for the A+ distributor changed when the Mini Metro Mk2 was introduced circa 1985.

First type
Pic 8
- Lucas type distributor.
- Fitted with points and condenser.

Second type
Pic 9
- Lucas type distributor.
- Fitted with points and condenser.
- Second type of vacuum unit.

ANATOMY OF THE CLASSIC MINI

Third type
- Ducellier type distributor.
- Fitted with points and condenser.

Fourth type
Pic 10
- October 1982 onward.

- Lucas electronic type.
- Fitted to MG Metro Turbo Mk1.
- Clip-on distributor cap.

Fifth type
Pics 11 & 12

- Lucas electronic type.
- Screw-on distributor cap.

Sixth type
Pic 13
- Circa 1992 onward.
- Mulitplug connector.

DISTRIBUTORS & DRIVES

Drives
First type Pre A+
Pic 14
- 2A139 became 1G2062.
- 2A847 became 1G2062.
- 1G2062.

Second type A+
Pic 15
- Mini Metro Oct 1980 onward.
- Allegro.
- Mini.
- Morris Ital.

Distributor retaining clamps
First type Pre A+
Pic 16
- 1951 to 1980.

Second type A+
Pic 17
- 1980 to circa 1985.
- Round bolt hole.

Third type A+
Pic 18
- Circa 1985 onward.
- Elongated bolt hole.

Distributor part numbers
These distributors listed below are just some of the many variations fitted to the A-Series engine.
   This will hopefully help when trying to choose the correct distributor for your engine.

948cc
12A165/12A62/12A415 These distributors were for use on high-compression engines.
- 12A165 became 12A415.
- 12A62 became 12A415.
- 12A415.

12A167/12A58/12A439 These distributors were for use on low-compression engines.
- 12A167.
- 12A58.
- 12A439.

848cc
- 2A995 became 12A423 for use with premium fuel. (Mini Van.)
- 12A169 became 12A423 for use with premium fuel.
- 12A423 for use with premium fuel.
- 12A97 became 12A129 for use with regular fuel.
- 12A129 for use with regular fuel. (Mini Van low octane fuel.)
- 12A417.

997cc
- 12A300.

1098cc Manual
12G144/12G261/12G443/12G701/12G802/12G918/12G1237 These distributors were for use on high-compression engines.
- 12G144 fitted up to change over to 12G261.
- 12G261 became 12G701.
- 12G443 became 12G701.
- 12G701.
- 12G802.
- 12G918.
- 12G1237.

12G38/12G259/12G439/12G697/12G800/12G1239 These distributors were for use on low-compression engines.
- 12G38 fitted up to change over to 12G259.
- 12G259 became 12G800.
- 12G439 became 12G800.
- 12G697 became 12G800.
- 12G800.
- 12G1239.

1098cc Automatic
- 12G909.
- 12G1218.

1098cc Automatic
- 12G1264 for French market.

998cc Manual
- 12A1187.

998cc Automatic
- 12G909.

1275cc
12G815/12G1260/12G1563/12G1967/12G2856/12G118 These distributors were for use on high-compression engines.
- 12G815 is for 12G coded engines.
- 12G1260 is for both 12H and 12G coded engines.
- 12G1563 is for 12H coded engines.
- 12G1967 is for 12H coded engines.
- 12G2856 is for 12H coded engines.
- 12G118 is for 12H coded engines.

12G1258/12G1117 These distributors were for use on low-compression engines.
- 12G1258 is for 12H coded engines.
- 12G1117 is for 12H coded engines.

Chapter 11
Engine block & upper stabiliser bars

UPPER STABILISER BARS

The 1965 onward automatic bar reappears on the 1990 onward vehicles (engine and gearbox moved forward by 0.375in).

The third type of upper engine stabiliser bar had two bushes and a steel sleeve fitted to the engine end. Pic 1
- 1959 onward. Part number 2A5874. (Three bush type.) Pic 2
- Part number 2A5874 replaced by 21A1020. (Three bush type.) See pic 2
- Modified stabiliser bar. Part number 21A1109. (Four bush type.) Pic 3
- 1965 onward, automatic. Part number 21A1817. (Four bush type.) Pic 4
- 1989 ERA turbo Mini. Part number ERA1020, adjustable. (Four bush type.) Pic 5

948CC ENGINE BLOCKS
Pre A+ engine blocks from 1959 to 1962

All blocks detailed must be considered as finished items. For example: fitted with their cam bearing/s, all oil galleries drilled and plugged, and badges or castings where applicable.

Note, when assembling the oil pump to the engine block it is essential that the bolt lengths are correct and the thread depth in the block is checked to ensure the pump is seated/clamped against the oil pump face in the block.
- All blocks can be identified by noting the casting at the back of the block as 950.
- Oil filter heads fitted, unless otherwise stated.
- All blocks have nine head studs, unless otherwise stated.
- All blocks have tappet chests, unless otherwise stated.
- All blocks have dipstick tubes, unless otherwise stated.

FRONT-WHEEL DRIVE
One-off Zagato-bodied Mini (believed based on Mini Van).

First type 948cc front-wheel drive
See Mighty Minis (ISBN 094660911X) page 10.
- Transverse main caps.
- One camshaft bearing.
- Four core plugs.
- No dipstick tube. Dipstick fits directly into block.

Second type 948cc front-wheel drive
Same as first type, but I was able to photograph this one. Pics 6-10
- Transverse main caps.
- One camshaft bearing.
- Four core plugs.
- No dipstick tube. Dipstick fits directly into block.

Third type 948cc big bore front-wheel drive
- Refer to flat-faced engine blocks.

848CC ENGINE BLOCKS
Pre A+ and A+ engine blocks from 1959 to 1982

All blocks detailed must be considered as finished items. For example: fitted with their cam bearing/s, all oil galleries drilled and plugged, and badges or

ENGINE BLOCK & UPPER STABILISER BARS

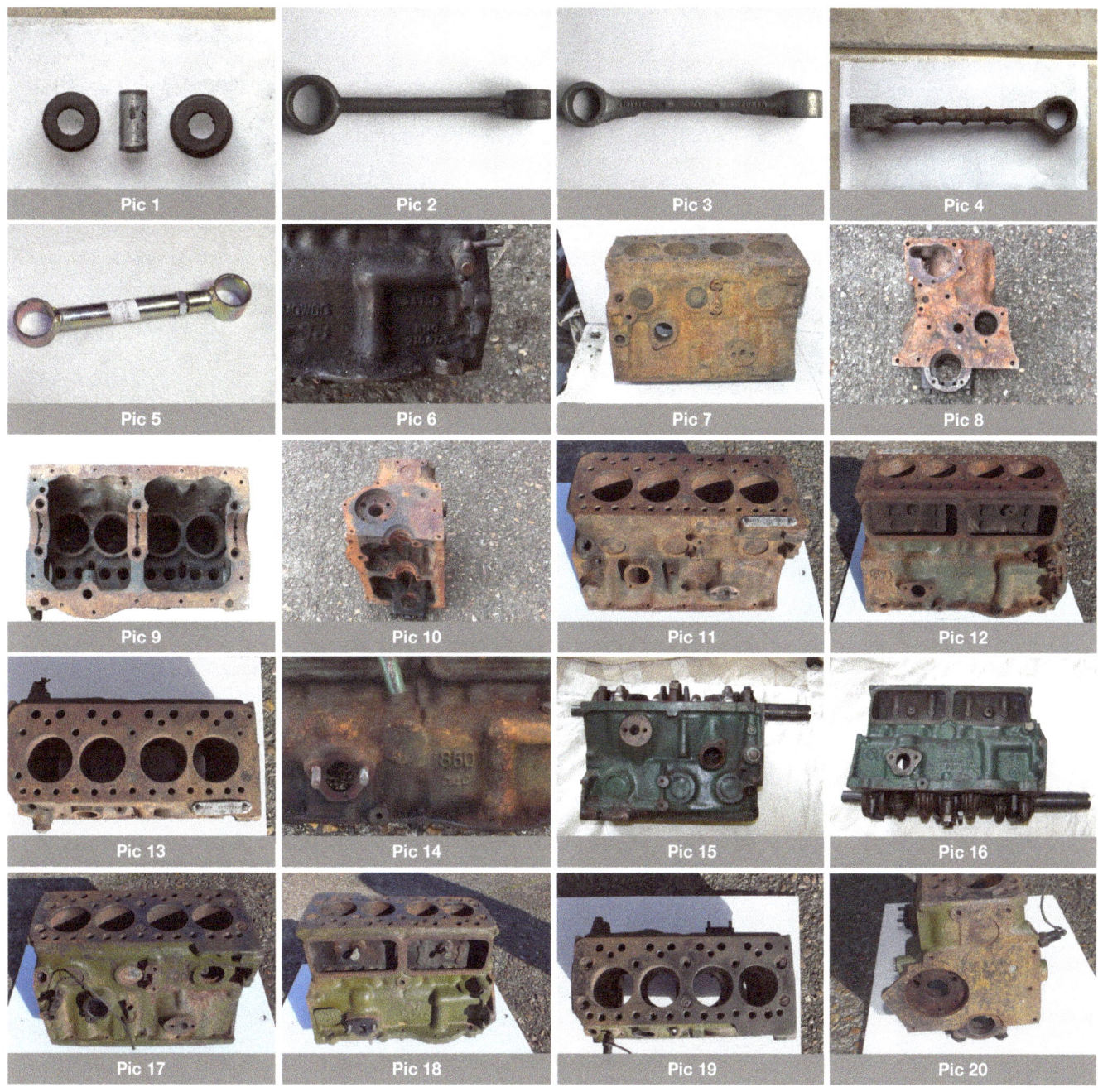

Pic 1 | Pic 2 | Pic 3 | Pic 4
Pic 5 | Pic 6 | Pic 7 | Pic 8
Pic 9 | Pic 10 | Pic 11 | Pic 12
Pic 13 | Pic 14 | Pic 15 | Pic 16
Pic 17 | Pic 18 | Pic 19 | Pic 20

castings where applicable.
Note, when assembling the oil pump to the engine block it is essential that the bolt lengths are correct and the thread depth in the block is checked to ensure the pump is seated/clamped against the oil pump face in the block.

- Oil filter heads fitted, unless otherwise stated.
- All blocks have nine head studs, unless otherwise stated.
- All blocks have tappet chests, unless otherwise stated.
- All blocks have dipstick tubes, unless otherwise stated.
- Some thin-flange transverse blocks have inline drillings, flywheel end of engine.
- Oil pump priming plug facility fitted, unless otherwise stated.

ANATOMY OF THE CLASSIC MINI

FRONT-WHEEL DRIVE MANUAL

First type 848cc front-wheel drive
Pics 11-13
- 850 cast into back of block by the engine front plate.
- Thin-flange.
- One camshaft bearing.
- Transverse rear main cap.
- Four core plugs.
- No dipstick tube. Dipstick fits directly into block.

Second type
Pic 14
- Two raised circles cast into back of block. One circle has 850 cast inside it. (This is actually a factory replacement using a 950 block.)
- Thin-flange.
- One camshaft bearing.
- Transverse rear main cap.
- Four core plugs.
- No dipstick tube. Dipstick fits directly into block.

Third type 848cc front-wheel drive
- Transverse rear main cap.
- Thick-flange.
- One camshaft bearing.
- Four core plugs.
- No dipstick tube. Dipstick fits directly into block.

Fourth type 848cc front-wheel drive (1969 onward)
- Transverse rear main cap.
- Facility for mechanical fuel pump.
- Thick-flange.
- One camshaft bearing.
- Four core plugs.
- No dipstick tube. Dipstick fits directly into block.

Fifth type 848cc front-wheel drive (late block)
Pics 15 & 16
- Casting number 12A 450 cast into back of the block.
- No oil priming plug facility fitted.
- Transverse rear main cap.
- Facility for mechanical fuel pump.
- Thick-flange.
- One camshaft bearing.
- Four core plugs.
- No dipstick tube. Dipstick fits directly into block.

Sixth type 848cc front-wheel drive
- Casting number 12A 450 cast into back of the block.
- No oil priming plug facility fitted.
- Transverse rear main cap.
- Facility for mechanical fuel pump.
- Thick-flange.
- One camshaft bearing.
- Four core plugs.
- No dipstick tube. Dipstick fits directly into block.
- One extra drilling to take fastening bolts on front face of block for timing chain tensioner. [1979 to 1980.]

Seventh type 848cc front-wheel drive (Authi Mini [Spanish factory])
Pics 17-20
- Pre A+.
- Thick-flange.
- Aluminium 850 badge riveted to back of block.
- Head gasket face (deck) different from UK.
- The Authi factory was in Spain (hotter climate).
- One camshaft bearing.
- Four core plugs.
- No dipstick tube. Dipstick fits directly into block.

A+ blocks 1980 onward
- All A+ blocks have nine head studs fitted from the factory.
- All blocks have oil filter heads in standard position, unless otherwise stated.
- All blocks have transverse main caps, unless otherwise stated.
- All A+ blocks were Thick-flange.
- All A+ blocks have dipstick fitted directly into block. No dipstick tube.

Eighth type 848cc front-wheel drive (Chilean Metro A+)
- Main bearing shells in caps have offset locating tangs.
- A+ distributor.
- External ribbing on block.
- Painted yellow from factory.
- Facility for mechanical fuel pump.
- Probably fitted with one camshaft bearing.
- No oil pump priming facility.
- One extra drilling to take fastening bolts on front face of block for timing chain tensioner.
- No dipstick tube. Dipstick fits directly into block.

Front-wheel drive automatic

848cc Automatic front-wheel drive
- 1965 onward.
- Thin-flange.
- Transverse rear main cap.
- Oil pump mounting face, unique to automatic.
- One camshaft bearing.
- Four core plugs.
- Dipstick fits into bellhousing.

997CC BLOCKS PRE A+ ENGINE BLOCKS FROM 1961 TO 1964

All blocks detailed must be considered as finished items. For example: fitted with their cam bearing/s, all oil galleries drilled and plugged, and badges or castings where applicable.

Note, when assembling the oil pump to the engine block it is essential that the bolt lengths are correct, and the thread depth in the block is checked to ensure the pump is seated/clamped against the oil pump face in the block.
- Oil filter heads fitted, unless otherwise stated.
- All blocks have nine head studs, unless otherwise stated.
- All blocks have tappet chests, unless otherwise stated.
- All blocks have dipstick tubes, unless otherwise stated.
- Some thin-flange transverse blocks have inline drillings, flywheel end of engine.

ENGINE BLOCK & UPPER STABILISER BARS

997cc front-wheel drive (Austin and Morris Cooper)
- Thin-flange.
- Transverse rear main cap.
- 1000 cast into back of block.
- One stud screwed into fuel pump casting boss.
- Three camshaft bearings.
- Four core plugs.
- No dipstick tube. Dipstick fits directly into block.

1098CC ENGINE BLOCKS
PRE A+ & A+ ENGINE BLOCKS FROM 1962 TO 1981

All blocks detailed must be considered as finished items. For example: fitted with their cam bearing/s, all oil galleries drilled and plugged, and badges or castings where applicable.

Note, when assembling the oil pump to the engine block it is essential that the bolt lengths are correct and the thread depth in the block is checked to ensure the pump is seated/clamped against the oil pump face in the block.
- Oil filter heads fitted, unless otherwise stated.
- All blocks have nine head studs, unless otherwise stated.
- All blocks have tappet chests, unless otherwise stated.
- 1098cc and 998cc blocks have the same bore size and the same deck height (except South African big bore 1098cc).
- Some thin-flange transverse blocks have inline drillings, flywheel end of engine.
- Oil pump priming plug facility fitted unless otherwise stated.
- 1098cc blocks were all fitted with dipstick location tubes in the block, Except for A+ blocks.

Front-wheel drive manual
First type 1098cc front-wheel drive (Morris 1100, AD016, etc. 1962 onward)
- Two circles cast into centre of rear of block.
- 1100 cast into block inside circle.
- Transverse rear main cap.
- Thin-flange.
- One stud screwed into fuel pump casting boss.
- 1.75in main bearings.
- Three camshaft bearings.
- Four core plugs.

Second type 1098cc front-wheel drive (AD016)
- Aluminium 1100 badge riveted to back of block.
- Transverse rear main cap.
- Thin-flange.
- One stud screwed into fuel pump casting boss.
- 1.75in main bearings.
- Three camshaft bearings.
- Four core plugs.

Third type 1098cc front-wheel drive (AD016) with positive crankcase ventilation (non-UK sales cars)
Pics 21-24
- Aluminium 1100 badge riveted to back of block.
- Transverse rear main cap.
- Thin-flange.
- 1.75in main bearings.
- Three camshaft bearings.
- Four core plugs.

Fourth type 1098cc front-wheel drive (Morris 1100cc, AD016 etc. Circa 1967 onward and Mini Clubman 1975 onward)
- Transverse rear main cap.
- Thick-flange.
- 1.75in main bearings.
- Aluminium 1100 badge riveted to back of block.
- Three camshaft bearings.
- Four core plugs.

Fifth type 1098cc front-wheel drive (AD016, Mini Clubman 1975 onward & Mini 1100 Special)
- When fitted to Clubman has facility for mechanical fuel pump.
- Transverse rear main cap.
- Thick-flange.
- 1.75in main bearings.
- Aluminium 1100 badge riveted to back of block.
- Three camshaft bearings.
- Four core plugs.
- No oil priming plug facility fitted at the back of the block.

Sixth type 1098cc front-wheel drive (late Mini Clubman)
- Transverse rear main cap.
- Thick-flange.
- 1.75in main bearings.
- Aluminium 1100 badge riveted to back of block.
- When fitted to Clubman has facility for mechanical fuel pump.
- Three camshaft bearings.
- Four core plugs.
- No oil priming plug facility fitted at the back of the block.
- One extra drilling to take fastening bolts on front face of block for timing chain tensioner.

Built in South Africa Mini Clubman (Marina Block derivative)
1098cc front-wheel drive (South African big bore 1098cc Mini)
- 2in non 'S' main caps.
- No tappet chests.
- Oil filter screwed to block below head.
- 1275 Marina block.
- No thread in block main oil gallery from gearbox.
- 'S' camshaft bearings (three).
- Five core plugs.
- 1098 embossed on main caps.
- Transverse main caps.

TRANSITIONAL/SEMI A+ PRE 1980 ALLEGRO
Seventh type 1098cc front-wheel drive
- Transverse rear main cap.
- One extra drilling in front face of block for timing chain tensioner.
- Thick-flange.

ANATOMY OF THE CLASSIC MINI

Pic 21

Pic 22

Pic 23

Pic 24

- 1.75in main bearings.
- Some external ribbing (not as much as A+).
- Facility for mechanical fuel pump.
- Three camshaft bearings.
- Four core plugs.

A+ blocks 1980 onward
- All A+ blocks have nine head studs fitted from the factory.
- All blocks have oil filter heads in standard position unless otherwise stated.
- All blocks have transverse main caps unless otherwise stated.
- 1098cc and 998cc blocks have the same bore size and the same deck height.
- All A+ blocks have dipstick fitted directly into block. No dipstick tube.

Eighth type 1098cc front-wheel drive (Mini Clubman Estate last of the 1098ccs used in Minis)
- Main bearing shells in caps have offset locating tangs.
- A+ distributor.
- 1.75in main bearings.
- External ribbing on block.
- Painted yellow from factory.
- Facility for mechanical fuel pump.
- Three camshaft bearings.
- Four core plugs.
- WFM1028 cast into back of block.

Front-wheel drive automatic
First type 1098cc automatic front-wheel drive (Morris 1100, AD016, etc, 1965 onward)
- Transverse rear main cap.

Pic 25

- Oil pump mounting face, unique to automatic.
- 1.75in main bearings.
- Three camshaft bearings.
- Four core plugs.
- Dipstick fits into bellhousing.
- Thin-flange block.

Second type 1098cc automatic front-wheel drive (Morris 1100, AD016, etc. Circa 1967 onward)
Pic 25
- Transverse rear main cap.
- Oil pump mounting face, unique to automatic.
- 1.75in main bearings.
- Three camshaft bearings.
- Four core plugs.
- Dipstick fits into bellhousing.
- Thick-flange block.

Third type 1098cc Automatic front-wheel drive
- Transverse rear main cap.
- Oil pump mounting face, unique to automatic.
- 1.75in main bearings.
- Three camshaft bearings.
- Four core plugs.
- Dipstick fits into bellhousing.
- Thick-flange block.
- No oil priming plug facility fitted at the back of the block.

Fourth type 1098cc automatic front-wheel drive
- Transverse rear main cap.
- Oil pump mounting face, unique to automatic.
- 1.75in main bearings.
- Three camshaft bearings.
- Four core plugs.
- Dipstick fits into bellhousing.
- Thick-flange block.
- No oil priming plug facility fitted at the back of the block.
- One extra drilling to take fastening bolts on front face of block for timing chain tensioner.

A+ blocks 1980 onward
- All A+ blocks have nine head studs fitted from the factory.
- All blocks have transverse main caps, unless otherwise stated.
- 1098cc and 998cc blocks have the same bore size and the same deck height.
- All A+ blocks have dipstick fitted directly into block. No dipstick tube.

Fifth type 1098cc automatic front-wheel drive (Mini Metro MkII)
- Central locating tangs on shells in main bearing caps.
- Oil pump mounting face unique to automatic.
- 1.75in main bearings.
- A+ distributor.
- External ribbing on block.
- Three camshaft bearings.
- Four core plugs.
- One extra drilling in front face of block for timing chain tensioner.
- Dipstick fits into bellhousing.
- WFM1028 cast into both back of

ENGINE BLOCK & UPPER STABILISER BARS

block and front of block below cylinder head.

998CC ENGINE BLOCKS
PRE A+ & A+ ENGINE BLOCKS FROM 1962 TO 1992

All blocks detailed must be considered as finished items. For example: fitted with their cam bearing/s, all oil galleries drilled and plugged, and badges or castings where applicable.

Note, when assembling the oil pump to the engine block it is essential that the bolt lengths are correct and the thread depth in the block is checked to ensure the pump is seated/clamped against the oil pump face in the block.
- Oil filter heads fitted, unless otherwise stated.
- All blocks have nine head studs, unless otherwise stated.
- All blocks have tappet chests, unless otherwise stated.
- All blocks have dipstick tubes, unless otherwise stated.
- 1098cc and 998cc blocks have the same bore size and the same deck height (except South African big bore 1098cc).
- Some thin-flange transverse blocks have inline drillings, flywheel end of engine.
- Oil pump priming plug facility fitted, unless otherwise stated.

Front-wheel drive manual

For images of 998cc blocks please see 1098cc blocks (except for the badging, the blocks are identical like for like).

First type 998cc front-wheel drive (Riley Elf and Wolseley Hornet also Mini)
- Transverse rear main cap.
- Thin-flange.
- Aluminium 1000 badge riveted to back of block.
- One stud screwed into fuel pump casting boss.
- Three camshaft bearings.
- Four core plugs.

Second type 998cc front-wheel drive with positive crankcase ventilation
- Transverse rear main cap.
- Thin-flange.
- One short bolt screwed into fuel pump casting boss.
- Aluminium 1000 badge riveted to back of block.
- Three camshaft bearings.
- Four core plugs.

Third type 998cc front-wheel drive
- Transverse rear main cap.
- Thick-flange.
- One short bolt screwed into fuel pump casting boss.
- Aluminium 1000 badge riveted to back of block.
- Three camshaft bearings.
- Four core plugs.

Fourth type 998cc front-wheel drive (1969 onward)
- Transverse rear main cap.
- Facility for mechanical fuel pump.
- Thick-flange.
- Aluminium 1000 badge riveted to back of block.
- Three camshaft bearings.
- Four core plugs.

Fifth type 998cc front-wheel drive
- Transverse rear main cap.
- Facility for mechanical fuel pump.
- Thick-flange.
- Aluminium 1000 badge riveted to back of block.
- Three camshaft bearings.
- Four core plugs.
- No oil pump priming facility.

Sixth type 998cc front-wheel drive
- Transverse rear main cap.
- Facility for mechanical fuel pump.
- Thick-flange.
- Aluminium 1000 badge riveted to back of block.
- Three camshaft bearings.
- Four core plugs.
- No oil pump priming facility.
- One extra drilling to take fastening bolts on front face of block for timing chain tensioner.

A+ blocks 1980 onward
- All A+ blocks have nine head studs fitted from the factory.
- All blocks have oil filter heads in standard position, unless otherwise stated.
- All blocks have transverse main caps, unless otherwise stated.
- 1098cc and 998cc blocks have the same bore size and the same deck height.
- All A+ blocks were Thick-flange.
- All A+ blocks have dipstick fitted directly into block, no dipstick tube.

Seventh type 998cc front-wheel drive (Allegro, Metro and Mini)
- Main bearing shells in caps have offset locating tangs.
- A+ distributor.
- External ribbing on block.
- Painted yellow from factory.
- Three camshaft bearings.
- Four core plugs.
- WFM1028 cast in back of block.
- One extra drilling to take fastening bolts on front face of block for timing chain tensioner.

Eighth type 998cc front-wheel drive (last of the 998 Mini only)
Pics 26-29
- Central locating tangs on shells in main bearing caps.
- A+ distributor.
- External ribbing on block.
- Painted yellow from factory.
- Three camshaft bearings.
- Four core plugs.
- WFM1028 cast into both back of block and front of block below cylinder head.
- One extra drilling to take fastening bolts on front face of block for timing chain tensioner.

ANATOMY OF THE CLASSIC MINI

Pic 26 · Pic 27 · Pic 28 · Pic 29
Pic 30 · Pic 31 · Pic 32 · Pic 33
Pic 34 · Pic 35 · Pic 36 · Pic 37

Front-wheel drive automatic

First type 998cc automatic front-wheel drive 1965 onward
- Transverse rear main cap.
- Oil pump mounting face unique to automatic.
- Aluminium 1000 badge riveted to back of block.
- Three camshaft bearings.
- Four core plugs.
- Dipstick fits into bellhousing.
- Thin-flange block.

Second type 998cc automatic front-wheel drive
- Transverse rear main cap.
- Oil pump mounting face unique to automatic.
- Aluminium 1000 badge riveted to back of block.
- Three camshaft bearings.
- Four core plugs.
- Dipstick fits into bellhousing.
- Thick-flange block.

Third type
- Transverse rear main cap.
- Oil pump mounting face unique to automatic.
- Aluminium 1000 badge riveted to back of block.
- Three camshaft bearings.
- Four core plugs.
- Dipstick fits into bellhousing.
- Thick-flange block.
- No oil pump priming facility.

Fourth type 998cc automatic front-wheel drive
Pics 30-37
- Transverse rear main cap.
- Oil pump mounting face unique to automatic.
- Aluminium 1000 badge riveted to back of block.
- Three camshaft bearings.
- Four core plugs.
- Dipstick fits into bellhousing.
- Thick-flange block.
- No oil pump priming facility.
- One extra drilling to take fastening bolts on front face of block for timing chain tensioner.

A+ blocks 1980 onward
- All A+ blocks have nine head studs fitted from the factory.
- All blocks have transverse main caps unless otherwise stated.
- 1098cc and 998cc blocks have the same bore size and the same deck height.
- All A+ blocks were Thick-flange.
- All A+ blocks have dipstick fitted directly into block, no dipstick tube.

Fifth type 998cc automatic front-wheel drive (Mini only)
- Oil pump mounting face unique to automatic.
- Main bearing shells in caps have offset locating tangs.
- A+ distributor.
- External ribbing on block.

ENGINE BLOCK & UPPER STABILISER BARS

- Three camshaft bearings.
- Four core plugs.
- Dipstick fits into bellhousing.
- One extra drilling to take fastening bolts on front face of block for timing chain tensioner.
- WFM1028 cast into back of block.

Sixth type 998cc automatic front-wheel drive (last of the 998cc automatics Mini only). Circa 1985 onward

- Central locating tangs on shells in main bearing caps.
- Oil pump mounting face unique to automatic.
- A+ distributor.
- External ribbing on block.
- Three camshaft bearings.
- Four core plugs.
- Dipstick fits into bellhousing.
- One extra drilling to take fastening bolts on front face of block for timing chain tensioner.
- WFM1028 cast into both back of block and front of block below cylinder head.

1071CC COOPER S ENGINE BLOCKS

All Cooper S blocks have a four-digit number stamped into the main bearing caps. This number can also be found on the water pump mounting face.

Pre A+ engine blocks from March 1963 to 1964

All blocks detailed must be considered as finished items. For example: fitted with their cam bearing/s, all oil galleries drilled and plugged, and badges or castings where applicable.
Note, when assembling the oil pump to the engine block it is essential that the bolt lengths are correct and the thread depth in the block is checked to ensure the pump is seated/clamped against the oil pump face in the block.
- Oil filter heads fitted, unless otherwise stated.
- All blocks have nine head studs, unless otherwise stated.
- All blocks have tappet chests, unless otherwise stated.
- All blocks have dipstick tubes, unless otherwise stated.
- 1071cc, 1275cc & 970cc 'S' type blocks all have same bore size.
- Some thin-flange transverse blocks have inline drillings, flywheel end of engine.
- Oil pump priming plug facility fitted, unless otherwise stated.

First type 1071cc 'S' front-wheel drive (Austin and Morris Cooper S)

Pics 38-42

DAS (David Scarbro) advises that all 1071cc 'S' had six main cap bolts from the factory.
- Thin-flange.
- 2in 'S' main caps.
- Drilled and tapped for ten head studs and one head bolt.
- Aluminium 1070 badge riveted to back of block.
- One stud screwed into fuel pump boss.
- Two raised bosses (rear of block) over main oil gallery.
- 'S' camshaft bearings (three).
- 'S' core plugs (four).
- AEG151 cast into back of block.

Second type 1071cc 'S' front-wheel drive with positive crankcase ventilation

Looks the same as block above except for bolt screwed into fuel pump casting boss.
- Thin-flange.
- 2in 'S' main caps.
- Drilled and tapped for ten head studs and one head bolt.
- Aluminium 1070 badge riveted to back of block.
- Two raised bosses (rear of block) over main oil gallery.
- One short bolt screwed into fuel pump casting boss.
- 'S' camshaft bearings (three).
- 'S' core plugs (four).
- AEG151 cast into back of block.

970CC COOPER S ENGINE BLOCKS

All Cooper S blocks have a four-digit number stamped into the main bearing caps. This number can also be found on the water pump mounting face.

Pre A+ engine blocks from 1964 to 1965

All blocks detailed must be considered as finished items. For example: fitted with their cam bearing/s, all oil galleries drilled and plugged, and badges or castings where applicable.
   Note, when assembling the oil pump to the engine block it is essential that the bolt lengths are correct and the thread depth in the block is checked to ensure the pump is seated/clamped against the oil pump face in the block.
- Oil filter heads fitted unless otherwise stated.
- All blocks have nine head studs, unless otherwise stated.
- All blocks have tappet chests, unless otherwise stated.
- All blocks have dipstick tubes, unless otherwise stated.
- 1071cc, 1275cc & 970cc 'S' type blocks all have same bore size.
- Some thin-flange transverse blocks have inline drillings, flywheel end of engine.
- Oil pump priming plug facility fitted, unless otherwise stated.

First type 970cc 'S' front-wheel drive (Austin and Morris Cooper S)

Pics 43-46
- 2in 'S' main caps.
- Drilled and tapped for ten head studs and one head bolt.
- Main caps retained by studs and nuts.
- One stud screwed into fuel pump boss.
- Two raised bosses (rear of block) over main oil gallery.
- Aluminium 970 badge riveted to back of block.
- 'S' camshaft bearings (three).
- 'S' core plugs (four).
- AEG151 cast into back of block.
- Thin-flange block.

ANATOMY OF THE CLASSIC MINI

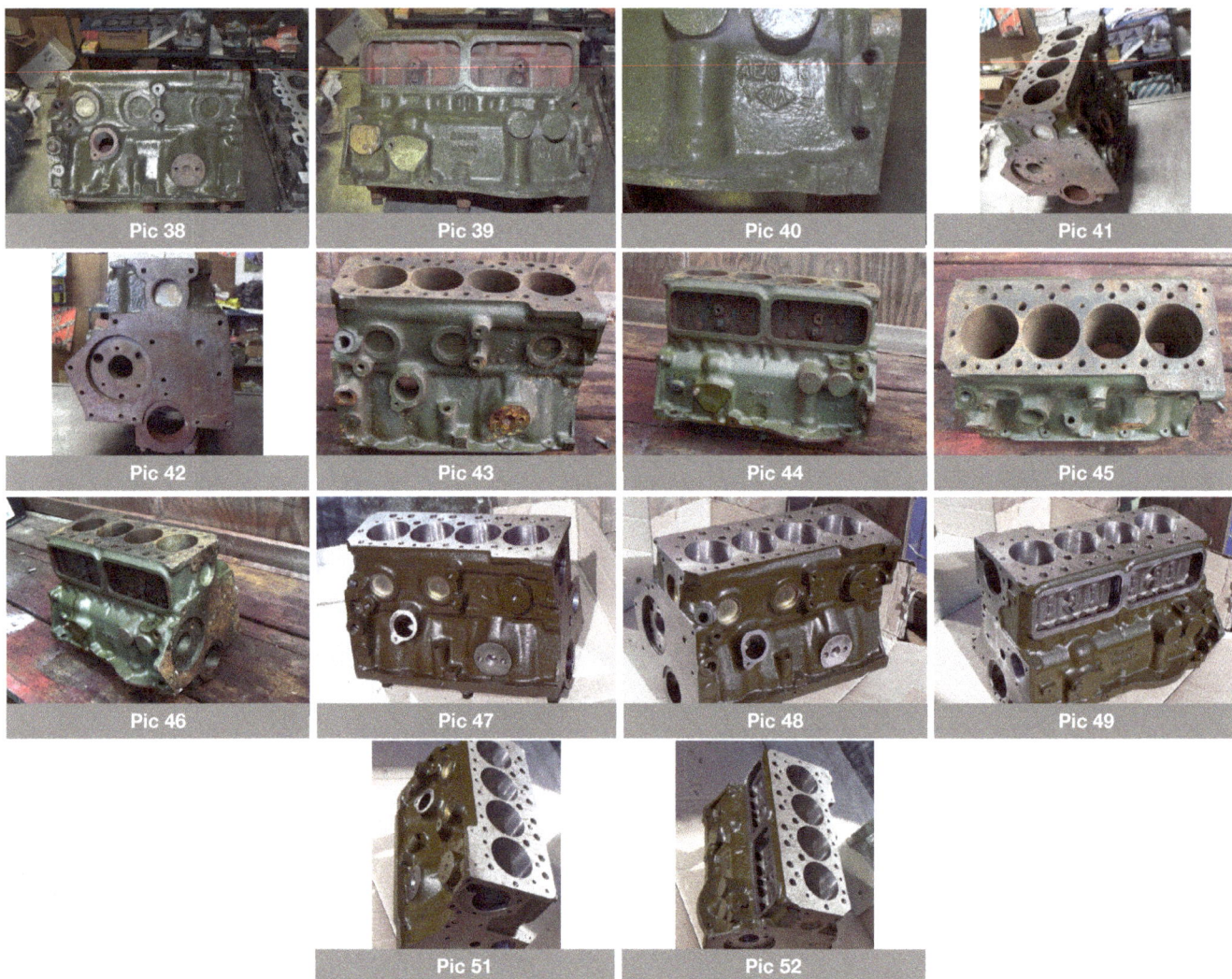

Second type 970cc 'S' front-wheel drive with positive crankcase ventilation

Looks the same as block above except for bolt screwed into fuel pump casting boss.
- 2in 'S' main caps.
- One short bolt screwed into fuel pump casting boss.
- Drilled and tapped for ten head studs and one head bolt.
- Main caps retained by studs and nuts.
- Two raised circular bosses (rear of block) over main oil gallery.
- Aluminium 970 badge riveted to back of block.
- 'S' camshaft bearings (three).
- 'S' core plugs (four).
- AEG151 cast into back of block.
- Thin-flange block.

Third type 970cc 'S' front-wheel drive

Pics 47-52

Engine block source: David A Scarbro
- Factory exchange unit.
- 2in 'S' main caps.
- Thick-flange (machined down 1275 thick-flange 'S' block).
- Two raised circular bosses (rear of block) over main oil gallery.
- Drilled and tapped for ten head studs and one head bolt.
- Main caps retained by studs and nuts.
- 'S' camshaft bearings (three).
- 'S' core plugs (four).
- Note, this particular block has a water jacket heater in the front core plug hole.

Fourth type 970cc 'S' front-wheel drive

Looks the same as 1275cc thick-flange block with horizontal reinforcing webs between front core plugs.
- Factory exchange unit.
- 2in 'S' main caps.
- Thick-flange (machined down Mk3 1275 thick-flange 'S' block).

ENGINE BLOCK & UPPER STABILISER BARS

- Two raised circular bosses (rear of block) over main oil gallery.
- Drilled and tapped for ten head studs and one head bolt.
- Main caps retained by studs and nuts.
- 'S' camshaft bearings (three).
- 'S' core plugs (four).
- Two horizontal reinforcing webs between front core plugs.

1275CC ENGINE BLOCKS PRE A+ & A+ ENGINE BLOCKS FROM 1964 TO 2000

All blocks detailed must be considered as finished items. For example: fitted with their cam bearing/s, all oil galleries drilled and plugged, and badges or castings where applicable.

Note, when assembling the oil pump to the engine block it is essential that the bolt lengths are correct and the thread depth in the block is checked to ensure the pump is seated/clamped against the oil pump face in the block.

- Oil filter heads fitted in standard position, unless otherwise stated.
- All blocks have nine head studs, tappet chests and dipstick tubes, unless otherwise stated.
- 1071cc, 1275cc & 970cc 'S' type blocks all have same bore size.
- Some thin-flange transverse blocks have inline drillings, flywheel end of engine.
- Oil pump priming plug facility fitted, unless otherwise stated.

Front-wheel drive manual

For all Cooper S blocks, first, second, third and fifth, please note the following.
- All Cooper S blocks have a four-digit number stamped into the main bearing caps. This number can also be found on the water pump mounting face.
- All post 1969 non 'S' 1275cc engine blocks fitted to the 1275GT Mini and Allegro have facility for mechanical fuel pump.

First type 1275cc 'S' front-wheel drive (Austin and Morris Cooper S)

- 2in 'S' main caps.
- Thin-flange.
- Oil pump retained by three bolts.
- Main caps retained by studs and nuts.
- Drilled and tapped for ten head studs and one head bolt.
- One stud screwed into fuel pump boss.
- Aluminium 1275 badge riveted to back of block.
- Two raised bosses (rear of block) over main oil gallery.
- 'S' camshaft bearings (three).
- 'S' core plugs (four).
- AEG312 cast into back of block.

Second type 1275cc 'S' front-wheel drive with positive crankcase ventilation

Looks the same as block above except for bolt screwed into fuel pump casting boss.
- 2in 'S' main caps.
- Thin-flange.
- Oil pump retained by three bolts.
- Main caps retained by studs and nuts.
- Drilled and tapped for ten head studs and one head bolt.
- One short bolt screwed into fuel pump casting boss.
- Aluminium 1275 badge riveted to back of block.
- Two raised bosses (rear of block) over main oil gallery.
- 'S' camshaft bearings (three).
- 'S' core plugs (four).
- AEG312 cast into back of block.

Third type 1275cc 'S' front-wheel drive with positive crankcase ventilation

Pics 53-62
- 2in 'S' main caps.
- Thick-flange.
- Oil pump retained by three bolts.
- Main caps retained by studs and nuts.
- Drilled and tapped for ten head studs and one head bolt.
- One short bolt screwed into fuel pump casting boss.
- Two raised bosses (rear of block) over main oil gallery.
- Aluminium 1275 badge riveted to back of block.
- 'S' camshaft bearings (three).
- 'S' core plugs (four).
- AEG312 and AEG634 cast into back of block.
- It is also possible to come across a Thick-flange 1275cc 'S' block with only AEG312 cast into the back of the block.

Fourth type 1275cc non 'S' front-wheel drive (Morris 1300 (AD016), etc)

Pics 63 & 64
- 2in non 'S' main caps.
- Oil pump retained by four bolts.
- No tappet chests.
- Two raised bosses (rear of block) over main oil gallery.
- Aluminium 1275 badge riveted to back of block.
- 'S' camshaft bearings (three).
- Five core plugs.
- Thin-flange.

Fifth type 1275cc 'S' front-wheel drive (last of the 1275 'S' blocks)

Pics 65-68 (Courtesy Peter Giffen)
- Horizontal reinforcement between front core plugs.
- 2in 'S' main caps.
- Drilled and tapped for ten head studs and one head bolt.
- Thick-flange.
- Oil pump retained by three bolts.
- Main caps retained by studs and nuts.
- Two raised bosses (rear of block) over main oil gallery.
- One short bolt screwed into fuel pump casting boss.
- Aluminium 1275 badge riveted to back of block.
- 'S' camshaft bearings (three).
- 'S' core plugs (four).

Sixth type 1275cc front-wheel drive

- 2in non 'S' main caps.
- Oil pump retained by four bolts.
- Window above centre main bearing in block.
- No tappet chests.

ANATOMY OF THE CLASSIC MINI

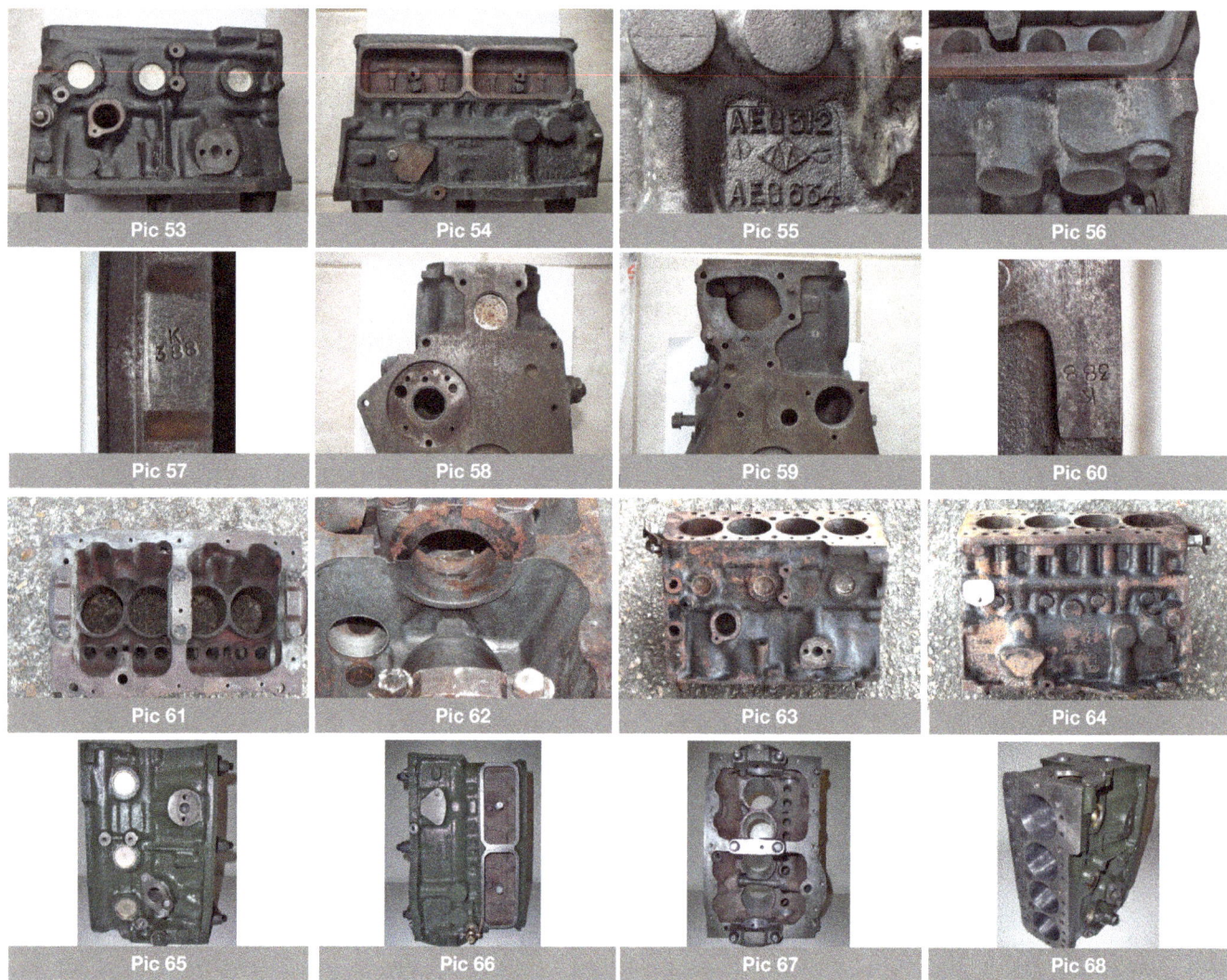

Pic 53 · Pic 54 · Pic 55 · Pic 56 · Pic 57 · Pic 58 · Pic 59 · Pic 60 · Pic 61 · Pic 62 · Pic 63 · Pic 64 · Pic 65 · Pic 66 · Pic 67 · Pic 68

- Two raised bosses (rear of block) over main oil gallery.
- Aluminium 1275 badge riveted to back of block.
- 'S' camshaft bearings (three).
- Five core plugs.
- Thick-flange.

Seventh type 1275cc front-wheel drive

- 2in non 'S' main caps.
- Oil pump retained by four bolts.
- Window above centre main bearing in block.
- No tappet chests.

- Two raised bosses (rear of block) over main oil gallery.
- Aluminium 1275 badge riveted to back of block.
- 'S' camshaft bearings (three).
- Five core plugs.
- Thick-flange.
- No oil pump priming facility.

Eighth type 1275cc front-wheel drive (Austin and Morris 1300 GT)

- 2in non 'S' main caps.
- Oil pump retained by four bolts.
- Window above centre main bearing in block.
- Ten head studs and one head bolt.

- No tappet chests.
- Two raised bosses (rear of block) over main oil gallery.
- Aluminium 1275 badge riveted to back of block.
- 'S' camshaft bearings (three).
- Five core plugs.
- Thick-flange.

Ninth type 1275cc front-wheel drive (Austin and Morris 1300 (AD016) GT)

Pics 69-76

- 2in non 'S' main caps.
- Oil pump retained by four bolts.
- Window above centre main bearing

ENGINE BLOCK & UPPER STABILISER BARS

in block.
- Ten head studs and one head bolt.
- No tappet chests.
- Two raised bosses (rear of block) over main oil gallery.
- Aluminium 1275 badge riveted to back of block.
- 'S' camshaft bearings (three).
- Five core plugs.
- Thick-flange.
- No oil pump priming facility.

Tenth type 1275cc front-wheel drive
Pics 77-82
- 2in non 'S' main caps.
- Oil pump retained by four bolts.
- No window above centre main bearing in block.
- No tappet chests.
- Two raised bosses (rear of block) over main oil gallery.
- Aluminium 1275 badge riveted to back of block.
- 'S' camshaft bearings (three).
- Five core plugs.
- Thick-flange.
- No oil pump priming facility.

Eleventh type 1275cc front-wheel drive (Austin and Morris 1300 GT (AD016))
- 2in non 'S' main caps.
- Oil pump retained by four bolts.
- No window above centre main bearing in block.
- Ten head studs and one head bolt.
- No tappet chests.
- Two raised bosses (rear of block) over main oil gallery.
- Aluminium 1275 badge riveted to back of block.
- 'S' camshaft bearings (three).
- Five core plugs.
- Thick-flange.
- No oil pump priming facility.

Twelfth type 1275cc front-wheel drive
- 2in non 'S' main caps.
- Oil pump retained by four bolts.
- No window above centre main bearing in block.
- No tappet chests.
- Two raised bosses (rear of block) over main oil gallery.
- Aluminium 1275 badge riveted to back of block.
- 'S' camshaft bearings (three).
- Five core plugs.
- Thick-flange.
- No oil pump priming facility.
- One extra drilling to take fastening bolt on front face of block for timing chain tensioner.

TRANSITIONAL/SEMI A+ PRE 1980 ALLEGRO
Thirteenth type 1275cc front-wheel drive
- 2in non 'S' main caps.
- Oil pump retained by four bolts.
- One extra drilling in front face of block for timing chain tensioner.
- No tappet chests.
- Some external ribbing (not as much as A+).
- Facility for mechanical fuel pump.
- 'S' camshaft bearings (three).
- Five core plugs.

A+ blocks 1980 onward
- All A+ blocks have nine head studs fitted from the factory.
- All blocks have oil filter heads in normal position, unless otherwise stated.
- All blocks have transverse main caps, unless otherwise stated.
- All A+ blocks have dipstick fitted directly into block, no dipstick tube.

Fourteenth type 1275cc front-wheel drive (Allegro, Metro) 1980 on
Pics 83-85
- Main bearing shells in caps have offset locating tangs.
- A+ distributor.
- No tappet chests.
- Rectangular raised casting on front of block.
- External ribbing on block.
- Painted red from factory.
- 'S' camshaft bearings (three).
- Five core plugs.
- WFM1024 cast in back of block.

Fifteenth type 1275cc front-wheel drive (Metro Turbo Mk1) 1982 on
Pics 86-89
- Central locating tangs on shells in main bearing caps.
- A+ distributor.
- No tappet chests.
- Rectangular raised casting on front of block.
- External ribbing on block.
- Painted red from factory.
- 'S' camshaft bearings (three).
- Five core plugs.
- WFM1024 cast in back of block.

Sixteenth type 1275cc front-wheel drive (Maestro and Montego) 1983 to circa 1985
- Main bearing shells in caps have offset locating tangs.
- Oil filter screwed to block below head.
- A+ distributor.
- No tappet chests.
- Rectangular raised casting on front of block.
- External ribbing on block.
- Painted red from factory.
- 'S' camshaft bearings (three).
- Five core plugs.
- Can be used as replacement transverse block for Mini, Allegro, Metro.
- WFM1024 cast in back of block.

Seventeenth type 1275cc front-wheel drive (Metro Mk2 and Metro Mk2 Turbo) Circa 1985 on
- Not the same block as Metro Turbo Mk1.
- Central locating tangs on shells in main bearing caps.
- A+ distributor.
- No tappet chests.
- External ribbing on block.
- Painted red from factory.
- 'S' camshaft bearings (three).
- Five core plugs.
- WFM1024 cast into both back of block and front of block below cylinder head.

ANATOMY OF THE CLASSIC MINI

Pic 69 | Pic 70 | Pic 71 | Pic 72
Pic 73 | Pic 74 | Pic 75 | Pic 76
Pic 77 | Pic 78 | Pic 79 | Pic 80
Pic 81 | Pic 82 | Pic 83 | Pic 84
Pic 85 | Pic 86 | Pic 87 | Pic 88
Pic 89 | Pic 90 | Pic 91 | Pic 92

ENGINE BLOCK & UPPER STABILISER BARS

Pic 93 | Pic 94 | Pic 95 | Pic 96
Pic 97 | Pic 98 | Pic 99 | Pic 100

Pic 101

Eighteenth type 1275cc front-wheel drive (Maestro and Montego). Circa '85 on
Pics 90-94
- Central locating tangs on shells in main bearing caps.
- Oil filter screwed to block below head.
- A+ distributor.
- No tappet chests.
- External ribbing on block.
- Painted red from factory.
- 'S' camshaft bearings (three).
- Five core plugs.
- Can be used as replacement transverse block for Metro and non-twin-point Mini, and the Allegro.
- WFM1024 cast into both back of block and front of block below cylinder head.

Nineteenth type 1275cc front-wheel drive (12A engine code. Last of the remote oil filter head type blocks, carburettor and SPI)
Pics 95 & 96
- Oil feed pipe from block to oil filter head has olive fitting instead of banjo bolt.
- Different thread (smaller) than any other 'A' series.
- Central locating tangs on shells in main bearing caps.
- A+ distributor.
- No tappet chests.
- External ribbing on block.
- Painted red from factory.
- 'S' camshaft bearings (three).
- Five core plugs.
- WFM1024 cast into both back of block and front of block below cylinder head.

Twentieth type 1275cc front-wheel drive twin-point Injection (MPI)
Pics 97-99
- Oil filter screwed to block below head.
- Central locating tangs on shells in main bearing caps.
- No hole in block for distributor.
- No tappet chests.
- External ribbing on block.
- Extra bosses cast onto outside of block.
- Painted black from factory.
- 'S' camshaft bearings (three).
- Five core plugs.

Front-wheel drive automatic
First type 1275cc automatic front-wheel drive (Morris 1300 (AD016), etc)
- 2in non 'S' main caps.
- Oil pump mounting face, unique to automatic.
- No tappet chests.
- Two raised bosses (rear of block) over main oil gallery.
- Aluminium 1275 badge riveted to back of block.
- 'S' camshaft bearings (three).
- Five core plugs.
- Dipstick fits into bellhousing.
- Thin-flange.

ANATOMY OF THE CLASSIC MINI

Second type 1275cc automatic front-wheel drive (Morris 1300 (AD016), etc)
- 2in non 'S' main caps.
- Window above centre main bearing in block.
- Oil pump mounting face, unique to automatic.
- No tappet chests.
- Two raised bosses (rear of block) over main oil gallery.
- Aluminium 1275 badge riveted to back of block.
- 'S' camshaft bearings (three).
- Five core plugs.
- Dipstick fits into bellhousing.
- Thick-flange.

Third type 1275cc automatic front-wheel drive (Morris 1300 (AD016), etc)
- 2in non 'S' main caps.
- No window above centre main bearing in block.
- Oil pump mounting face, unique to automatic.
- No tappet chests.
- Two raised bosses (rear of block) over main oil gallery.
- Aluminium 1275 badge riveted to back of block.
- 'S' camshaft bearings (three).
- Five core plugs.
- Dipstick fits into bellhousing.
- Thick-flange.

Fourth type 1275cc automatic front-wheel drive (Morris 1300 (AD016), etc)
- 2in non 'S' main caps.
- No window above centre main bearing in block.
- Oil pump mounting face, unique to automatic.
- No tappet chests.
- Two raised bosses (rear of block) over main oil gallery.
- Aluminium 1275 badge riveted to back of block.
- 'S' camshaft bearings (three).
- Five core plugs.
- Dipstick fits into bellhousing.
- Thick-flange.

- No oil pump priming facility.

A+ blocks 1980 onward
- All A+ blocks have nine head studs fitted from the factory.
- All blocks have transverse main caps, unless otherwise stated.
- All A+ blocks have dipstick fitted directly into block, no dipstick tube.

Fifth type 1275cc automatic front-wheel drive (Allegro and Metro) 1980 on
- Oil pump mounting face, unique to automatic.
- Main bearing shells in caps have offset locating tangs.
- A+ distributor.
- No tappet chests.
- Rectangular raised casting on front of block.
- External ribbing on block.
- Painted red from factory.
- 'S' camshaft bearings (three).
- Five core plugs.
- Dipstick fits into bellhousing.
- WFM1024 cast into back of block.
- Metal plate fitted to front of block, where oil filter head would normally be.

Sixth type 1275cc automatic front-wheel drive (Metro and Mini. Last of the English automatics). Circa 1985 on
Pics 100 & 101
- Oil pump mounting face, unique to automatic.
- Central locating tangs on shells in main bearing caps.
- A+ distributor.
- No tappet chests.
- External ribbing on block.
- Painted red from factory.
- 'S' camshaft bearings (three).
- Five core plugs.
- Dipstick fits into bellhousing.
- WFM1024 cast into both back of block and front of block below cylinder head.

1275cc Front-wheel drive automatic Mini (Japanese spec SPI)
- Similar to twin-point manual block but not the same.
- Oil pump mounting face, unique to automatic.
- Oil filter casting left blank.
- Central locating tangs on shells in main bearing caps.
- No hole in block for distributor.
- No tappet chests.
- External ribbing on block.
- Extra bosses cast onto outside of block.
- Painted black from factory.
- 'S' camshaft bearings (three).
- Five core plugs.
- Dipstick fits into bellhousing.

FLAT FACED ENGINE BLOCKS
- These engine blocks can trace their origins back to Formula Junior single-seater racing cars.
- The casting below the oil pressure relief valve nut is flat, not sculpted.
- These blocks were cast in this manner for strength to take an end-on mounted gearbox.

Front-wheel drive
First type 948cc (prototype 1071cc 'S' block)
I believe that this engine block is pre-August 1962. This is based on the fact that the block has 950 cast into the back of it. When the Morris 1100 (AD016) was launched in August 1962 the engine block was fitted with an aluminium badge. This 1100 engine was the first A-series to be fitted with an aluminium badge as opposed to casting. Pics 102-105

- The 948cc A-series engine first came out in 1956 and had 950 cast into the back of the block.
- The 848cc A-series engine first came out in 1959 and had 850 cast into the back of the block.
- The 997cc A-series engine first came out in 1961 and had 1000 cast into the back of the block, this was the last engine to have its capacity cast into the back of the block.
- Drilled and tapped for ten head studs and one head bolt.

106

ENGINE BLOCK & UPPER STABILISER BARS

Pic 102 Pic 103 Pic 104 Pic 105
Pic 106 Pic 107 Pic 108 Pic 109
Pic 110 Pic 111 Pic 112

- Thin-flange.
- 'S' sized bores.
- 2in 'S' main caps.
- Facility for scavenge pump on back of block (fuel pump take off position).
- Two raised circular bosses (rear of block) over main oil gallery.
- No thread in oil gallery from gearbox.
- Main caps retained by bolts (six).
- 'S' camshaft bearings (three).
- Four Cooper core plugs.
- 950 cast into back of block.
- AEG151 cast into back of block.

Second type 1071cc Cooper S
Pics 106-112
- Thin-flange.
- 'S' sized bores.
- 2in 'S' main caps.
- Drilled and tapped for ten head studs and one head bolt.
- Aluminium 1070 badge riveted to back of block.
- One stud screwed into fuel pump boss.
- Two raised bosses (rear of block) over main oil gallery.
- 'S' camshaft bearings (three).
- Four Cooper core plugs.
- AEG151 cast into back of block.

Chapter 12
Exhaust & inlet manifolds

EXHAUST MANIFOLDS PRE A+ 2A89602
Pic 1
- Combination inlet and exhaust manifold.
- Made of cast iron.
- Fitted with a sidedraught 1.25in SU carburettor.
- When this item was produced, Austin and Morris (BMC) were using only SU (Skinners Union) carburettors (see Carburettors).

12A104702
Pics 2 & 3
- Combined inlet and exhaust manifold which accepts a 1.25in SU carburettor.
- Made of cast iron.
- Three raised bosses as part of the casting.
- Centre boss is for a positive crankcase ventilation valve fitted to re-circulate crankcase gasses.
- This manifold was probably fitted to a non-UK car.
- Morris 1100 FWD (ADO16) also fitted to 998CC engine.

12A1141
Pic 4
- Combined inlet and exhaust manifold to accept the 1.25in SU carburettor.
- Made of cast iron.
- Original Minis, Riley Elves, Wolseley Hornets and Morris 1100 range (AD016), etc.
- Austin A35/A40, Morris Minors.

997cc Mini-Cooper/1071 Cooper 'S'/998cc Cooper and 970cc Cooper 'S'
Pic 5
- Fabricated steel.
- Part number 12A271.
- Fitted from the factory.
- Originally fitted to the 997cc Mini-Cooper, it was also fitted to the 1071 Cooper 'S,' 998cc Cooper and 970cc Cooper 'S.'
- This particular part comes from an October 1963 built 1071cc Cooper 'S,' and is 0.375in shorter in height than the 1275 Cooper 'S' version.

12G235 and 12G421
Pic 6
- Austin Morris 1100 range fitted with twin carburettors (ADO16).
- Fabricated steel.
- This manifold was probably fitted to a non-UK car.
- (CN) G16S16008M to 23407M and (CN) G162S11405M to 135592M.
- These manifolds were fitted before the 12G545.

12G545
Pic 7
- MG 1100, etc, fitted with twin carburettors (ADO16).
- Fabricated steel.
- This extractor manifold does not go 'round the bend' below the toeboard and floor of the car.
- Can be fitted to the original Mini, but would require modification to the standard exhaust system to make it fit.

1275 Cooper 'S'
Pic 8
- Part number for original 12G615.
- Non-genuine fabricated 1275 Cooper 'S' exhaust manifold, instead of the metal being rolled over on the vertical

EXHAUST & INLET MANIFOLDS

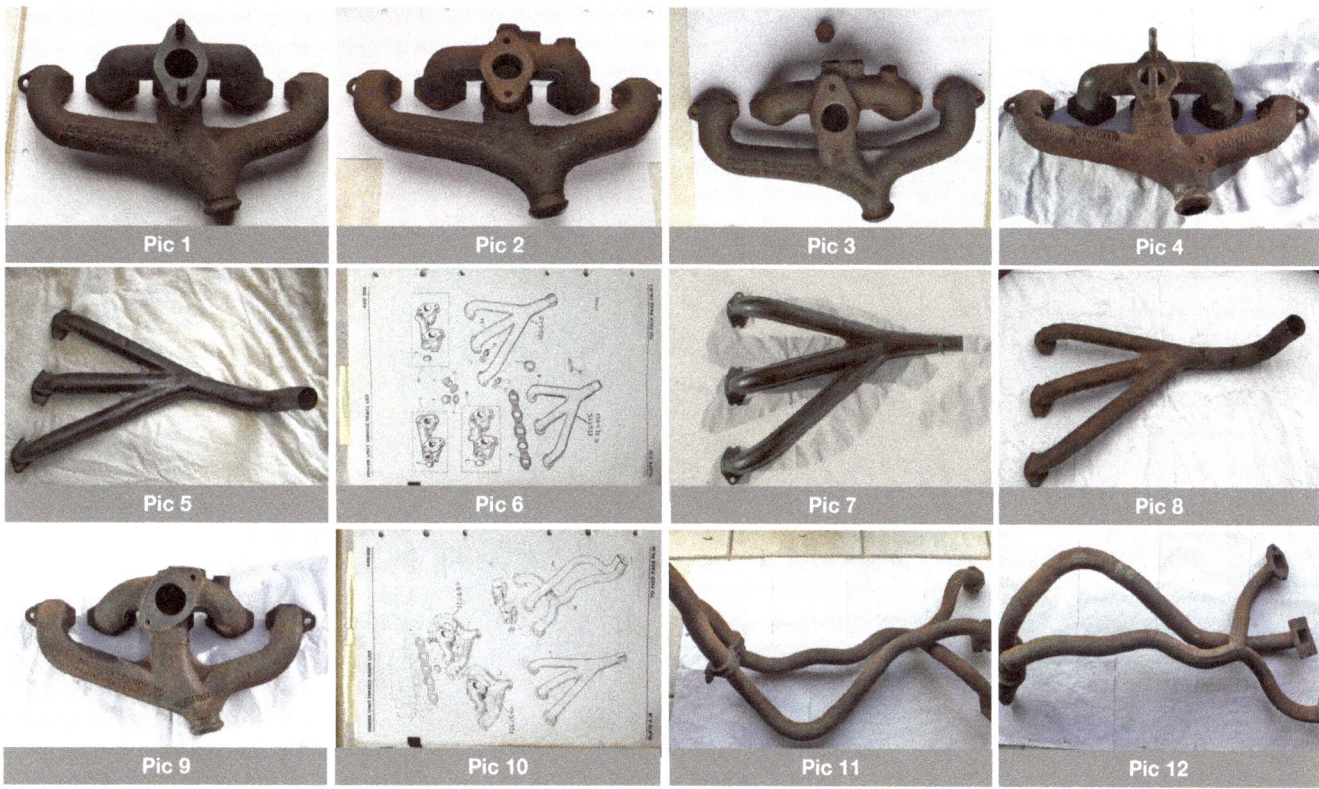

Pic 1 | Pic 2 | Pic 3 | Pic 4 | Pic 5 | Pic 6 | Pic 7 | Pic 8 | Pic 9 | Pic 10 | Pic 11 | Pic 12

seams, as the original, it is gas welded.
- 0.375in taller for the 1275cc engine only (see Engine Blocks).

12G787
Pic 9
- 1.5in SU carburettor.
- Made of cast iron.
- First appearing on the optional 848cc automatic Mini in 1965 also the Morris 1100 (FWD) ADO16 automatic.
- Standard equipment on the Austin/Morris 1300 range (AD016), manual gearbox models, circa 1967.
- Good source of a performance modification for the original Mini.

12G1540
Pic 10
- Combined inlet and exhaust manifold to accept the 1.5in SU carburettor.
- Made of cast iron.
- 1275cc (AD016) anti-smog.
- This manifold was probably fitted to a non-UK car.

Austin Morris 1300 range fitted with twin carburettors (ADO16)
See image of 12G545 above.
- 12G545 (Same part number as MG 1100).
- Fabricated steel.
- This extractor manifold does not go 'round the bend' below the toeboard and floor of the car.
- I believe the additional 0.375 was built into the exhaust pipe for the 1300 engined cars.
- Can be fitted to the original Mini but would require modification to the standard exhaust system to make it fit.

Late Austin Morris 1300GT fitted with twin carburettors
Pics 11 & 12
- Fabricated steel.
- Manifold shaped to clear pot joint inner constant velocity joints.

12G787 (to take servo)
Pic 13
- To accept 1.5in SU (HS4).
- Made of cast iron.
- Mini Clubman 1275GT 1969 onward.
- Austin Allegro Estate 1300cc, 1975 onward.
- Allegro 'A' series saloons, 1977 onward.
- 1300cc, Morris Marina Coupé/Saloon/Pickup and Van with front disc brakes.
- Servo attachment.
- If you wish to fit a servo to your automatic 850/998cc original Mini, it would be far quicker and easier to acquire and fit one of these manifolds, than to modify the existing one.

EXHAUST MANIFOLDS A+
Similar to 12G787 type manifold
- Combined inlet and exhaust manifold

ANATOMY OF THE CLASSIC MINI

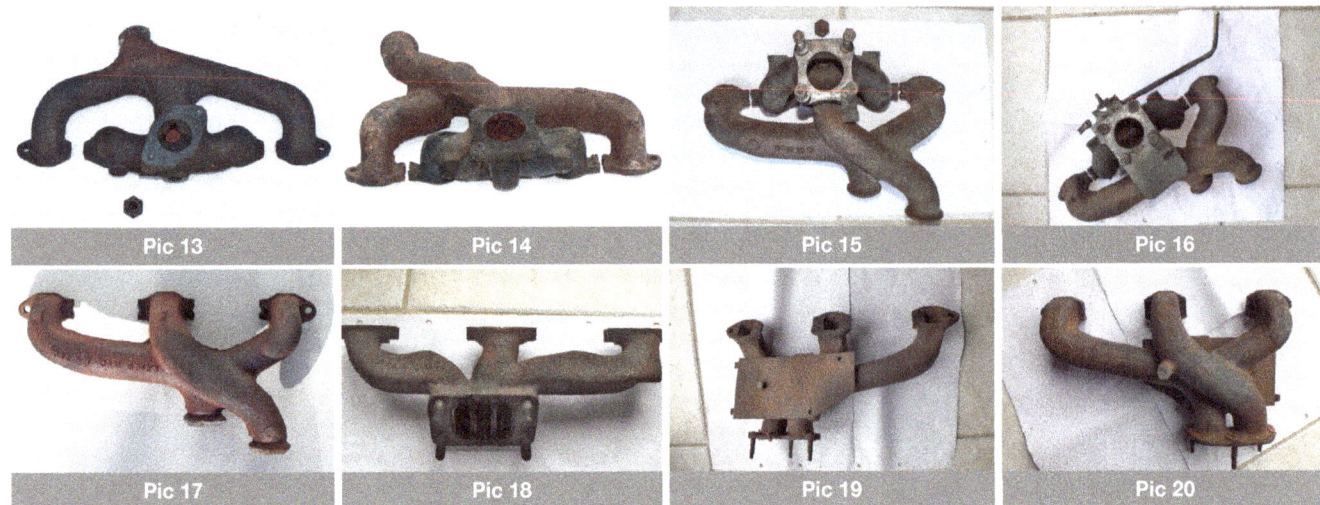

Pic 13　Pic 14　Pic 15　Pic 16
Pic 17　Pic 18　Pic 19　Pic 20

is almost identical to the two 12G787 items shown.
- Made of cast iron.
- Raised boss on the number one and two inlet tract, which is drilled and threaded and then fitted with a blanking plug.
- Austin Mini Metro 998cc low-compression models with single exhaust downpipe.
- Two-stud diagonal carburettor fixing, fitted with an HIF38 (38mm) carburettor. See Carburettors.
- The plug fitted to the inlet tract could be removed, an adaptor fitted with a vacuum pipe leading to an air temperature control flap (if fitted) in the air cleaner assembly. The most common source of this item would be the Austin Mini Metro Van.

Twin downpipe without servo

Pic 14
- WFM1047 cast into exhaust manifold.
- Made of cast iron.
- Early Austin Mini Metro without servo.
- Combined inlet and exhaust manifold, twin downpipe.
- 998cc high-compression engine fitted with HIF38 (38mm) SU carburettor.
- 1275cc non-MG/VDP (Vanden Plas) cars fitted with HIF44 (44mm) SU carburettor.

Twin downpipe with blanking plug

Pic 15
- WFM1047 cast into exhaust manifold.
- Made of cast iron.
- Can be used for vehicles without/with servo.

Twin downpipe with servo

Pic 16
- WFM1047 cast into exhaust manifold.
- Made of cast iron.
- Fitted with banjo bolt to take servo attachment.
- Early Austin Mini Metro with servo.
- Combined inlet and exhaust manifold, twin downpipe.
- 998cc high-compression engine fitted with HIF38 (38mm) SU carburettor.
- 1275cc non-MG/VDP (Vanden Plas) cars fitted with HIF44 (44mm) SU carburettor.

CAM6745

Pic 17
- Separate twin downpipe exhaust manifold.
- Made of cast iron.
- Originally fitted to 1275cc MG and Vanden Plas Metros from May 1982 onward.
- 1275cc RSP (Rover Special Products) Mini Cooper non fuel-injection.

1275cc MG Metro turbo and Era Turbo Mini

I believe the difference between the two types is to do with where the exhaust gasses enter the turbo, the casting is different.
　Not sure which of the two types is pictured. Pic 18
- Two types.
- Made of cast iron.
- Turbo exhaust manifold, first appearing in 1982 on the MG Metro Turbo.
- Used on the Era Turbo Mini launched in 1989.

Maestro 1300/Montego 1300

Pics 19 & 20
- Maestro 1275cc 1983 onward.
- Montego 1275cc 1984 onward.
- Made of cast iron.

LKC1009 1275cc injection

Pic 21
- Single-point fuel injected and twin-point fuel injected cars (known as TBI, Throttle Body Injection by Rover).
- Made of cast iron.
- Separate exhaust manifold.

EXHAUST & INLET MANIFOLDS

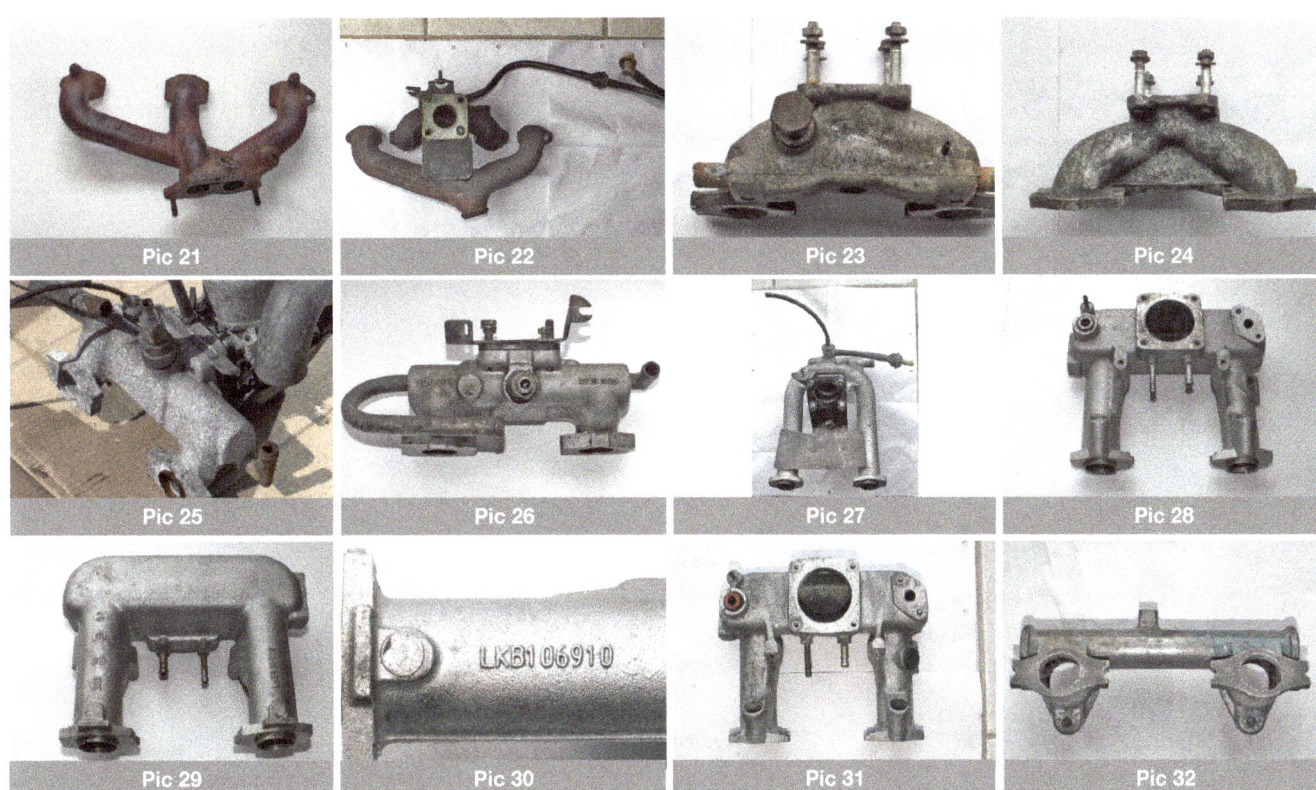

Pic 21 Pic 22 Pic 23 Pic 24
Pic 25 Pic 26 Pic 27 Pic 28
Pic 29 Pic 30 Pic 31 Pic 32

- Shown here with unboltable heat shield.
- Built-in facility for the Lambda exhaust gas probe.
-

12G3538 1275cc May 1992 onward including Mayfair and Sprite
Pic 22
- 1275cc cars (ie Mayfair and Sprite) from May 1992 onward.
- Made of cast iron.
- Fitted from the factory with an HIF38 (38mm) carburettor.
- Larger bore downpipe, requiring a larger exhaust.
- Combined inlet and exhaust manifold.
- Can be fitted with the larger HIF44 (44mm) carburettor, if required.
- If considering the use of an exhaust manifold which accepts an HiF carburettor, it is useful to bear in mind two problem areas. The May 1992 onward cars with this type of carburettor had their engine moved forward by 0.375in. Modification to the front bulkhead above the east/west box section will be needed on Mk1, 2, 3 and 3.5 bodyshells to enable fitting.

SEPARATE INLET MANIFOLDS FOR SINGLE CARBURETTOR AND TURBO; ALSO FUEL-INJECTION CAM6618
Pics 23 & 24
Finding good secondhand inlet manifolds is getting harder. The two steel pipes that connect to the coolant system rot out.
- 1982 onward.
- Aluminium alloy inlet manifold to accept single HIF44 (44mm) SU carburettor.
- Originally fitted to the MG Metro.
- Also fitted to Mini Metro Vanden Plas.
- Later reappeared on the Mini Cooper RSP.

1983 onward
Pics 25 & 26
- Aluminium alloy inlet manifold.
- Originally fitted to the MG Metro Turbo.
- Later reappeared on the ERA Turbo Mini.

CAM6763
Pic 27
- 1983 onward.
- Aluminium alloy inlet manifold.
- 1275cc Austin Maestro.
- 1275cc Austin Montego.

October 1991 onward
Pics 28 & 29
- Aluminium alloy inlet manifold.
- Originally fitted to the single-point injection 1990s Minis.
- Also fitted to Mini automatics.

LKB106910
Pics 30 & 31
- 1996 onward.

111

ANATOMY OF THE CLASSIC MINI

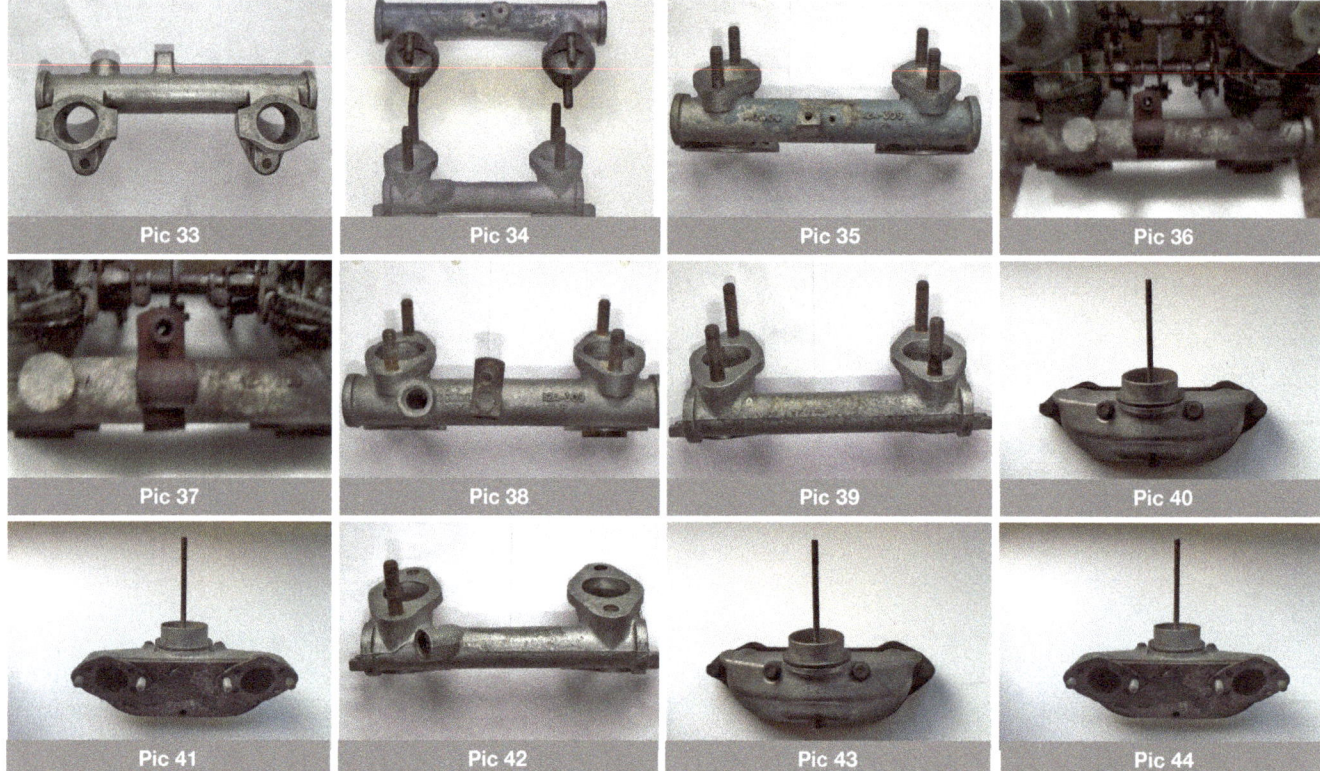

Pic 33 Pic 34 Pic 35 Pic 36
Pic 37 Pic 38 Pic 39 Pic 40
Pic 41 Pic 42 Pic 43 Pic 44

- Aluminium alloy inlet manifold.
- Originally fitted to twin-point injection Minis.

TWIN CARBURETTOR FRONT-WHEEL DRIVE INLET MANIFOLDS 1961 ONWARD

All numbers on twin carburettor inlet manifolds are cast into manifold bodies, unless otherwise stated.
The purpose of this image is to show the 'ear' type of inlet manifold fitting.
Pic 32
The purpose of this image is to show the 'non-ear' type of fitting inlet manifold. Pic 33
Top: 12A309 997cc Cooper first type. Bottom: 12G242 MG1100 (AD016) FWD, etc. Pic 34
The purpose of this image is to show the difference between a Mini Cooper and Cooper 'S' inlet manifold and that of the MG 1100 FWD (AD016) range.

Whilst the inlet manifold will bolt to the cylinder head without a problem. It's not possible to fit the Mini Cooper and Cooper 'S' twin air box because the carburettors are too close together.
Therefore, all four versions of the inlet manifold listed below for the MG1100 (AD016) FWD range are not suitable for the Mini.

12A309 P
Pic 35
- Originally fitted to the 997cc Mini Cooper.
- Single raised boss positioned in middle of manifold for throttle linkage.
- This item does not have locating rings to align the manifold with the cylinder head. It relies on the extended 'ears' and locating washers for fitment.

12A309 P
Pics 36 & 37
- 997cc Mini Cooper post March 1963.
- The 997cc Mini Cooper was not fitted with a servo. This casting has an extra blank boss, so was made around the time of the 1071 Cooper 'S.'
- Twin raised bosses.
- One boss for throttle linkage.
- Second boss left plain (undrilled).

12A309 P
Pic 38
- 997cc Mini Cooper.
- The 997cc Mini Cooper was not fitted with a servo. This casting has an extra blank boss, so was made around the time of the 1071 Cooper 'S.'
- Twin raised bosses.
- One boss for throttle linkage.
- Second boss drilled and tapped for servo vacuum attachment.
- Probably fitted with a blanking plug.

12G242
Pics 39-41
- Fitted to MG 1100/Riley Kestrel/Wolseley, 1100cc front-wheel drive. (ADO16)

EXHAUST & INLET MANIFOLDS

- This item does not have locating rings to align the manifold with the cylinder head. It relies on the extended 'ears' and locating washers for fitment.
- Also shown is air inlet tract.

12G242/12G352
Pics 42-44
- 12G352 cast into inlet manifold on back of servo boss.
- Fitted to MG 1100/Riley Kestrel / Wolseley, 1100cc front-wheel drive. (ADO16)
- This item does not have locating rings to align the manifold with the cylinder head. It relies on the extended 'ears' and locating washers for fitment.
- Also shown is air inlet tract.

12G242/12G352
Pics 45-47
- 12G352 cast into inlet manifold on back of servo boss.
- Fitted to MG 1100/Riley Kestrel / Wolseley, 1100cc front-wheel drive. (ADO16)
- Also shown is air inlet tract.

12G 299
Pics 48-50
- Manifold to take valve for positive crankcase ventilation.
- Fitted to MG 1100/Riley Kestrel / Wolseley, 1100cc front-wheel drive. (ADO16)
- Also shown is air inlet tract.

AF383 P (1004)
Pics 51 & 52
- Formula junior engine fitted to Mini.
- Prototype 1071cc Mini Cooper 'S.'
- Twin 1.5in SU carburettors (H4).

AEG179
Pic 53
- The number AEG179 is engraved on the manifold, not cast.
- Originally fitted to the 1071cc Mini Cooper 'S.'
- March 1963 onward.

12A661
The 12A661 inlet manifolds were the first type to have an extra raised boss to take the valve for positive crankcase ventilation on the Mini. Pic 54 Top: 12A661 P2 (1004); middle: 12A661 P (1004); bottom: 12A661 P (1008).

12A661 P (1008)
Pics 55 & 56
- This item has both extended 'ears' and locating rings to align the manifold with the cylinder head.
- Early 998cc Mini Cooper.

12A661 P (1004)
- 998cc Mini Cooper. Pic 57

12A661 P2 (1004)
- 998cc Mini Cooper. Pic 58
- Reinforced.

AEG347 (12A661 P)
Pic 59
- The number AEG347 is engraved on the manifold, not cast.
- 1071cc/1275cc and 970cc Mini Cooper 'S' with PCV valve.

AEG573
- Non-reinforced (not reinforced between PCV valve boss and throttle cable anchorage boss). Pic 60

AEG573
- Reinforced raised bosses. (Reinforced between PCV valve boss and throttle cable anchorage boss.) Pic 61

12G2463
See photographs of 12G2463 reinforced.
- 1969 to 1971 Austin Morris 1300GT (AD016).
- Non-reinforced (not reinforced between PCV valve boss and throttle cable anchorage boss.)
- Drilled and tapped for one way valve (to take servo pipe).

12G2463
Pics 62 & 63
- Reinforced raised bosses. (Reinforced between PCV valve boss and throttle cable anchorage boss.)
- Drilled and tapped for one way valve (to take servo pipe).

12G2464
Pic 64
- Reinforced raised bosses. (Reinforced between PCV valve boss and throttle cable anchorage boss.)
- No thread tapped for PCV valve.
- Drilled and tapped for one way valve (to take servo pipe).

AEG489
Pics 65 & 66
- Special tuning part.
- To take twin HS4 SU carburettors. (Note diagonal configuration securing studs.)

1989 998cc Mini Cooper
- Offered as part of a kit to modify a 998cc Mini, probably aimed at the Mini 30.

ANATOMY OF THE CLASSIC MINI

Pic 45 / Pic 46 / Pic 47 / Pic 48 / Pic 49 / Pic 50 / Pic 51 / Pic 52 / Pic 53 / Pic 54 / Pic 55 / Pic 56 / Pic 57 / Pic 58 / Pic 59 / Pic 60 / Pic 61 / Pic 62 / Pic 63 / Pic 64 / Pic 65 / Pic 66

Chapter 13
Hydraulics & pedal box assemblies

BRAKE MASTER CYLINDERS

The single-line brake master cylinders first appeared on the Mk1 Austin A40 Pininfarina-styled car launched by BMC in 1958. These then made their way onto the first Minis.

Single-line system
- 1958 onward Austin A40. Pressed steel cylindrical single-line brake master cylinder. These are easily identified by the large nut fitted to the top of the master cylinder. The cylinders were made like this for easy major servicing. For example, the master cylinder did not require removal from the vehicle to replace the hydraulic rubbers.
- Mk2 Austin A40 948cc 1961 onward. Original part number 2A5649.

SINGLE-LINE SYSTEM 1959 ONWARD MINI AND AUSTIN MORRIS 11/1300 (ADO16) RANGE

All single-line master cylinders are short (2.25in), unless otherwise stated. Listed mainly for information.

First type
Pic 1
(Image from a left-hand drive car. Left (as viewed from cockpit): Brake master cylinder. Right: Clutch master cylinder).
- 848cc Mini.
- Part number 21A1237 became GMC153.
- Pressed steel cylindrical, easily identified by the large nut fitted to the top of the master cylinder.
- The cylinders were made like this for easy major servicing. For example, the master cylinder did not require removal from the vehicle to replace the hydraulic rubbers.
- 0.750in bore.

Second type
Pic 2
- Part number 2A5649.
- Similar to the first type of cylinder, but with a pressing that looks like a nut but does not unscrew. Therefore, the master cylinder has to be removed from the vehicle for major servicing.

Third type
- This cylinder does not have a nut-shaped pressing at the top of its tower.
- Has recess below brake pipe.

Fourth type
- This is the most common type to be fitted, different from the second type (it has no pressed-in nut shape). Again, it has to be removed from the vehicle for major servicing.
- Slight taper on tower below brake pipe.

Fifth type
- 997cc Cooper.
- This master cylinder was fitted in conjunction with a brake intensifier valve, part number 21A655.
- Part number 21A800.
- I think the current part number for this item is GMC103 (use GMC153).
- 0.750in bore.

Sixth type
- 997cc Cooper.
- Current part number GMC104.

115

ANATOMY OF THE CLASSIC MINI

Pic 1

Pic 2

Pic 3

Pic 4

Pic 5

Pic 6

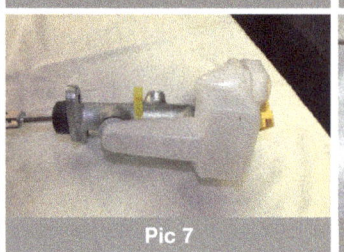
Pic 7

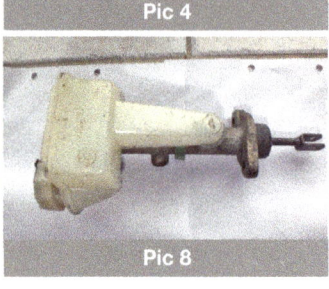
Pic 8

Seventh type
- 997cc Cooper and 998cc Cooper.
- This master cylinder was fitted in conjunction with second type of brake calipers, part numbers 27H4654 and 27H4655.
- Current part number GMC171.

Eighth type
When replacing the BCA4727 brake master cylinder two items are required. These are the master cylinder (part number 13H819), and pushrod (part number 17H6786).
- 1962 onward.
- Part number BCA4727.
- Morris 1100 front-wheel drive (ADO16).
- Different bore size to Mini.
- Different rod length to Mini.

Ninth type
- Morris 1100 front-wheel drive (ADO16).
- Part number 13H819.
- Different bore size to Mini.
- Different rod length to Mini.

Tenth type
- Morris 1100 front-wheel drive (ADO16).
- Part number 13H1541 with plastic cap.
- Different bore size to Mini.
- Different rod length to Mini.

Eleventh type
Pic 3
(Left: Brake master cylinder. Right: Clutch master cylinder.)
- March 1963 onward.
- Current part number GMC172.
- Cooper 'S' type brake master cylinder (1071cc, 1275cc, 970cc) plus 1275GT Mini Clubman with single-line system 1974 to 1977.
- Taller than cylinders fitted to other models and are not to be confused with the master cylinder fitted to the Morris 1300 front-wheel drive range (ADO16).
- The cylinders are not only a different bore size; they also have different rod lengths.

Twelfth type
Pic 4
- 1967 onward.
- Current part number GMC175.
- Morris 1300 (ADO16) front-wheel drive (tall) brake master cylinder.
- Different to the Cooper 'S' as explained in the previous text.

REPLACEMENT BRAKE MASTER CYLINDER
- This brake master cylinder is sometimes referred to as the 'Euro' cylinder. It replaces the single-line short (2.25in) non-Cooper 'S' cylinder.
- Easily identified by its plastic fluid tank.
- Part number GMC171.

TANDEM BRAKE SYSTEM 1974 ONWARD
First type
Pic 5
- Part number GMC160.
- 1974 to 1975.
- 1275GT diagonal split.

Second type
Pic 6
- Failure switch on body.
- Part numbers GMC167 and GMC173, square reservoir.
- 1975 to 1980.
- GMC167 fits 1275GT, diagonal split, 1977 to 1978, metric pipe unions.
- GMC173 front to rear, 1978 to 1980.
- GMC173 became GMC198.
- Use GMC227 to replace GMC173/GMC198.

Third type
Pics 7 & 8
- Failure switch on cap.
- Part numbers GMC192 and GMC195, front to rear.
- 1980 to 1985.
- Use GMC227 to replace GMC192/GMC195. (GMC227 1985 onward.)

116

HYDRAULICS & PEDAL BOX ASSEMBLIES

Pic 9   Pic 10   Pic 11   Pic 12
Pic 13   Pic 14   Pic 15   Pic 16

Fourth type (two types of repair kit)
Pic 9
- 'F' registered (1989) onward.
- Horizontal tandem brake master cylinder.
- This is the last type of UK spec brake master cylinders to be fitted.

BRAKE SERVOS
- Mk1, Mk2 Mini Cooper 'S.' Pic 10
- Mk3 Mini Cooper 'S' and 1275GT Clubman with 10in wheels. Pic 11
- 1989 onward (all models) horizontally-mounted servo. Pic 12 (Courtesy Mini Spares, Potters Bar)

BRAKE SERVO HOSE
Pic 13
- Original Works type.

CLUTCH MASTER CYLINDERS
The single-line clutch master cylinders first appeared on the Mk1 Austin A40 Pininfarina-styled car launched by BMC in 1958. These cylinders then made their way onto the first Minis.

Single-line system
- 1958 onward Austin A40.
- Pressed steel cylindrical single-line clutch master cylinder.
- These are easily identified by the large nut fitted to the top of the master cylinder. The cylinders were made like this for easy major servicing. For example, the master cylinder did not require removal from the vehicle to replace the hydraulic rubbers.
- Part number 2A5650 becomes 21A1836.

Single-line system 1959 onward Mini and Austin Morris 11/1300 range
Listed mainly for information.

First type
Pic 14 Left (as viewed from cockpit): Brake. Right: Clutch (Image from a left-hand drive car. Left: Brake master cylinder. Right: Clutch master cylinder.)
- Part number 2A5868.
- 848cc Mini, 848cc Mini Van, 997cc Cooper.
- Pressed steel cylindrical, easily identified by the large nut fitted to the top of the master cylinder.
- The cylinders were made like this for easy major servicing. For example, the master cylinder did not require removal from the vehicle to replace the hydraulic rubbers.

Second type
- Similar to the first type of cylinder, but with a pressing which looks like a nut but does not unscrew. Therefore, the master cylinder has to be removed from the vehicle for major servicing.

Third type
When replacing the BCA4777 clutch master cylinder two items are required. These are the master cylinder (part number 13H1539), and pushrod (part number 17H6786).
- 1962 onward.
- Part number BCA4777.
- Morris 1100 (ADO16).

Fourth type
- Morris 1100 (ADO16).
- Part number 13H820.

Fifth type
- Morris 1100 (ADO16).
- Part number 13H1539.

Sixth type
Pic 15 (Courtesy Mini Spares, Potters Bar)
(Also see photo of type eleven brake master cylinder with clutch master cylinder.) See pic 3
- This is the most common type to be fitted. It differs from the second type in that it has no pressed-in nut shape. Again, it has to be removed from the vehicle for major servicing.

117

ANATOMY OF THE CLASSIC MINI

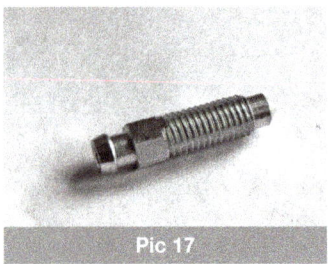
Pic 17

Pic 18

Pic 19

Pic 20

REPLACEMENT CLUTCH MASTER CYLINDER
Pic 16 (Courtesy Mini Spares, Potters Bar)
- Part number GMC1008.
- This clutch master cylinder is sometimes referred to as the 'Euro' cylinder.
- Easily identified by its plastic fluid tank.

FRONT BRAKE WHEEL CYLINDERS
Listed mainly for information.

First type
- Single twin leading cylinder.
- Looks like a rear wheel cylinder.
- Only type of single front cylinder.
- Part numbers for cylinders 17H7624 and 17H7768 (both became 17H2478).
- Only part number available these days is GWC101.

Second type
- Two x twin front wheel cylinders.
- For 17H8145/17H8159 backplates.
- Single piston cylinders.
- Requires different backplate from first type.
- Part numbers for cylinders GWC102 x two and GWC103 x two.

Third type
- Similar to second type.
- For 13H2013/13H2014 backplates.
- Larger piston single cylinders.
- Requires different backplate from second type.
- Part numbers for cylinders GWC126 x two and GWC127 x two.

REAR BRAKE WHEEL CYLINDERS
Part numbers 17H7614, 17H7767, 17H7861 all three replaced by 17H6993. Part number 17H6993 was replaced by 17H8088.
Part number 17H8088 was replaced by 17H8773.
The purpose of this listing is to demonstrate the problems that they had with the first type of rear wheel cylinder and rear brakes on early cars.
Five types of rear brake wheel cylinders for the English market.

First type
Pic 17
- 0.750in bore size.
- Small bleed nipple.
- Part number GWC1102.

Second type
- Part number GWC1101.
- 0.625in bore size.
- Small bleed nipple.

Third type
- Part number GWC1129.
- 0.6875in bore size.
- Small bleed nipple.
- 1275 GT Clubman 1974 to 1976.

Fourth type
- Part number GWC1126.
- 0.500in bore size.
- Small bleed nipple.
- 1275 GT Clubman 1976 to 1978.

Fifth type
Pic 18
- Part number GWC1131.
- 0.5625in bore size.
- Large bleed nipple.
- Diagonal split brake system 1977 to 1978, except Pickup and Van.
- Fitted to ERA Turbo Mini.

FRONT BRAKE CALIPER SECURING BOLTS
- All disc-braked models from 1961 to 2000, except ERA Turbo. Pic 19
- ERA Turbo. Pic 20

FRONT BRAKE CALIPERS
All brake calipers have two pistons unless otherwise stated.

First type
- 1961 onward.
- 997cc Cooper.

Second type
Pic 21
- March 1963 onward.
- 997cc Cooper modified type.
- 998cc Cooper Mk1/2.
- Part numbers 27H4654 and 27H4655.

Third type
Pic 22 (Left: Third type. Right: Fourth type.)
- 1963 to 1974.
- 1071cc/1275cc/970cc Cooper 'S.'
- 1275 GT with 10in wheels.

Fourth type
See picture shown under Third type.
- 1275 GT with 12in wheels.
- All 12 and 13in wheeled Minis except ERA turbo

Fifth type
Pics 23 & 24
- 1275cc ERA turbo Mini.
- Brake calipers came from the Mini

HYDRAULICS & PEDAL BOX ASSEMBLIES

Metro Mk2.
• Four-piston caliper.

CLUTCH SLAVE CYLINDERS
First type

• First type (13H395): Cylinder for six-spring and diaphragm type.
• Second type (13H461, chassis number 8AM-U-H28001 onward): Has internal circlip to prevent piston coming out of cylinder. Pic 25

Second type
Pic 26
• Cylinder for diaphragm type.
• Can be used for six-spring type.
• No internal circlip.

Third type
Pic 27
• Cylinder for verto type clutch.
• Mounts at an angle on flywheel and clutch bellhousing cover.

BRAKE COMPENSATING VALVES
This valve was fitted to the rear subframe.

First type
The image of this particular item is a modified standard item done by my good friend John Meale.
Pic 28
• 848cc Saloon, Seven Van, 997cc Cooper.
• Part number 2A5893.
• Fitted with spring part number 17H7632.
• Also fitted to Morris disabled person's vehicle. Chassis number M-A2S4-169036 onward.

Second type
See first type as externally the same.
• Morris disabled person's vehicle.
• Part number 21A1010.
• Morris chassis number M-A2S4-101 to 169035.

Third type
See first type as externally the same.
• Austin chassis number A-A2S7-359771 onward right-hand drive.
• Austin chassis number 358923 left-hand drive.
• Morris chassis number M-A2S4-170654 (plus 16994 to 170000) onward.
• Part number 21A1201.
• Fitted with spring part number 17H8063.

Fourth type
See first type as externally the same.
• Mk1/2 Mini.
• Mk3 Cooper 'S.'
• Part number 21A1774.

Fifth type
See first type as externally the same.
• 1969 onward.
• Mk3 Mini, 850cc and 998cc.
• Part number 21A2031.

Sixth type
Pic 29
• Tandem braking system.
• 1978 onward.
• Part number FAM7821.
• This valve was fitted under the bonnet on the east-west front subframe mounting box section.
• Vehicles fitted with the horizontal brake servo and master cylinder have the valve moved to a slightly different position on the box section.

BRAKE INTENSIFIER VALVE
• 1961 onward to February 1962. Part number 12A655.
• 997cc Cooper only.
• Fits under bonnet on offside (right-hand) inner wing.

REDUCING VALVE
• Only fitted to the ERA Turbo Mini. Part number ERA1053.
• Fitted in front to rear brake line to reduce pressure to rear brakes.

PEDAL BOX ASSEMBLIES
• Mk1/2. Steel bracket part number 2A5859. Pic 30
• Mk3. 1969 onward. Pic 31
• Part number FAM4368 became NAM8670. These are listed for tandem brake master cylinders. Similar to Mk3 1969 onward.
• 1988 to 1996, with horizontal brake servo and master cylinder. Part number SKU10043. Similar to Mk3 1969 onward.
• 1996 onward. Part number SKU101220. Pic 32

Brake pedals
• Mk1 to Mk3.5 not including Cooper 'S.' Part number 21A318.
• Cooper February 1962 onward and Mk1, two and three Cooper 'S.'
• Mk4 onward. 1976 to 1989. Part number NAM3112.
• 1989 onward. Part number NAM8539. Link bar is not detachable from brake pedal unless you use either a drill or grinder. Pic 33
• Somewhere between 1989 and 2000 they reverted to a separate brake pedal and link bar. Pic 34

Clutch pedals
• Mk1 to Mk3.5. Part number 2A5866.
• Mk4 1976 onward. Part number NAM3116.

METAL BASE PLATES FOR MASTER CYLINDERS
• 1959 to 1976 part number 14A6733. Pic 35 (Courtesy Mini Spares, Potters Bar)
• 1976 to circa 1988 part number ALA6505. Larger hole for tandem brake master cylinder. Pic 36 (Courtesy Mini Spares, Potters Bar)
• Circa 1988 onward part number CRC8664. Pic 37

ACCELERATOR PEDALS
Listed in fuel system chapter.

119

ANATOMY OF THE CLASSIC MINI

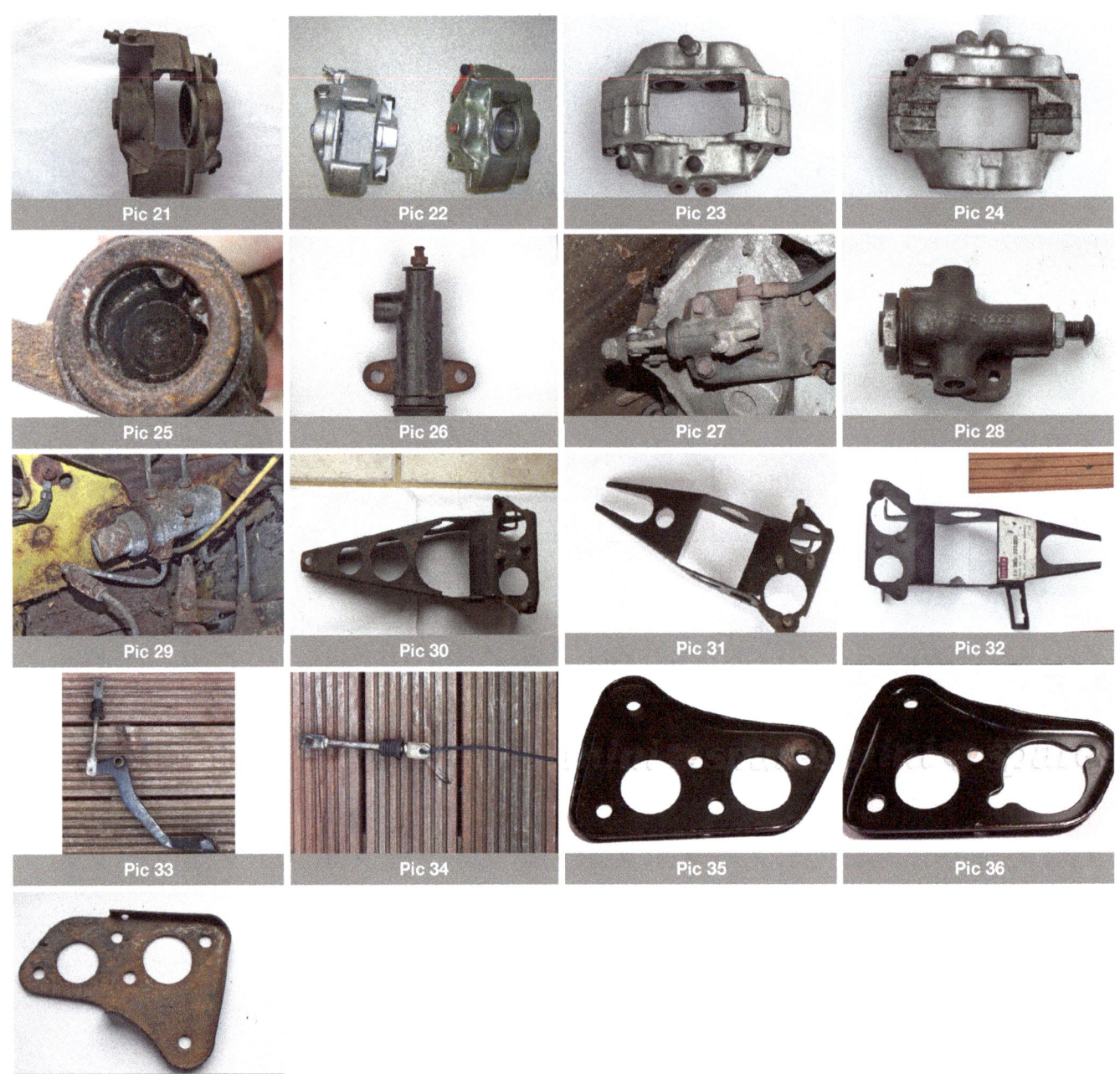

Pic 21 | Pic 22 | Pic 23 | Pic 24
Pic 25 | Pic 26 | Pic 27 | Pic 28
Pic 29 | Pic 30 | Pic 31 | Pic 32
Pic 33 | Pic 34 | Pic 35 | Pic 36
Pic 37

Chapter 14
Fuel system

FUEL TANKS
Fuel tank (Saloon) (ARA90, ARA104) (ARA104 997cc Cooper)
Pic 1
- 1959 onward.
- Fuel tank sender fastened to tank by six screws.
- 5.5-gallon capacity.

Fuel tank (Saloon)
Pic 2
- Fuel tank sender fastened to tank by six screws.
- Tank fitted with fuel drain facility.
- 5.5-gallon capacity.

Fuel tank (Riley Elf and Wolseley Hornet)
Also see image of later Riley Elf and Wolseley Hornet which looks the same except for fuel tank sender fixings.
Pic 3
- 1961 onward.
- Part number ARA144.
- Fuel tank sender fastened to tank by six screws.
- Tank fitted with fuel drain facility.
- 5.5-gallon capacity.

Fuel tank (Saloon)
Pic 4
- Fuel tank sender fastened to tank by locking ring.
- Tank fitted with fuel drain facility.
- 5.5-gallon capacity.

Fuel tank (Saloon)
Pic 5
- Fuel tank sender fastened to tank by locking ring.
- 5.5-gallon capacity.

Fuel tank (Riley Elf and Wolseley Hornet)
Pics 6 & 7
- Fuel tank sender fastened to tank by locking ring.
- Tank fitted with fuel drain facility.
- 5.5-gallon capacity.

Fuel tank (Saloon Cooper 'S')
Pic 8 (Courtesy Peter Giffen)
Available initially as an option, made available as standard fit from January 1966 onward.
- Right-hand fuel tank.
- No fuel tank sender fitted.
- 5.5-gallon capacity.
- Part number 21A2183.

Fuel tanks (Saloon) (ARP1043, WFE10093, WFE10420, WFE10401)
Pic 9
- Fuel tank sender fastened to tank by locking ring.
- Recess in tank for strap.
- 7.5-gallon capacity.

Fuel tank (Saloon)
Same tank as above but without recess in tank for strap.
- Fuel tank sender fastened to tank by locking ring.
- 7.5-gallon capacity.

Fuel tank (Saloon)
Pic 10
- Fuel tank sender fastened to tank by screws.
- 7.5-gallon capacity.

ANATOMY OF THE CLASSIC MINI

- Fuel pump immersed in tank for petrol injection models.

Fuel tank (Saloon)
Pic 11
- Fuel tank sender fastened to tank by screws.

- 7.5-gallon capacity.
- Fuel pump immersed in tank for petrol injection models.

Fuel tank (Saloon)
Pics 12-14
- Unusual early 5.5-gallon capacity.

- Fuel tank sender fastened to tank by six screws.
- Also note petrol tank lower securing bracket.
- These photographs were taken in April 2010 at Gaydon Heritage Motor Museum.

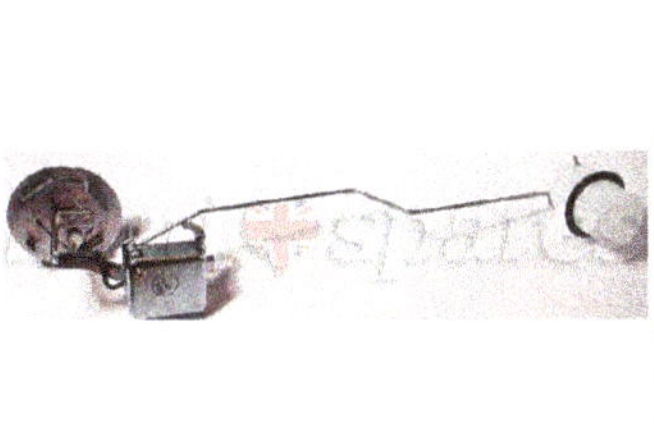

FUEL SYSTEM

Pic 21  | Pic 22 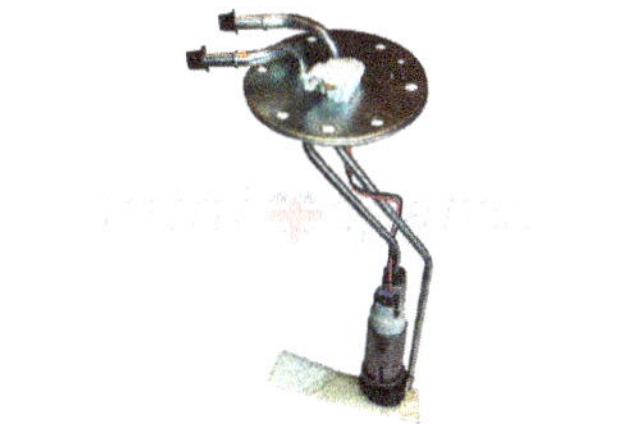 | Pic 23  | Pic 24

Pic 25  | Pic 26  | Pic 27 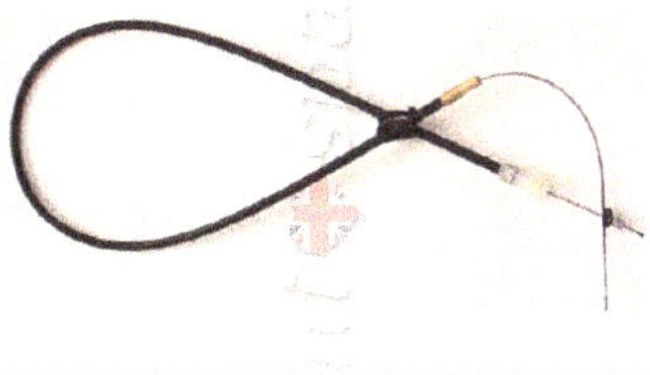 | Pic 28

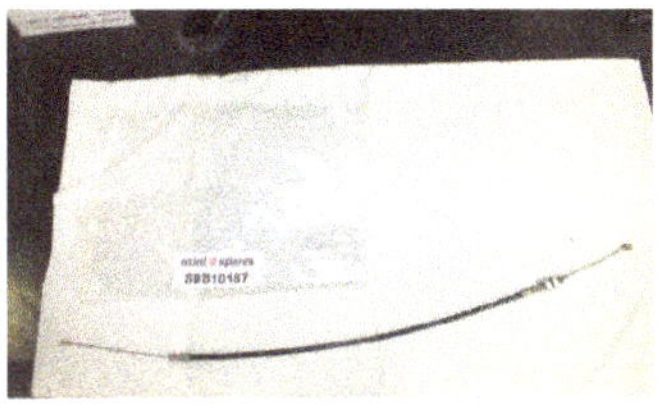

Pic 29 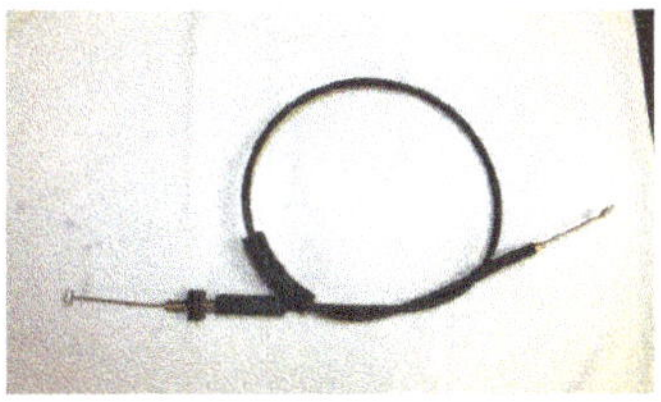 | Pic 30 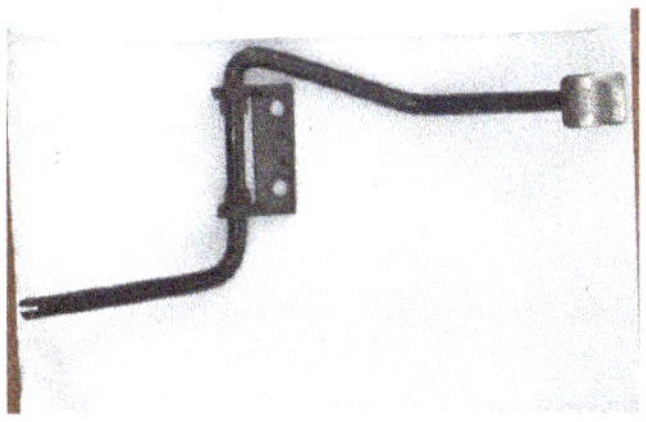 | Pic 31 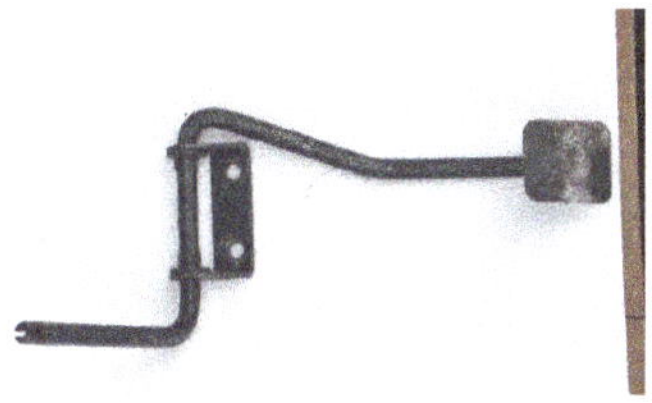 | Pic 32

Fuel tank (Moke)
Pics 15-18
- Mini Moke.
- 1965 onward.
- Fuel tank sender fastened to tank by six screws.

FUEL TANK SENDERS
- 848cc Mini Saloon, 997cc Cooper, Riley Elf, Wolseley Hornet. Six screw type part number 2A2163. Pic 19

- 1964 to 1992 part number AHU1029 became XNB10007. Pic 20 (Courtesy Mini Spares, Potters Bar)
- 1992 onward 1275cc with catalytic converter part number XNB100380. Pic 21 (Courtesy Mini Spares, Potters Bar)

FUEL PUMPS (ELECTRIC)
Electric fuel pump
- 1959 onward.

The earlier SU fuel pump (type PD).

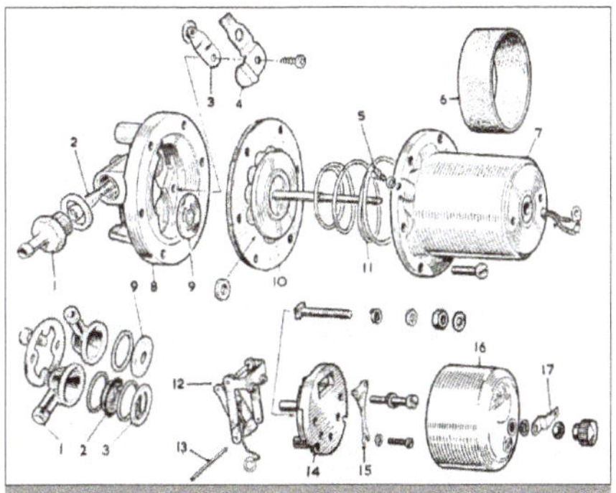

Later SU fuel pump (type SP).

- AUA103.
- PD pump.

Electric fuel pump
- SU pump.
- AUA83/AUB83.

Electric fuel pump
Pic 22 (Courtesy Mini Spares, Potters Bar)
- SU pump.
- AUF200.

Electric fuel pump
Pic 23 (Courtesy Mini Spares, Potters Bar)
- Part number WFX10045 became WFX100810.
- Fits both SPI and MPI.

Mechanical fuel pump
- 1969 onward.
- AUF705 original type.

ANATOMY OF THE CLASSIC MINI

Pic 33 | Pic 34 | Pic 35 | Pic 36
Pic 37 | Pic 38 | Pic 39 | Pic 40
Pic 41 | Pic 42 | Pic 43 | Pic 44

Mechanical fuel pump
Pic 24 (Courtesy Mini Spares, Potters Bar)
- AZX1818.
- 998cc.

ERA TURBO
- 1989 onward.
- Electric fuel pump. Part number AUU1649

Mechanical fuel pump
Pic 25 (CourtesyMini Spares, Potters Bar)
- AZX1817.
- For HIF44 carburettor.

Mechanical fuel pump
Pic 26 (CourtesyMini Spares, Potters Bar)
- WND10005.
- 1275cc with HIF38 carburettor.

ACCELERATOR CABLES
- 1.25in and 1.5in SU carburettor, part number 21A95. Pic 27 (CourtesyMini Spares, Potters Bar)
- 1990s Mini, 1275cc with carburettor, part number SBB10099. Pic 28 (CourtesyMini Spares, Potters Bar)
- Single-point part number SBB10187. Pic 29
- Twin-point part number SBB103400. Pic 30

ACCELERATOR PEDALS
- 1959 onward, manual. Pic 31
- Automatic 1965 onward.
- 1976 onward part number NAM3108. Pic 32
- Twin-point, right-hand drive, part number SAB101220MUN Pic 33
- Cooper 'S' works (1999).

CHOKE CABLES
- Part number 2A2241. Pic 34
- Part number 21A1202 required when fresh air heater is fitted. Says 'Choke.' Pic 35 (CourtesyMini Spares, Potters Bar)
- Early Cooper says 'Choke and lock,' part number 21A1204. Pic 36 (CourtesyMini Spares, Potters Bar)
- Up to 1987 rubber type, part number 21A2329. Pic 37
- Up to 1990 32in long, part number SBF10027. Pic 38
- 1990 onward 36in long, part number SBF10031. Pic 39

CARBURETTOR
SU 1.25in (HS2)
- 1959 onward.
- Solidly-mounted float chamber.
- Brass dashpot nut.
- Brass float.

SU 1.25in (HS2)
Pics 40 & 41 (CourtesyMini Spares, Potters Bar)
- Carburettor crankcase ventilation.

Twin 1.25in SU's
Pic 42
- First fitted to the 997cc Mini Cooper.

FUEL SYSTEM

Pic 45 | Pic 46 | Pic 47 | Pic 48
Pic 49 | Pic 50 | Pic 51 | Pic 52
Pic 53 | Pic 54 | Pic 55 | Pic 56

Twin 1.25in SU's
Pic 43
- Carburettor crankcase ventilation.

SU 1.5in (HS4)
Only difference between 850cc and 1098cc would have been the jet and needle.
Waxstat carburettor shown.
Pic 44 (CourtesyMini Spares, Potters Bar)
- First fitted on the 850cc automatic.
- Also fitted to the Morris 1100 (ADO16) automatic.

SU 1.5in (HS4)
Pic 45
- Carburettor crankcase ventilation.

SU 38mm (HIF38)
For image please refer to SU 44mm (HIF44) RSP Cooper.
- 38mm bore.
- Fitted to 1275cc Mini Sprite.

SU 44mm (HIF44)
Pic 46
- ERA Turbo Mini.
- 44mm bore.

SU 44mm (HIF44)
Pic 47
- First fitted to RSP Cooper.
- 44mm bore.

ANTI-RUN ON VALVE
Pic 48
- Part number MAV10021. First appeared on the MG Metro.

AIR INTAKE FILTER CASINGS FOR SINGLE CARBURETTORS (MINI) Downdraught Zenith type
- Rectangular type.
- Originally fitted to Austin A30/A35 with Zenith carburettor.
- This application fitted to a single 1.25in SU (HS2).
- Photos can be found on page 9 and 10 of *Mighty Minis* by Chris Harvey, ISBN 094660911X.

Frying pan type
- Air intake positioned toward radiator.
- Fits a single 1.25in SU (HS2).
- All metal.
- Photo can be found on page 11 of *Mighty Minis* by Chris Harvey, ISBN 094660911X.

Two-position type (2A989, 12A51, 12A131, 12A622)
For photograph please refer to page 27 of *Amazing Mini* by Peter Filby, ISBN 08566140600.
- By releasing the retaining wing nut the air filter casing can be moved for winter or summer positions.
- Fits a single 1.25in SU (HS2).
- All metal.

ANATOMY OF THE CLASSIC MINI

Pic 57 Pic 58 Pic 59 Pic 60
Pic 61 Pic 62 Pic 63 Pic 64
Pic 65 Pic 66 Pic 67 Pic 68

Two-position type
- By releasing the retaining wing nut the air filter casing can be moved for winter or summer positions.
- Fits a single 1.25in SU (HS2).
- Metal with plastic top.

1.5in SU (HS4) type (12G732, 12A1275)
Pic 49
- First fitted to 850cc automatic Mini.
- All metal.

1.5in SU (HS4) type
Pic 50
- First fitted to 850cc automatic Mini.
- Metal with plastic top.

All plastic
- HS4 carburettor, pre-horizontal servo, part number 12G4298. Part number on air filter plastic case is 12G4299. Pics 51 & 52
- HS4 carburettor when horizontal servo fitted, part number TAM2138. The plastic part of this assembly is a 12G4299 but the other item is shorter to clear the horizontal servo.
- HIF38 air cleaner, part number CAM6037. Pics 53 & 54
- HIF44 air cleaner, part number PHB10092.
- HIF44 commemorative Cooper air cleaner. Refer to page 108 of *Original Mini Cooper* by J Parnell, ISBN 187097932X.
- HIF44 mainstream Cooper air cleaner. Refer to page 108 of *Original Mini Cooper* by J Parnell, ISBN 187097932X. Pic 55
- Single-point air cleaner part number PHB10081. Refer to page 109 of *Original Mini Cooper* by J Parnell, ISBN 187097932X.
- Twin-point air cleaner part number PHB101910.

AIR INTAKE ELBOWS
- HS2 single. Part number 27H1389. Pic 56
- HS2 twin. Pic 57
- HS4 single. Part number 12G1812. Pic 58 (CourtesyMini Spares, Potters Bar)
- ERA turbo HIF44. Casting number WFM 1142. Pic 59
- HIF38. Part number CAM4598. Pics 60 & 61
- HIF44. Part number CAM4694. Similar to CAM4598 but with larger airway near butterfly.

AIR INTAKE FILTER CASINGS FOR TWIN CARBURETTORS
Front filter is nearest to radiator, rear filter is furthest from radiator.
The Irish seem to be the experts on twin SU metal air boxes, especially the 1071cc Cooper 'S.' I think this has something to do with the Mini's rallying heritage. My thanks to Neville Smythe. The Mk1/2 Coopers and Cooper 'S' metal air boxes are taller (deeper) than that of the Mk3 Cooper 'S'

FUEL SYSTEM

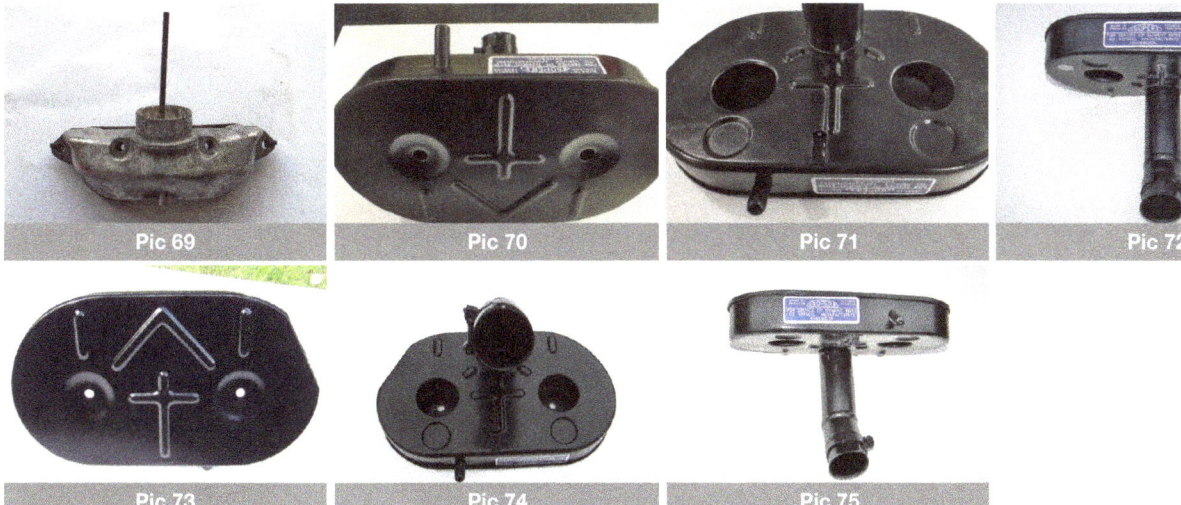

- 997cc and early 1071cc Cooper 'S' fitted with two pancake filters. Part number front filter 12A221, rear filter 12A222. Pics 62-65
- Later 997cc and early 1071cc Cooper 'S' fitted with metal air box, no recesses on underside for SU dash pot tops. First position for breather pipe.
- 1071cc Cooper 'S,' fitted with metal air box, no recesses on underside for SU dash pot tops. Second position for breather pipe, with large internal bore.
- 1071cc Cooper 'S,' fitted with metal air box, no recesses on underside for SU dash pot tops. Second position for breather pipe with standardised breather pipe. Pics 66 & 67
- First type 1098cc Morris 1100cc (AD016) FWD range with twin carburettors.
- Second type 1098cc Morris 1100cc (AD016) FWD range with twin carburettors. Pics 68 & 69
- Later 1071cc Cooper 'S'/1275cc Cooper 'S'/970cc Cooper 'S.' (Two recesses on under side for SU dashpot tops). Pics 70-72
- Late Mk2 1275cc Cooper 'S' (Looks externally like Mk3 'S') deeper than Mk3 'S.'
- Austin/Morris 1300cc range with twin carburettors and Mk3 Cooper 'S.' (Two recesses on under side for SU dashpot tops). Part number 12G2294. Pics 73-75

Chapter 15
Gauges & mounting pods

For a more in-depth analysis of Mk1/2/3 Coopers please refer to John Parnell's book *Mini Cooper* (1993). Pages 29, 30 and 62. ISBN 187097932x.

ROUND, CENTRALLY-MOUNTED SPEEDOMETERS

Speedometers gained an additional warning light in 1964 to indicate a blocked oil filter.

Speedometers fitted with 0.1 mile facility, unless otherwise stated.

Mk1 gauges had a tapered chrome bezel fitted. Pic 1

Mk2 onward gauges had a rounded chrome bezel fitted.

The Works rally cars with the centrally-mounted speedometer were fitted with the Morris Minor speedo needle (the see-through item with the red tip).

Mk1 Mini
- 1959 Austin with old English white face (no 0.1 mile facility). Fitted with thin red needle.
- 1959 Morris with silver face (no 0.1 mile facility). Fitted with see-through needle with red tip.
- 90mph Austin with old English white face.
- 90mph Morris with silver face. Pics 2 & 3
- 90mph with black face (Austin and Morris 1961 onward). Pic 4
- Cooper with black face.
- Cooper 'S' with black face.

Mk2/3 Mini with curved chrome bezel
- 90mph. Pic 5
- Cooper. Pic 6
- Cooper 'S' (non-genuine). Pic 7

Mk4
- 90mph centrally-mounted speedo (as Mk2/3 Mini). See image for Mk2/3.
- 90mph (Clubman type) twin-gauge. Pic 8

SMITHS GAUGES
Smiths water temperature gauges (Cooper, Super and Cooper 'S')
- Mk1. Red square under letter H. Pic 9
- Mk1.
- Mk2/3 with curved chrome bezel. Pic 10

Smiths oil pressure gauges (Cooper, Super and Cooper 'S')
- Mk1. Pic 11
- Mk1. Pic 12
- Mk2/3 with curved chrome bezel. Pic 13

Clubman type Smiths gauges (Twin gauges)
See image for Mk4, 90mph (Clubman type).
- 1969 onward. Mounted in front of steering wheel.

Clubman type Smiths gauges (Triple gauges)
Pic 14
- 1275GT first type.
- Note: Fuel gauge, temperature gauge and rev counter.

Clubman type Smiths gauges (Triple gauges)
Pics 15 & 16

GAUGES & MOUNTING PODS

ANATOMY OF THE CLASSIC MINI

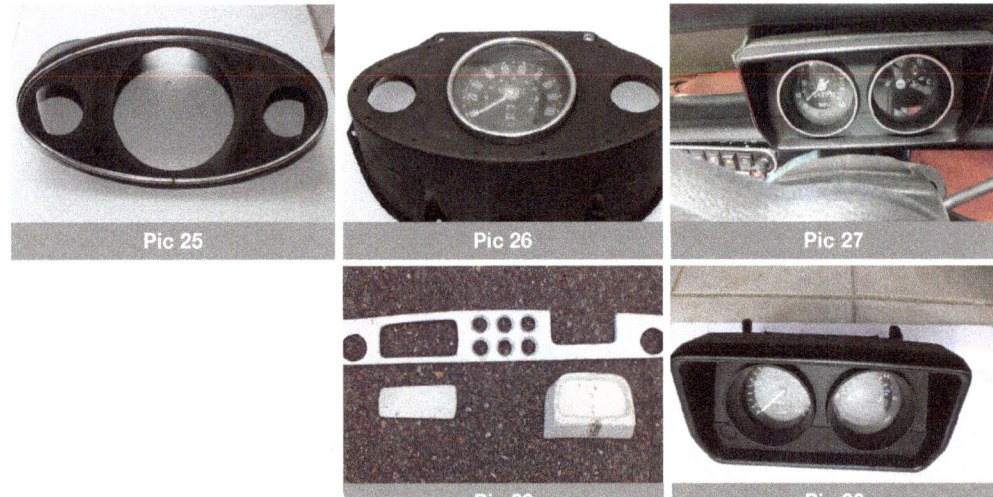

Pic 25 Pic 26 Pic 27 Pic 28
Pic 29 Pic 30

- 1275GT second type.
- Note: Fuel gauge, temperature gauge and rev counter.

NIPPON-SEIKI (TWIN GAUGES)
Pic 17
- Same plastic surround as Mini Clubman (gauges of Nippon-Seiki manufacture).

NIPPON-SEIKI (TWIN GAUGES)
- Flashing built-in LED for alarm.
- Same plastic surround as Mini Clubman (gauges of Nippon-Seiki manufacture).

NIPPON-SEIKI (TRIPLE GAUGES)
Pics 18 & 19
- Same plastic surround as Mini Clubman (gauges of Nippon-Seiki manufacture).

MOUNTING PODS Mk1 for 90mph speedometer
- 1959 to circa October 1960 non-plastic (cardboard), finished in old English white. Pic 20
- Plastic finished in old English white. Pic 21
- Plastic finished in black (this pod was also used on Mk2/3/4 Mini Pickup and Mini Van). Pic 22

Mk1 Cooper and Super also Cooper 'S'
Pics 23-25
- Combined pod to take centrally-mounted speedometer with water temperature gauge and oil pressure gauge.
- Multi-piece (plastic pod, metal backplate, four screws to mount pod to backplate, two long screws with spacers and two metal brackets to attach speedometer to metal backplate).

Mk2/3 (except base models)
Pic 26
- Black plastic pod, non-multi-piece (gauges fit directly into pod).
- Combined pod to take centrally-mounted speedometer with water temperature gauge and oil pressure gauge.

Mk4
- Black plastic for centrally-mounted speedo only. See photograph of Mk1, third type. Pic 22
- Black plastic for 90mph (Clubman type) twin-gauge. Pic 27

Mini Clubman
- Black plastic for 90mph twin-gauge. See photograph of Mk4, second type. Pic 27
- Black plastic for 120mph triple gauge. Pic 28

ERA turbo Mini dashboard
- Made of fibreglass, this is what it looks like without its trim. Pic 29

Late Mini
- Black plastic for 90mph (Clubman type) twin-gauge, less alarm. Pic 30
- Black plastic for 90mph (Clubman type) twin-gauge, with alarm.

Chapter 16
Glass & lighting

Whilst it is generally accepted that the height and width of the front windscreen did not change between 1959 and 2000, the thickness of the glass did.

FRONT WINDSCREEN
- Non-toughened glass.
- Toughened glass. Part number 14A5894.
- Laminated glass. Part number 14A5895. Pic 1
- Sundym light green tint glass. Part number CZH4048.
- Front windscreen for twin-point injection models. (Has pad stuck to screen for rear view mirror.) Part number CMB100920. Pic 2 (Courtesy Mini Spares, Potters Bar)

FRONT WINDSCREEN RUBBER
- Part number 14A6809 for toughened glass. Pic 3
- Part number 14A6842 for laminated glass. (Slot that accepts windscreen is wider because of the thicker glass.)
- Part number CCB10011 (wider rubber) vehicles from 1991 to 2000. Pic 4

DOOR GLASS
Sliding glass (front half)
- Glass without any holes, rectangular glass handle bonded to sliding glass. Photo can be found on page 70 of *Mighty Minis* by Chris Harvey, ISBN 094660911X.
- Single-hole type glass. Pic 5
- Double-hole type glass. Pics 6 & 7

Sliding glass (rear half)
- Glass without any holes, rectangular glass handle bonded to sliding glass. Photo can be found on page 70 of *Mighty Minis* by Chris Harvey, ISBN 094660911X.
- Single-hole type glass. See sliding glass (front half) single hole picture above.
- Double-hole type glass. Pics 8 & 9

Drop glass
- Riley Elf, Wolsely Hornet and Mk3 Mini 1969 onward. Pic 10 (Courtesy Mini Spares, Potters Bar). This particular dropglass is tinted.
- English Mini Cabriolet. Pics 11 & 12

QUARTER LIGHT GLASS
Mk1/2 (non-opening)
- 1959 onward. Pic 13 (Courtesy Kevin Palmer)

Mk1 (opening)
- 1959/60 piano hinge type (chrome frame). First type of window latch. Pics 14-16 (Courtesy Gaydon Heritage Motor Museum)
- Piano hinge type. (Chrome frame.) Pics 17-19
- Non-piano hinge type. (Late Mk1.) Pic 20 (Courtesy Scott Turner)

Mk2
See image for non-piano hinge type. (Late Mk1.)
- Non-piano hinge type.
- Frame split in two places: upper and lower horizontal.
- Stainless steel frame.

Mk3 onward
Pic 21
- Non-piano hinge type.
- These rear quarter lights are physically larger than those fitted to Mks1/2.

ANATOMY OF THE CLASSIC MINI

GLASS & LIGHTING

Pic 25 | Pic 26 | Pic 27 | Pic 28
Pic 29 | Pic 30 | Pic 31 | Pic 32
Pic 33 | Pic 34 | Pic 35 | Pic 36

- Stainless steel frame.

English Mini Cabriolet
Pic 22
- Wind down into rear quarter panel.

REAR WINDSCREEN
Pic 23 (Top: small, bottom: large), Pic 24 (Large heated).
- Small rear screen. (Mk1 Mini plus all Riley Elf and Wolseley Hornet models.) Pic 25
- Heated small rear screen. (Mk1 Mini/Riley Elf/Wolseley Hornet, optional in UK.)
- Large rear screen. (Mk2 onward) Pic 26
- Large heated rear screen. Pic 27
- Large heated rear screen. December 1970 onward. Heating element stuck to inside of rear screen.

REAR WINDSCREEN RUBBER
- Small screen, Mk1 Mini and all Riley Elves and Wolseley Hornets. Pic 28

- Large screen, Mk2 Mini until 2000. Pic 29

LIGHTING
Circa 1980 Cibie headlamps could be found on original Mini and Clubman. These headlamps require a Cibie headlamp bowl and, in the case of the non-Clubman, a Cibie headlamp bezel.

Front headlamps
- Bulb type. Part number 47H5354. Pics 30 & 31
- Sealed beam type. Non-Clubman. Part number 13H3471A. Pics 32 & 33
- Mini Clubman type. (Does not have facility for sidelight, sidelight is below bumper with indicator.) Pics 34 & 35
- Cibie type.
- Quadoptic. Part number XBC104430. Pic 36 (Courtesy Mini Spares, Potters Bar)

Headlamp bowls
- Metal type. Pic 37 (Courtesy Mini Spares, Potters Bar)

- Cibie type.
- Plastic type. Non self-levelling. Pics 38 & 39
- Plastic type. Self-levelling headlamps. Pic 40 (Courtesy Mini Spares, Potters Bar)

Front indicator lamps
- Small (orange lens, glass). Pic 41
- Small (orange lens, plastic). Pic 42 (Courtesy Mini Spares, Potters Bar)
- 1986 onward. Large (orange lens, plastic). Pic 43 (Courtesy Mini Spares, Potters Bar) & Pic 44
- Large (white lens with orange bulb). Pic 45 (Courtesy Mini Spares, Potters Bar)

Front indicator and side lamps
- Riley Elf, Wolsely Hornet. Pic 46
- Mini Clubman. Pic 47

Front spot lamps
- 90s Cooper. Pic 48 (Courtesy Mini Spares, Potters Bar)

ANATOMY OF THE CLASSIC MINI

Front fog lamps
- English Mini Cabriolet. Pic 49

Side repeaters on front wing
- 1979 Mini 1100 Special, rectangular. (Same as Morris 1300 FWD ADO16 ETC) Pic 50 (Courtesy Mini Spares, Potters Bar)
- 1986 onward (orange lens). Pic 51

Rear companion bin lamps (early 850)
- Fitted to deluxe models. Pic 52

Rear lamps
The Mk2/3 rear lamp was used on the base model car until 1980.
- Mk1 type. Pic 53 (Courtesy Mini Spares, Potters Bar)
- Riley Elf, Wolsely Hornet. Pics 54 & 55
- Mk2/3 type. Pic 56

GLASS & LIGHTING

Pic 57 | Pic 58 | Pic 59 | Pic 60
Pic 61 | Pic 62 | Pic 63 | Pic 64
Pic 65 | Pic 66

- Mk4 target type with Leyland logo. (With built-in reversing lamps.) 1976 onward except base model. Pic 57
- Mk4 non target type. (With built-in reversing lamps.) 1976 onward except base model. Pic 58 (Courtesy Mini Spares, Potters Bar)

Rear numberplate lamps

- One bulb, one lens. (Mounted on swinging numberplate plinth.)
- Two bulbs, one lens. (Mounted on swinging numberplate plinth.) Pic 59
- Two lamps. Riley Elf, Wolsely Hornet. Pic 60
- Two lamps (Mk3 onward). Pic 61

Rear foglamp

- 1980 onward. Pic 62 (Courtesy Mini Spares, Potters Bar) & Pic 63

Roof interior light

- Part number 13H192. Alternative to 14A9148.
- Part number 13H4398.
- Part number 14A9148. Alternative to 13H192.
- Part number 13H8919. 1974 onward, clear lens.
- Part number EAM1650. 1974 onward, white lens. Pic 64 (Courtesy Mini Spares, Potters Bar)
- Part number AFU4092. 1975 onward. Pic 65 (Courtesy Mini Spares, Potters Bar) & 66

Chapter 17
Oil system

DIPSTICKS (MANUAL PRE A+ AND A+)
All of these dipsticks are A Series, one of them is a 12A116. Pic 1
- 848cc front-wheel drive, part number 12A116.
- 997cc, part number 12A116.
- 1098cc front-wheel drive (AD016), part numbers 12A116, 12A1263.
- 998cc, part number 12A1263.
- 1275cc front-wheel drive, non 'S' part numbers 12G1782 became 12A1263, which then became LQM100380. Pic 2 (Courtesy Mini Spares, Potters Bar) & Pic 3
- 1275cc Austin Maestro/Montego. This dipstick is the longest of all A Series and A+ sticks.
- 1275cc twin-point Mini part number LQM100630. Pic 4 (Courtesy Mini Spares, Potters Bar)

DIPSTICKS (AUTOMATIC PRE A+, METAL)
Pic 5
- 848cc.
- 1098cc, part number 22A750.
- 998cc, part number 22A750.
- 1275cc, part number 22A750.

DIPSTICKS (AUTOMATIC A+)
- October 1980 onward.
- Blue plastic. Become brittle, break up, and can end up in the gearbox!

OIL FEED PIPE TO TURBO
Mini Metro Mk1/2 Turbo plus ERA Turbo Mini. Pic 6

OIL PUMP DRIVES
The Woodruff key disappeared circa 1981/82. See pic 11
- Pin drive non-Cooper 'S' with Woodruff key. Pic 7
- Pin drive Cooper 'S' with Woodruff key. Longer than standard item.
- Spider drive with Woodruff key. Pic 8
- A+ drive with Woodruff key. Pic 9
- Pin drive without Woodruff key.
- Spider drive without Woodruff key. Pic 10
- A+ drive without Woodruff key. Pic 11
- Odd ball spider drive with Woodruff key. Pic 12

OIL PUMPS (MANUAL)
- Burman. Sliding-vane type. Pic 13
- Concentric (early). Three-vane impeller. Pic 14
- Concentric three-bolt fixing. Five-vane impeller. Pic 15
- Concentric three-bolt fixing, Cooper 'S.'
- Concentric three-bolt fixing. A+ drive. Pic 16
- Concentric four-bolt fixing. Spider drive. Refer to pic 8
- Concentric four-bolt fixing. A+ drive. Pics 17 & 18
- Hobourn-Eaton. Pin drive. Pics 19-22
- Hobourn-Eaton. Spider drive. Pics 23 (with Woodruff key) & 24 (no Woodruff key)
- Hobourn-Eaton. Non-turbo. Pic 25
- Hobourn-Eaton. Turbo type. Pics 26 & 27
- Hobourn-Eaton. Flat steel plate type. Pics 28 & 29
- British Leyland Rover. Pin drive. Pics 30 & 31
- British Leyland Rover. Spider drive and A+ drive. Pic 32

OIL PUMPS (AUTOMATIC)
- Spider drive. Pics 33 & 34

OIL SYSTEM

# OIL SYSTEM

ANATOMY OF THE CLASSIC MINI

Pic 25 | Pic 26 | Pic 27 | Pic 28
Pic 29 | Pic 30 | Pic 31 | Pic 32
Pic 33 | Pic 34 | Pic 35 | Pic 36
Pic 37 | Pic 38 | Pic 39 | Pic 40
Pic 41 | Pic 42 | Pic 43 | Pic 44

- A+ drive. Different drive, refer to spider drive for image.

OIL FEED PIPES (MANUAL)

- Banjo part is made of brass soldered to steel pipe. Part number 2A712 became 8G734. Pic 35
- Non 'kettle' type. Part number TAM2106. Pic 36
- Pipe for 'kettle' type. (MG Metro, Metro Vanden Plas.) Pic 37
- 12A type. Part number LQP10033. Pics 38 & 39

OIL FEED PIPE BANJO BOLTS

- Banjo bolt for non-oil cooler engines. Pic 40
- Banjo bolt to fit automatic Mini Metro, MG Metro turbo and ERA Turbo Mini, manual RSP Rover Cooper. Pic 41

OIL SYSTEM

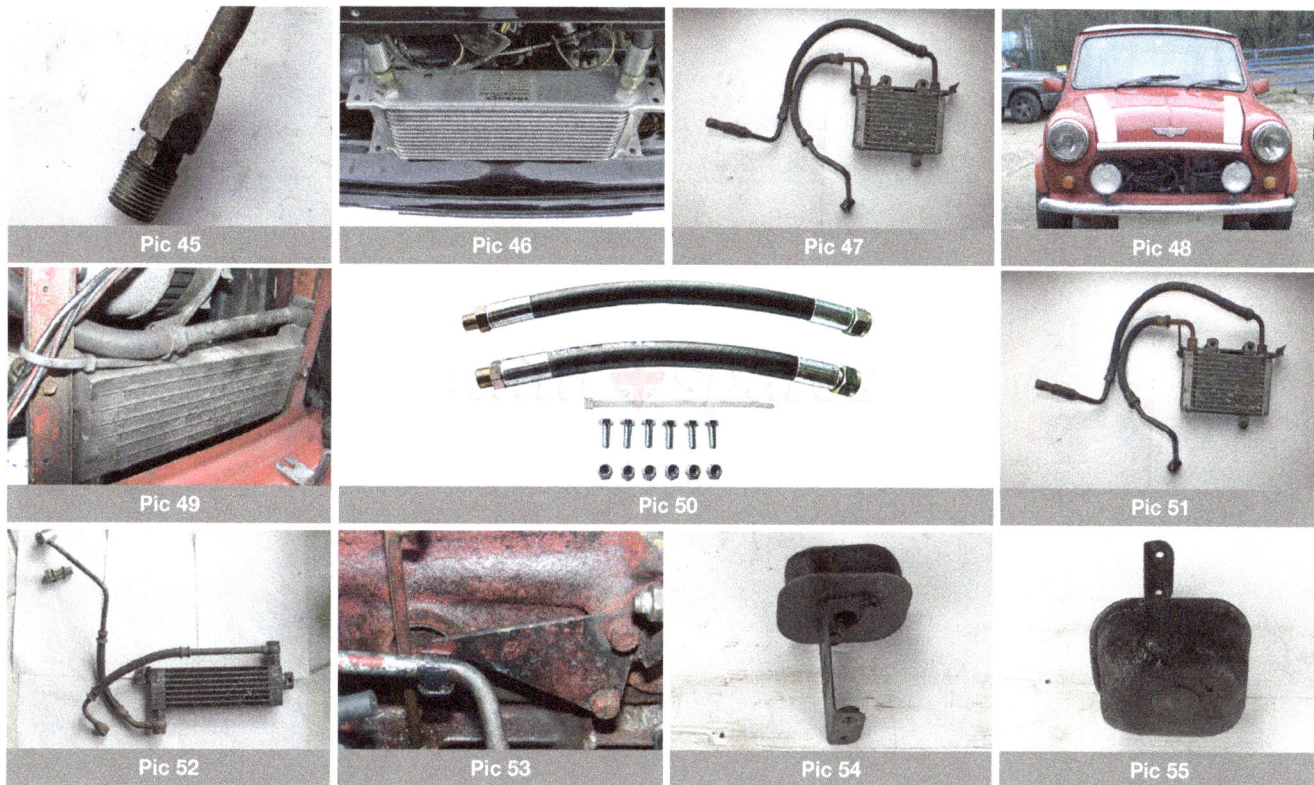

Pic 45　Pic 46　Pic 47　Pic 48
Pic 49　Pic 50　Pic 51
Pic 52　Pic 53　Pic 54　Pic 55

OIL FEED PIPES (AUTOMATIC)

- 1098cc (AD016). First part numbers 22A1248 and 22G710. (Pipe from engine block to transmission case.)
- 998cc and 1275cc. Part number 22G792. (Pipe from engine block to transmission case.) Pic 42
- 1992 onward 12A coded 1275cc.

OIL FILTER HEAD ADAPTERS (MANUAL)

- Tapered thread. Part number TCZ106. Pic 43
- Straight thread. Part number TAM2119. Pic 44

OIL FEED PIPE ADAPTERS (AUTOMATIC)

- 1098cc (AD016). First part number 22A1210, second part number 22G791.
- 998cc and 1275cc. Part number 22G791. Pic 45

OIL COOLERS

The oil coolers listed were standard fit from the factory, unless otherwise stated.
- Pre-1966 Mini Cooper 'S' not fitted from factory. Refer to *Original Mini Cooper* by John Parnell, ISBN 187097932X, page 36.
- This is a non-genuine oil cooler. An original would not have had the upper fixing bracket. Source John Meale.
- 1966 onward Mini Cooper 'S.' Pic 46
- MG Metro Turbo and Metro Automatic. Pic 47
- RSP Cooper. Part number PBC10057. (Eight-row.) Pics 48 & 49

OIL COOLER PIPES

- 1966 onward Mini Cooper 'S.' Pic 50 (Courtesy Mini Spares, Potters Bar)
- MG Metro Turbo and Metro Automatic. Pic 51
- RSP Cooper. Part numbers PBP10019 and PBP10020. Pics 52 & 53

OIL STRAINERS MINI

- Part number 2A3603. Pics 54 & 55
- Part number 22A335. Pic 56

OIL STRAINER PIPES MINI

- Narrow. Part number 2A3608. To fit oil strainer 2A3603.
- Wide. Part number 22A337. Pic 57

OIL FILTER HEAD SPACER

Pic 58

- Steel spacer, 562 thousandths of an inch thick. (MG Metro and Metro Vanden Plas.)
- Fitted with first type of spin-on oil filter head (1275cc Austin-Healey Sprite/ MG Midget).

OIL FILTER HEADS 1959 TO 1996 (MANUAL)

Two makes of oil filter head were fitted by Austin and Morris Motors, these being Tecalemit and Purolator. The Tecalemit was an option on the Austin Seven Van.
- All factory fitted oil filter heads had oil pressure relief valves fitted.

ANATOMY OF THE CLASSIC MINI

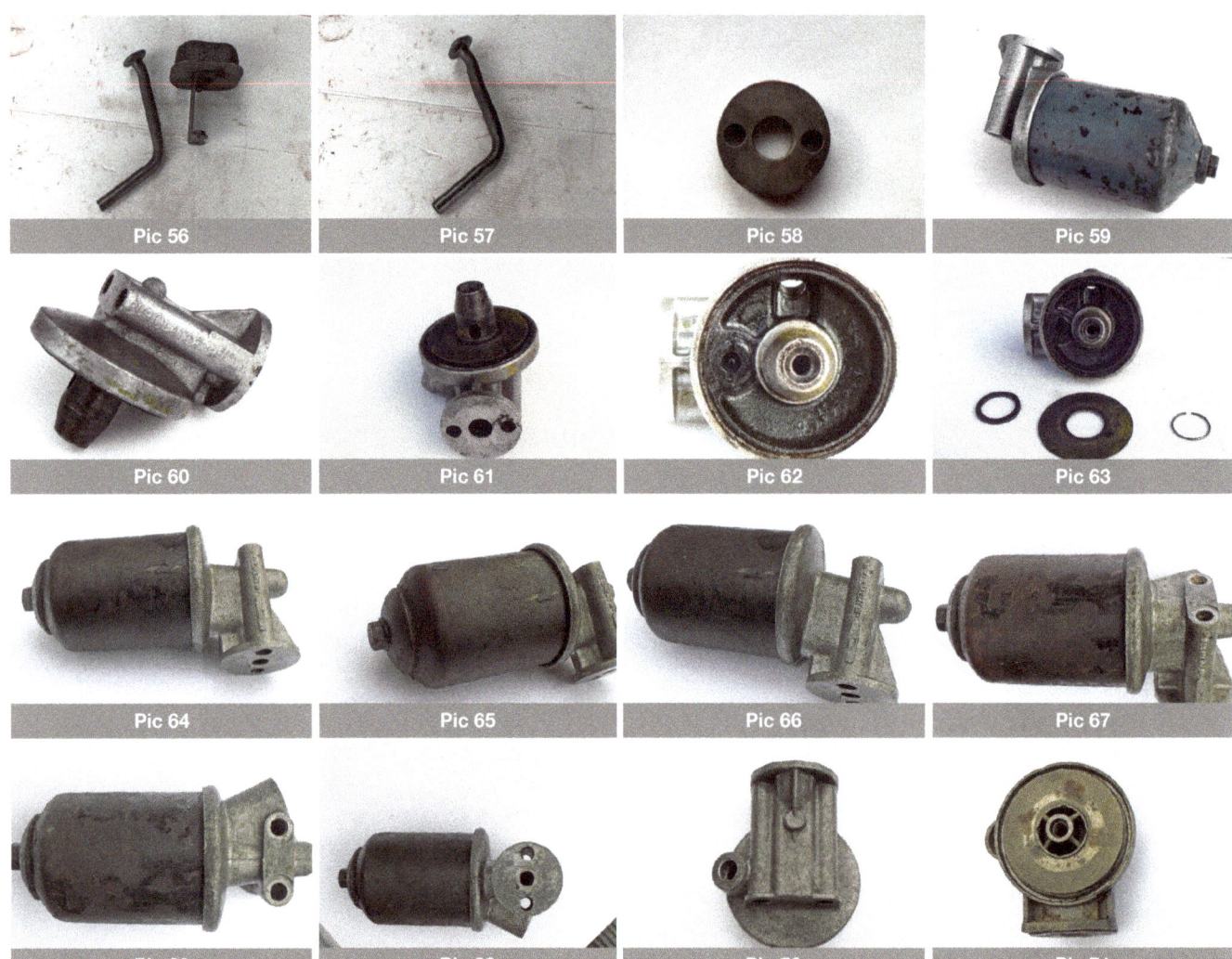

First type
Pics 59-63
- Part number 17H1170 (848cc Mini and Seven Van) for oil filter head.
- Part number 27H1717 (848cc Mini and Seven Van) for oil filter sump.
- Purolator.
- Head fitted with relief valve.
- Replaceable element type.

Second type
Pics 64-69
- Part number 17H945 (848cc Seven Van) for oil filter head.
- Part number 17H944 (848cc Seven Van) for oil filter sump.
- Tecalemit.
- Replaceable element type.

Third type
Pics 70 & 71
- Part number 37H690 (848cc Mini) for oil filter head. Chassis number 8AM-U-H103195 onward.
- Part number 17H2279 (848cc Mini) for oil filter sump in aluminium. To aid cooling.
- Part number 17H1169 (848cc Mini) for oil filter sump in steel. Chassis number 8AM-U-H103195 onward.
- Purolator.
- Replaceable element type.

Fourth type
Pics 72 & 73
- Part number 37H1226.
- Purolator.
- Replaceable element type.
- Gasket fitted between electrical switch and oil filter head.
- This type has an electrical switch fixed to one side by two bolts (Morris 1098cc (AD016) front-wheel drive, etc).

Fifth type
Pic 74
Whilst similar to the head listed above, this was the improved version incorporating a slightly modified switch.

OIL SYSTEM

Pic 72 | Pic 73 | Pic 74 | Pic 75
Pic 76 | Pic 77 | Pic 78 | Pic 79
Pic 80 | Pic 81 | Pic 82 | Pic 83
Pic 84 | Pic 85 | Pic 86 | Pic 87

Fitted with two O-rings.
- Part number 17H8891.
- Purolator.
- Replaceable element type.
- This type has an electrical switch fixed to one side by two bolts (Morris 1098cc (AD016) front-wheel drive, etc).

Sixth type
Pics 75 & 76
- Part numbers 27H3496, 27H6503, 37H1528.
- Purolator.
- Replaceable element type.
- Head fitted with electrical connector for oil filter blockage warning light.

Seventh type
Pic 77
- Purolator.
- Replaceable element type.
- Head cast for electrical connector but it is not fitted.

Eighth type
Pics 78-80
- Part number TAM2097 cast on front of head.
- Spin-on filter type head.
- Thread for oil filter attachment made of aluminium cast as part of head.
- Plain head.

Ninth type
Pic 81 (left to right: 12A2032, TAM1093, LPX10001), pics 82 & 83. Refer also to pic 80

The same head as used on the 1275cc Sprite and Midget, but used in conjunction with a spacer on MG Metro and variants, 1982 onward.
- Part number for oil filter head 12A2032.
- Purolator.
- Spin-on filter type head.
- Thread for oil filter attachment made of steel.
- Plain head.
- Additional steel spacer.

ANATOMY OF THE CLASSIC MINI

Pic 88

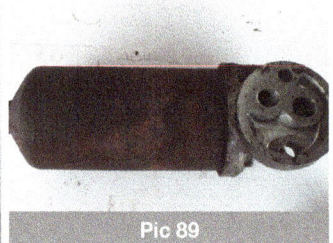
Pic 89

Pic 90

Pic 91

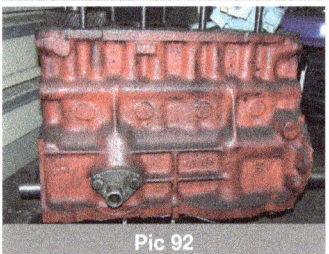
Pic 92

Tenth type
Pic 84 Refer also to pic 80

This head replaces the 1275cc Sprite/Midget type and no longer requires the spacer by virtue of the fact that the head casting is longer.
- Part number TAM1093 cast on front of head.
- Purolator.
- Spin-on filter type head.
- Thread for oil filter attachment made of steel.
- Plain head.
- Tapered thread to accept metal oil pipe adaptor.
- Fitted to MG Metro and Metro Vanden Plas.

Eleventh type
Pic 85 Refer also to pic 80

- Part number LPX10001 cast on front of head.
- Purolator.
- Spin-on filter type head.
- Thread for oil filter attachment made of steel.
- Fitted to MG Metro and Metro Vanden Plas.
- Plain head.
- Straight thread to accept metal oil pipe adaptor.

Twelfth type
Pics 86 & 87

This oil filter head was fitted to the post 1992 1275cc engines with code 12A.
- Part number LPX10026.
- Spin-on filter type head.
- Thread for oil filter attachment made of aluminium cast as part of head.
- Plain head.

OIL FILTER HEADS 1965 TO 1996 (AUTOMATIC)
- First type 1965 onward, 850, 1100, 1300 (AD016). Pic 88
- Second type, smaller diameter. Pics 89 & 90

SUPER-DUPER OIL FILTER (SPIN-ON)
Pic 91

I lay no claim to this but saw this on a Minicross car at Croft in 2007.

If you are running a competition classic Mini and you have a spin-on type oil filter head, it's a good idea to fit one of these. In the unfortunate circumstances that you damage the front of your car very badly and bend the front subframe beam, it will miss this oil filter due to its lack of height. And will probably save your engine.

Note: For competition use it is advisable to use an oil filter head with a steel thread.

TURBO OIL RETURN PLATE
Pic 92

Chapter 18
Steering

STEERING COLUMNS
First type
Pics 1-5
- 1959 to 1967.
- Mk1 steering column.
- Column drilled down the centre to allow electrical wire to pass through to horn push.
- Part number 21A1871 (inner column).

Second type
Pics 6 & 7 (Outer column)
- 1967 onward.
- Mk2 steering column.
- Inner column without drilled hole. (Horn push moved from centre of steering wheel to a stalk.)
- Part number 21A2069 (inner column without steering lock).

Third type
Pic 8
- Steering lock fitted.
- Part number 21A2437 (inner column with steering lock).

Fourth type
Pics 9 & 10
- 1976 to 1985.

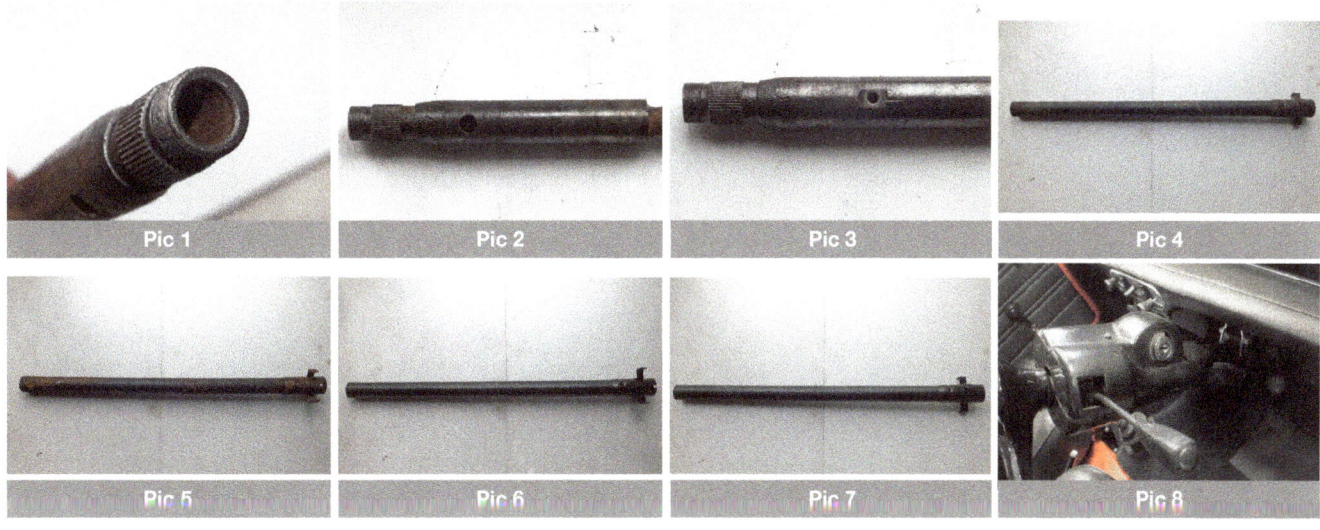

ANATOMY OF THE CLASSIC MINI

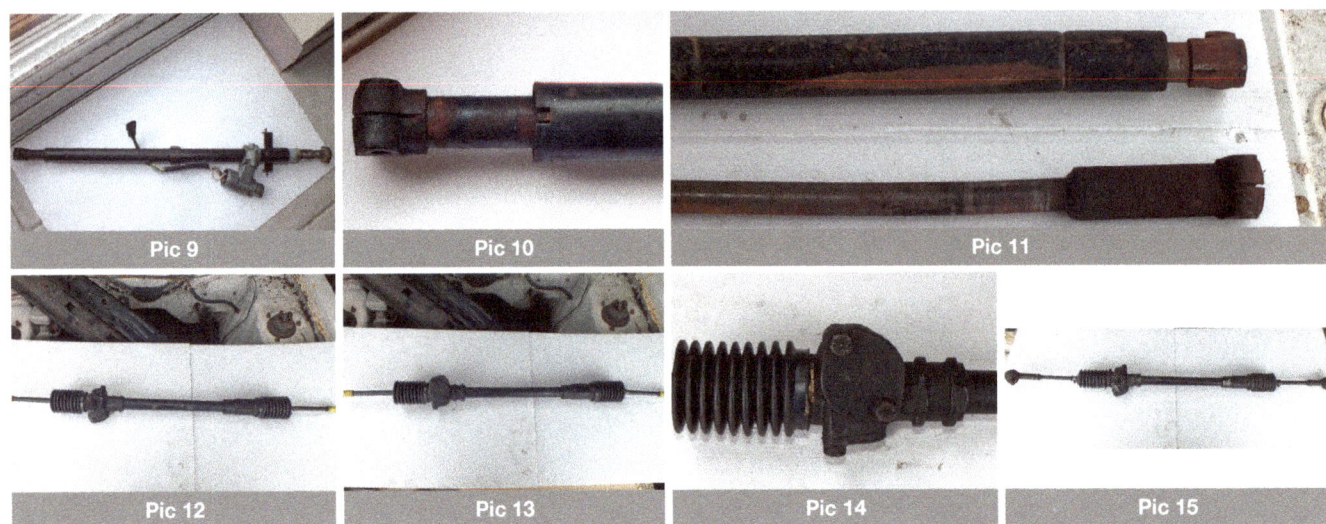

Pic 9 Pic 10 Pic 11
Pic 12 Pic 13 Pic 14 Pic 15

- Mk4 onward.
- Part number FAM5285 (inner column).

Fifth type
Pic 11 top: Mk1/2/3 inner and outer; bottom: inner shaft from an SPI Mini.
- 1985 to 1996.
- Part number NAM8527 (inner and outer column).
- Non-airbag.

Sixth type
- 1996 onward.
- Part number QMB101550PMA (inner and outer column).
- With airbag.

STEERING RACKS (RIGHT-HAND DRIVE) Mk1
There are four different part numbers listed for the Mk1 steering rack. 2A6205, 21A368, 21A715 and 21A1422.
- 1959 to 1967.
- Manufactured by Camgears.
- Identified by one Phillips screw on nearside aluminium housing to which the rack gaiter attaches.

2A6205
- 848cc Mini Saloon only.
- Austin chassis numbers A-A2S7-101 to 9799.
- Morris chassis numbers M-A2S4-101 to 8011.
- Pinion part number 17H6300.
- Rack part number 17H6301.
- Austin chassis numbers A-A2S7-101 to 536.
- Morris chassis numbers M-A2S4-101 to 1960.
- Rack part number 17H6377.
- Austin chassis numbers A-A2S7-537 to 9799.
- Morris chassis numbers M-A2S4-1961 to 8011.
- Tie rods part number 17H6288 (Two per rack).
- Trackrod ends part number 2A6207 (Two per rack).
- Pad damper part number ACA5244.
- Spring damper part number ACA5248.

21A368
- 848cc Mini Saloon only.
- Austin chassis numbers A-A2S7-9800 to 119433.
- Morris chassis numbers M-A2S4-8012 to 72655.
- Pinion part number 17H6300.
- Rack part number 17H6376.
- Tie rods part number 17H6288 (Two per rack).
- Trackrod ends part number 2A6207 (Two per rack).
- Pad damper part number ACA5244.
- Spring damper part number ACA5248.

21A715
- 848cc Mini Saloon, 848cc Riley Elf/Wolseley Hornet and 997cc Mini Cooper.
- Austin chassis numbers A-A2S7-119434 to 453263, 451964M.
- Morris chassis numbers M-A2S4-72656 to 221439 (less 220357 to 221000).
- Pinion part number 17H6300.
- Rack part number 17H6376.
- Tie rods part number 17H6288 (Two per rack).
- Trackrod ends part number 8G8625 (Two per rack).
- Pad damper part number ACA5244.
- Spring damper part number ACA5248.

21A1422
This is the final incarnation of the Mk1 steering rack, the previous three are externally the same except for the bottom plate under the pinion.
Pics 12-14
- Austin chassis numbers A-A2S7-453264 on, 451965M on.
- Morris chassis numbers M-A2S4-221440 on, plus 220357 to 221000.
- Pinion part number 17H6300.

STEERING

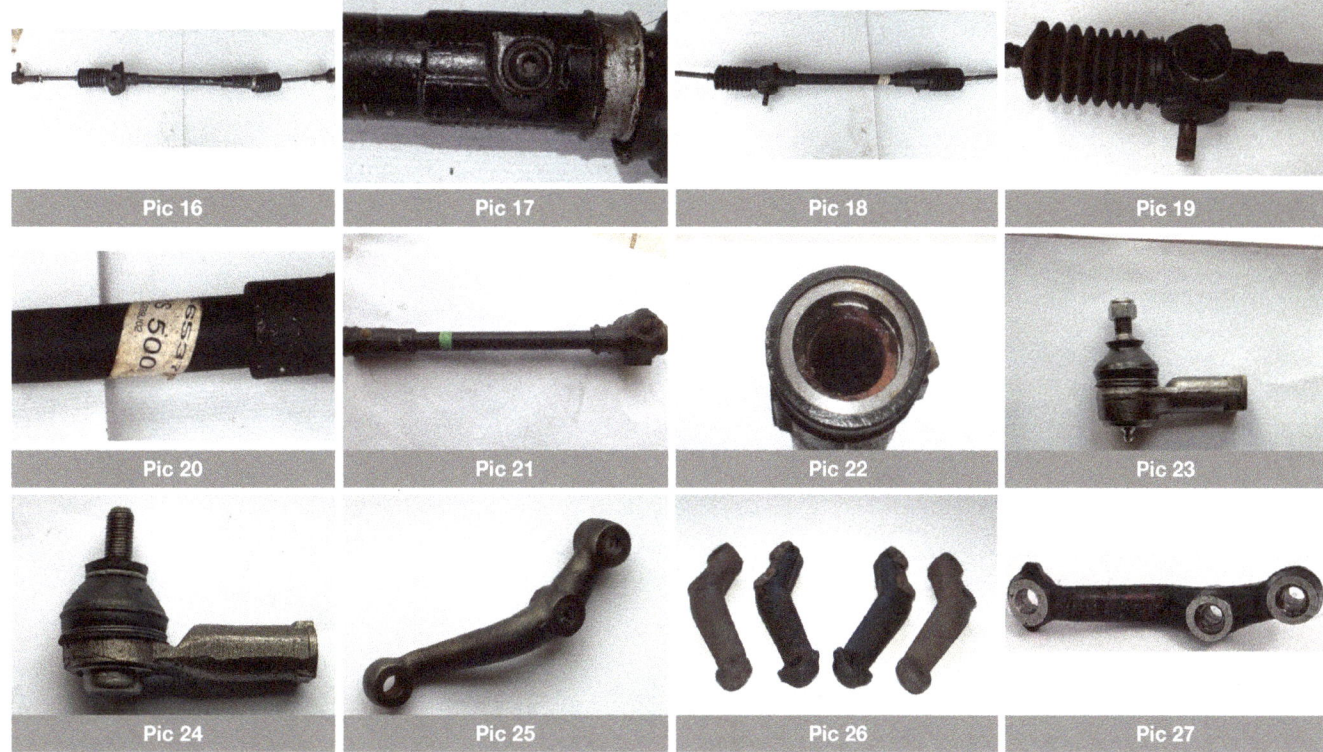

- Rack part number 17H6376.
- Tie rods part number 17H8864 (2 per rack).
- Trackrod ends part number 8G8625 (Two per rack).
- Rack support part number 17H8264.
- Plate cover part number 17H8265.
- Spring disc part number 17H8266.

Mk2
Pic 15
October 1968 onward rack housing drilled to allow centring pin to be used.
- 1967 to 1969.
- Manufactured by Camgears.
- Identified by one raised boss on nearside aluminium housing to which the rack gaiter attaches.
- Plastic plug pushes into raised boss.

Mk3 onward
Images of two different Mk3 onward steering racks.
Pics 16 & 17 Nylon allen screw
Pics 18-20

- 1969 onward.
- Manufactured by Camgears.
- Identified by one raised boss on nearside aluminium housing that rack gaiter attaches to.
- Plastic plug screws into raised boss (require allen key).

Mk7 (twin-point injection cars) with 13in wheels
Pics 21 & 22
- First offered as an option pre 1996.
- 1996 onward.
- Manufactured by TRW.
- Two collars fitted to rack, one each end to restrict turning circle.

TRACKROD ENDS
First type
Pic 23
- 1959 onward.
- Grease nipple fitted on underside.
- Part number 2A6207.

Second type
Pic 24
- Non-grease nipple type.
- Part number 8G8625.

STEERING ARMS
First type
Pic 25 (Right-hand)
- 1959 to 1967.
- Mk1.
- Non-Cooper 'S.'
- This steering arm could also be found on early 1071cc 'S' cars but was then changed to a specific Cooper 'S' arm listed below.
- Left-hand part number 21A73.
- Right-hand part number 21A74.

Second type
Pic 26 (Outer pair: steering arms Mk1 'S.' Inner pair: steering arms Mk2/3 'S')
- Cooper 'S' type.

Third type
Pics 27 & 28 (Courtesy Mini Spares,

ANATOMY OF THE CLASSIC MINI

Potters Bar)
- 1967 onward.
- Mk2 to Mk 7.
- Non-Cooper 'S.'
- Right-hand part number BTA896.
- Left-hand part number BTA897.

Fourth type
Pic 29 (Nearside)
- 1967 to 1971.
- Mk2/3.
- Cooper 'S.'
- Right-hand part number BTA894.
- Left-hand part number BTA895.

STEERING ARM SPACER
Pic 30
- Fitted between the steering arm and the swivel hub.
- ERA Turbo Mini only.
- Requires longer bolts.

STEERING ARM FIXING BOLTS
- Everything except ERA Turbo.

- ERA Turbo.

STEERING WHEELS
These are just some of the myriad steering wheels available from the factory.
- Mk1. Pics 31 & 32 (Hole to access screw holding horn push into position)
- Mk2/3. (Looks externally the same as Mk1 but does not have hole drilled to pass screwdriver through to get to screw holding in horn push.) See photograph of Mk1.
- 1969 onward Mini Clubman three-spoke. Pic 33
- 1976 onward plain padded two-spoke. Pic 34
- 1979 Mini 1100 Special. Pic 35
- 1980 onward four-spoke. Pic 36
- 1984 Mini 25. Pic 37
- 1989 Mini 30 and 90 onward, Mini Cooper. Pics 38 & 39
- 1990 Cooper. Pic 40 (Monte Carlo Special Edition with wrong insert)
- 1992 Mini British open classic. (Cream leather steering wheel.) Pic 41

SWIVEL HUBS
The 1275GT Mini Clubman was the first production Mini to be fitted with Denovo and then 12in wheels. I believe that the disc brake swivel hub was the post-1984 type.

Drum brake swivel hubs
The first drum brake swivel hub had a different ball seat spring than the later.

Ball seat spring
- Part number 2A4243 fitted to swivel hubs chassis number A-A2S7-101 to A-A2S7-16249.
- Standardised ball seat spring. Pic 42

First type
- 1959 onward.
- Right-hand swivel hub part number 2A4312.
- Left-hand swivel hub part number 2A4320.
- These swivel hubs were fitted from chassis number A-A2S7-101 to A-A2S7-16249.

STEERING

Pic 40 | Pic 41 | Pic 42 | Pic 43
Pic 44 | Pic 45 | Pic 46 | Pic 47
Pic 48 | Pic 49

Second type
Pic 43
- These swivel hubs were fitted from chassis number A-A2S7-16250 onward.
- Right-hand swivel hub part number 21A371.
- Left-hand swivel hub part number 21A372.

Disc brake swivel hubs
If you have a car fitted with 10in wheels and require a replacement swivel hub, the only items available new are part numbers FAM2390 and FAM2391. Some fettling with a grinder will be required, though, as they differ slightly to part numbers BTA186 and BTA187.

First type
Pics 44 & 45
- 1961 onward.
- 997cc/998cc Cooper.
- 1071cc/1275cc/970cc Cooper 'S.'
- 10in-wheeled 1275GT Clubman.
- Right-hand part number BTA186.
- Left-hand part number BTA187.

Second type
Pic 46
- 12- and 13in-wheeled cars.
- Right-hand part number FAM2390.
- Left-hand part number FAM2391.

BALL JOINTS
First type
- 1959 onward.
- This ball joint was short-lived in production.
- Part number 2A4235.
- Austin chassis numbers A-A2S7-101 to 420777 right-hand drive.
- Austin chassis number A-A2S7-418508 left-hand drive.

Second type
Pic 47
- Standardised ball joint.
- Common to all but very early Mini.
- Part number BTA445.

BALL JOINT SEAT
Part number 2A4236
- Austin chassis numbers A-A2S7-101 to 44383 right-hand drive.
- Austin chassis number A-A2S7-43674 left-hand drive.
- Morris chassis numbers M-A2S4-101 to 37222.

Part number 21A615
- Follows on after 2A4236. Pic 48

BALL JOINT RETAINER
Part number 2A4237
- Austin chassis numbers A-A2S7-101 to 44383 right-hand drive.
- Austin chassis number A-A2S7-43674 left-hand drive.
- Morris chassis numbers M-A2S4-101 to 37222.

Part number 21A616
- Follows on after 2A4237. Pic 49

Chapter 19
Subframes & suspension

Original subframes had the letters 'Mowog' stamped into them.

FRONT DAMPER/ SHOCK ABSORBER TOP MOUNTS

- Thin pin top mount. Part numbers 21A4 right-hand, 21A6 left-hand. These mounts were changed because the pin used to bend even with standard dampers (shock absorbers). Pics 1-3
- Thick pin top mount. Part numbers 21A471 right-hand, 21A474 left-hand. Pics 4 & 5

FRONT SUBFRAME MOUNTINGS 1976 ONWARD

- Turret bolts and rubbers. (Two per vehicle.) Pic 6
- Front teardrop. (Two per vehicle.) Pic 7
- Rear legs. (Two per vehicle.) Pics 8 & 9

FRONT SUBFRAMES (2A5820, 21A1613, 21A2570)

- All front subframes have two locating bolts passing through the front panel into the subframe, unless otherwise stated. Please refer to first type of front subframe.
- All front subframes are affixed to bodyshell by ten fixings, unless otherwise stated.
- Austin cars secured the front subframe to the underbonnet box section with four bolts. (Mk1 to Mk3.5.) Pic 10
- Morris cars used four bolts (chassis numbers M-A2S4-101 to 32083), then went over to four studs with nuts to retain the front subframe to the front box section. (Mk1 to Mk3.5.) Pic 11
- Turret, top ten fixing frame. Pic 12
- Turret, top hydrolastic frame. Pic 13
- Turret, top 1976 onward frame. Pics 14 & 15
- Inside turret, dry suspension. Pic 16
- Inside turret, hydrolastic suspension. Pic 17
- Straight front beam, pre-1990 manual. Pic 18
- Shaped front beam, automatic 1965 onward and 1990 onward manual. Pics 19-21
- Lower rear legs, ten fixing frame. Pic 22

Offside lower rear leg, eight fixing frame. Pic 23
Offside front lower forward facing stabiliser bar location bracket, 1976 onward. Pic 24
- First type of front subframe had two bolts and two locating dowels fastening the frame to the front panel. It also had two elongated holes to take the two bolts into the toe board. Photo can be found on page 12 of *Mighty Minis* by Chris Harvey, ISBN 094660911X.
- 1959 onward. Spring type suspension. (Common type.)
- 1964 onward. Hydrolastic type suspension, manual gearbox saloon models.
- 1965 onward. Automatic saloon models. Hydrolastic type suspension. Part number 21A1733/1773.
- Circa January 1965 onward. Hydrolastic front subframes strengthened. This photo is of the inside front turret, opposite the bump stop. Part number 21A1846. Pic 25
- 1969 onward. Automatic saloon models, spring type suspension. Part number 21A1816.
- 1973 onward. Rod-change type manual gearbox, spring type suspension.

SUBFRAMES & SUSPENSION

ANATOMY OF THE CLASSIC MINI

Pic 25 • Pic 26 • Pic 27 • Pic 28
Pic 29 • Pic 30 • Pic 31 • Pic 32
Pic 33 • Pic 34 • Pic 35 • Pic 36

- 1976 onward. Eight-bolt spring type suspension, manual gearbox models. Part number KGB10022.
- 1976 onward. Automatic gearbox models. Eight-bolt spring type suspension. Part number KGB10024.
- 1989 ERA turbo Mini. Eight-bolt spring type suspension. The ERA Mini had two lower rearward facing stabiliser bars. Part number ERA1062. Pics 26-28
- 1990s manual gearbox models, eight-bolt spring type suspension, engine moved forward by 0.375in. Part number KGB10027.
- 1990s automatic gearbox models, eight-bolt spring type suspension, cut out in front beam to clear inhibitor switch (Japanese spec). Engine moved forward by 0.375in.
- 1996 onward. All models. Manual gearbox eight-bolt spring type suspension, engine moved forward by 0.375in, with facility to fit front-mounted radiator. Part number KGB100500. Pics 29-31

FRONT SUBFRAME SPACERS

I believe that there were no spacers fitted between the turret top and bulkhead box section on hydrolastic cars.
- First type. Pics 32 & 33
- Second type. Pic 34

FRONT SUBFRAME BUMP STOPS

- Mk 1-3.5 (dry 2A4332).
- Mk 1/2 Hydrolastic 21A1598.
- M4 onward FAM2764.

REAR SUBFRAME BRACKET

- Early non-reinforced. Pic 35
- Reinforced. Effectively doubling the thickness of the bracket where the radius arm pin passes through it. Pic 36 (Courtesy Mini Spares, Potters Bar)

REAR SUBFRAMES (2A5776, 21A406, 21A779, 21A1655)

Original rear subframes had MOWOG stamped into them.
An original dry suspension type rear subframe does not have two holes punched in the rear beam. (These two holes are for the later hydrolastic type.)
Topside of rear subframe: Pic 37
Underside of rear subframe: Pic 38
- Spring type suspension. Pics 39 & 40
- Hydrolastic type suspension. Part number 21A2160. Pic 41 Image of front locking ring same as back locking ring.
- 1976 onward. Fitted with steel bump stop. Pic 42
- Spring type suspension with inner rear bump stop (ERA Turbo).
- Spring type suspension with exhaust mounting brackets welded to frame. Part number KHB10024. Pics 43-46
- Sports pack. Reinforced. (13in-wheeled cars.) Part number KHB100590. Pic 47

SUBFRAMES & SUSPENSION

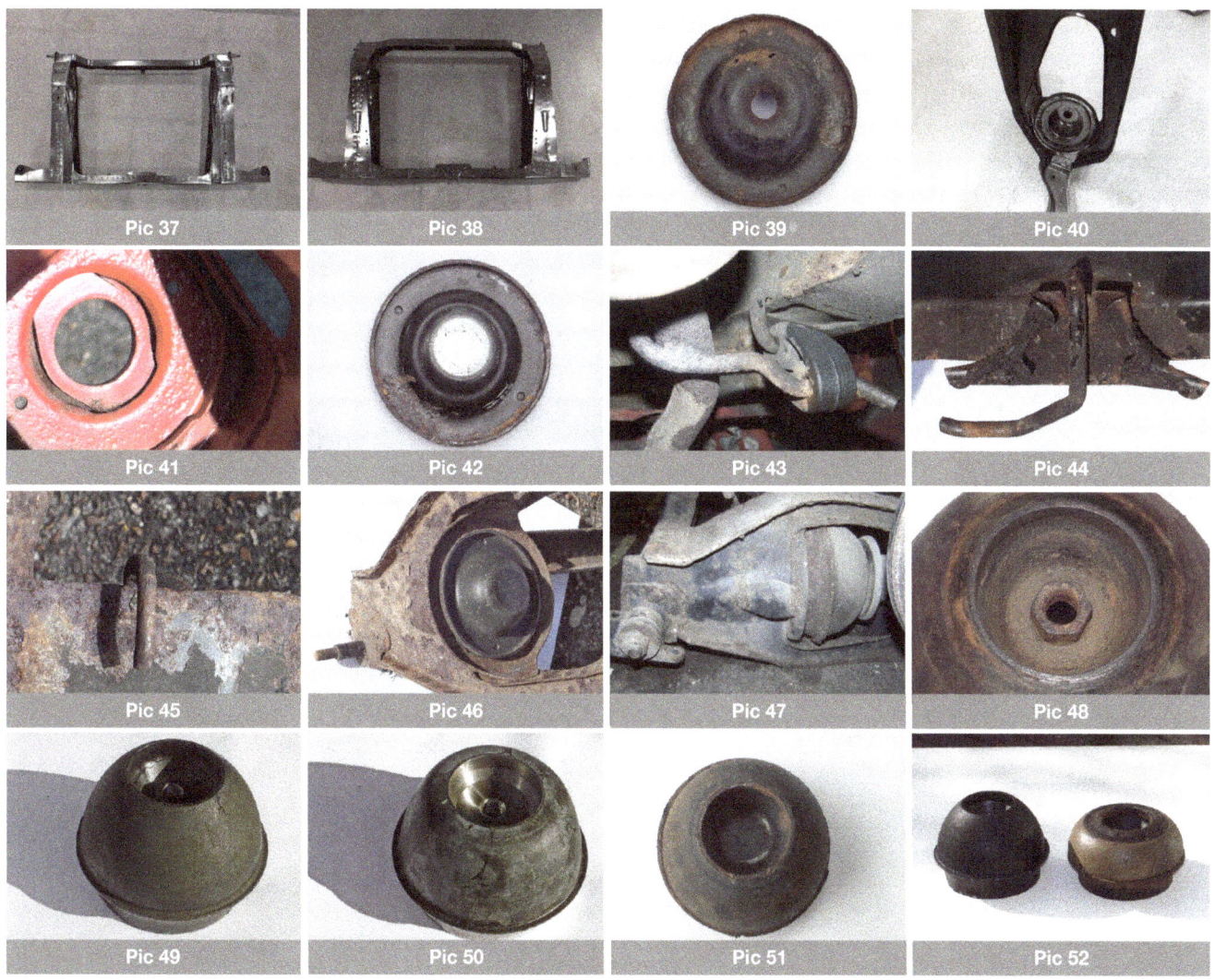

Pic 37 Pic 38 Pic 39 Pic 40
Pic 41 Pic 42 Pic 43 Pic 44
Pic 45 Pic 46 Pic 47 Pic 48
Pic 49 Pic 50 Pic 51 Pic 52

SUSPENSION SPRINGS

Believe it or not collapsed springs do actually have a use when no longer any good for a road car. The class one grass trackers use them on the front of their Minis to get a lower ride height.
- Imperial nut. Fine thread. Part number 2A4342. Pic 48
- Metric nut. Coarse thread. Pic 49
- Innocenti 90 (998cc) and 120 (1275cc) 1974 to 1980. Pic 50
- No nut. (Rear only.) Pic 51
- Collapsed metric nut spring. Pic 52 (left, new; right, collapsed).

HYDROLASTIC DISPLACER UNITS
Front
Pic 53
- Non colour coded.
- One yellow band.
- One red band.
- One orange band.
- One green band.
- Two orange bands.
- One blue band.
- Two silver bands.

Rear
See image for front Non-colour coded.
- Non-colour coded.
- One yellow band.
- Two red bands.
- One orange band.
- One green band.
- Two orange bands.
- Two blue bands.
- Two silver bands.

HYDROLASTIC REAR BUMP STOPS
- First type. Bolts to top of radius arm. Pic 54
- Second type. Fits behind radius arm, bolts to rear subframe. Pics 55 & 56

ANATOMY OF THE CLASSIC MINI

Pic 53 | Pic 54 | Pic 55 | Pic 56
Pic 57 | Pic 58 | Pic 59 | Pic 60
Pic 61 | Pic 62 | Pic 63 | Pic 64
Pic 65 | Pic 66 | Pic 67 | Pic 68

SUSPENSION SPRING BUMP STOPS (REAR ONLY)
- Metal type. Pics 57 & 58
- Mini ERA turbo. (Metal and rubber.) Part number ERA1190 plus ERA1191 Cap bolt. Pic 59

SUSPENSION STRUTS
Front
- Front fabricated steel type. Part number 2A4355. Pic 60
- Front fabricated steel type. Part number 2A4355 plus special washer part number 21A463. Knuckle and washer. Pic 61
- Front cast aluminium type. Part number 21A530. Pic 62

Rear
Note. The long wheelbase suspension struts are listed here for information.
- Rear fabricated steel type. (Saloon) part number 2A7375. Pic 63
- Rear fabricated steel type. (Saloon) part number 2A7375 plus special washer part number 21A463. Knuckle and washer. Pic 64
- Rear cast aluminium type. (Saloon) part number 21A1031. Pics 65 & 66
- Rear cast aluminium type, wider platform. (LWB and 1976 onward saloons.) Pics 66 & 67

SUSPENSION KNUCKLES AND CUPS
- Mushroom type knuckle. Pic 68
- Mushroom type knuckle with special washer. Pic 69
- Knuckle without built-in spacer. September 1962 onward. Pic 70
- 1990 onward. Knuckle with built-in spacer. (Front only). Pic 71

SUSPENSION FRONT UPPER ARM
Part numbers 2A4316 right-hand, 2A4322 left-hand
- Front arm for spring type suspension.

SUBFRAMES & SUSPENSION

Pic 69 | Pic 70 | Pic 71 | Pic 72
Pic 73 | Pic 74 | Pic 75 | Pic 76
Pic 77 | Pic 78 | Pic 79 | Pic 80
Pic 81 | Pic 82 | Pic 83 | Pic 84

• Austin chassis numbers A-A2S7-101 to 44383 right-hand drive.
• Austin chassis number A-A2S7-43694 left-hand drive.
• Morris chassis numbers M-A2S4-101 to 37222.

Part numbers 21A611 right-hand, 21A613 left-hand

• Dry (spring-type suspension). Pic 72 (Left, dry; right, wet, hydrolastic.)
• Front arm for spring type suspension.

Hydrolastic

See Pic 72 for dry and wet upper arms. Part numbers 21A1479 (right-hand), 21A1482 (left-hand).
• Front arm for hydrolastic type suspension.

SUSPENSION FRONT UPPER ARM THRUST WASHERS

• Copper-faced thrust washer. (Early.) Pic 73
• Non copper-faced thrust washer. (Very common.) Pic 74 (Courtesy Mini Spares, Potters Bar)

SUSPENSION FRONT LOWER ARM

• Lower arm to accept plain top-hat type rubber bushes. Part numbers 2A4318 right-hand, 2A4324 left-hand. Pics 75-77
• Lower arm to accept bushes with steel insert. Part numbers 21A1879 right-hand, 21A1881 left-hand. Pics 78-80
• Mini ERA turbo. (Longer arm to achieve slight negative camber.) Part numbers ERA1038 right-hand, ERA1039 left-hand. Pics 81-83

SUSPENSION FRONT LOWER ARM RETAINING PIN AND WASHER
First type

• Accepts top-hat type bushes, thick

ANATOMY OF THE CLASSIC MINI

pin where bushes fit.
• Straight pin. Part number 2A4362. Right-hand drive A-A2S7-101-32945, M-A2S4-101-25550 and left-hand drive A-A2S7-101-32232.
• Washer to go with straight pin. Part number AJD7232. Right-hand drive A-A2S7-101-9800, M-A2S4-101-14763 and left-hand drive A-A2S7-101-9368.

Second type
• Wiggly pin accepts top-hat type bushes, thick pin where bushes fit.

Third type
• Accepts bushes with steel insert, thin pin where bushes fit.
• Wiggly pin. Pic 84

Fourth type
• Accepts bushes with steel insert, thin pin where bushes fit.
• Wiggly pin with welded on washer. Part number 21A1889. Pic 85

SUSPENSION FRONT TIE BAR
The first two tie bars 21A263 and 21A448, I describe these as 'Staple type.' If you view the tie bar where it affixes to the lower wish bone they are shaped like a staple. These tie bars were weak, and the design was changed with the introduction of part number 21A450.

Part number 21A263
• Staple type.
• Austin chassis numbers A-A2S7-101 to 32945 right-hand drive.
• Austin chassis number 32232 left-hand drive.
• Morris chassis numbers M-A2S4-101 to 25550.

Part number 21A448
• Staple type.
• Shorter than part number 21A263.
• To achieve three degrees of caster.

Part number 21A450
Pic 86 Top: Longer tie bar, Bottom: 21A450
• Non staple type.
• Same length as part number 21A448.
• Austin chassis numbers A-A2S7-72808 onward right-hand drive.
• Austin chassis number 70901 left-hand drive.
• Morris chassis numbers M-A2S4-57210 onward.

13in-wheeled cars
See image for 21A450 that shows both tie bars together.
• Longer tie bar for 13in-wheeled cars.

REAR RADIUS ARMS
• First type of fabricated rear radius arm. (Non handbrake quadrant type.) Fitted with two bushes. Pic 87
• Second type of fabricated rear radius arm. (Handbrake quadrant type.) Fitted with two bushes. Pic 88
• Cast iron for spring type suspension.

SUBFRAMES & SUSPENSION

Fitted with one needle roller and one bush. Pics 89-92
- Cast iron for hydrolastic type suspension. (Saloon only.) Fitted with one needle roller and one bush. Pic 93

- 1992 onward. Small recess in wheel bearing stub shaft boss to accept rubber ring to prevent water ingress. Fitted with one needle roller and one bush. Pic 94

REAR RADIUS ARM STUB AXLES

- Dry type. Pic 95
- Wet type. (Hydrolastic.) Pic 96

Chapter 20
Transmission & lower stabiliser bars

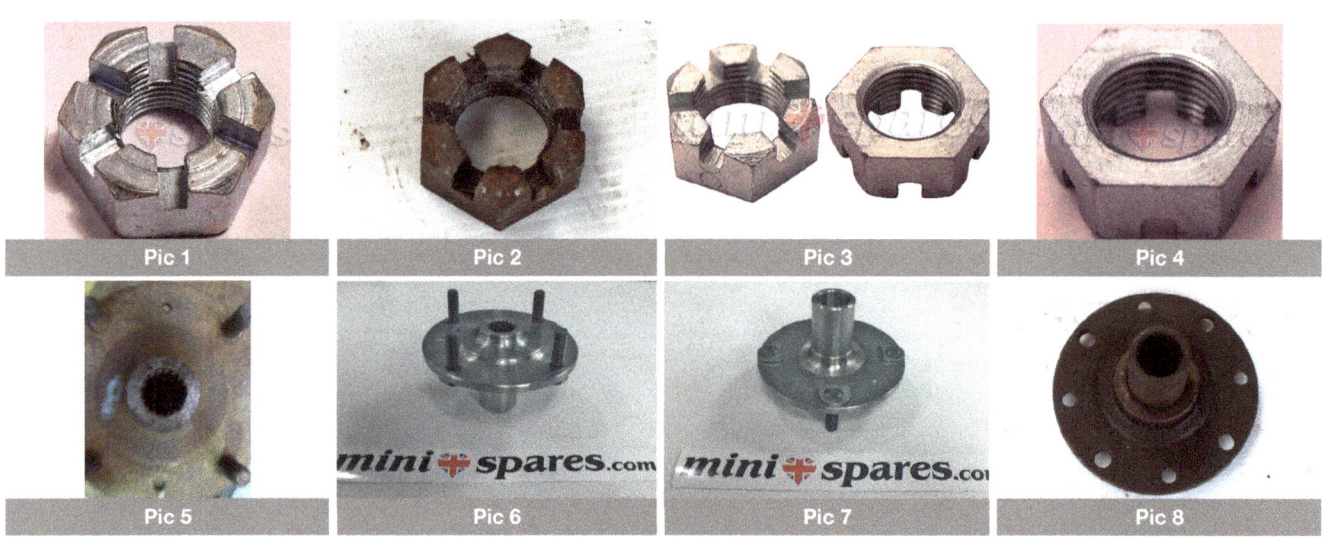

Pic 1   Pic 2   Pic 3   Pic 4
Pic 5   Pic 6   Pic 7   Pic 8

CONSTANT VELOCITY JOINT NUTS
- Drum-brake cars and 997/998 Cooper. Part number 21A79. Pics 1 (Courtesy Mini Spares, Potters Bar) & 2
- Cooper 'S.' Part number BTA249. Pics 3 & 4 (Courtesy Mini Spares, Potters Bar)

Parts behind CV nuts
- 2A7323 washer for drum brakes and 997/8 Cooper
- 'S' outer tapered collar and 8.4in disc brakes (FAM9270A). Always lubricate tapered collar faces before doing up nuts.

Drive flanges
Drum brake
Refer also to 'Drum-brake outer constant velocity joints' below.

Part number 2A4244
Pic 5
- 1959.

TRANSMISSION & LOWER STABILISER BARS

Pic 9 | Pic 10 | Pic 11 | Pic 12
Pic 13 | Pic 14 | Pic 15 | Pic 16
Pic 17 | Pic 18 | Pic 19 | Pic 20

- Drive flange square splines.
- This flange fitted the early outer constant velocity joint with the eighteen-spline driveshaft and early wheel bearing.
- Austin chassis numbers A-A2S7-101 to 26590, right-hand drive.
- Austin chassis numbers A-A2S7-26708, left-hand drive.
- Morris chassis numbers M-A2S4-101 to 24831, right-hand drive.

Part number 21A231
Pics 6 & 7
- Involute splines.
- Austin chassis numbers A-A2S7-26591 on, right-hand drive.
- Austin chassis numbers A-A2S7-26709 on, left-hand drive.
- Morris chassis numbers M-A2S4-24832 on, right-hand drive.

Disc brake
- 997cc/998cc Cooper drive flange. Part number BTA191. Pics 8 & 9

- Early 1071cc Cooper 'S' two-piece drive flange. (Parts obtained from P Giffen.) Pics 10 (also shows inner tapered collar, part number BTA663) & 11
- Later 'S' type and 10in 1275GT drive flange, one-piece. Part number 21A1270. Pics 12 & 13
- 12in 1275GT and all models 1984 onward drive flange. Part number 21A2695. Pic 14 (Courtesy Mini Spares, Potters Bar)
- ERA turbo drive flange. Part number NAM6450F. Pic 15 (Courtesy Mini Spares, Potters Bar)

Wheel bearings
Front wheel bearings
- Ball fitted to early models with drive flange 2A4244. Part number 13H107.
- Ball with spacer. Part number 21A234.
- Ball with built-in spacer. Part number GHB211. Pics 16 & 17 (Courtesy Mini Spares, Potters Bar)

- Taper roller with spacer. Pic 18
- Taper roller with built-in spacer.

Rear wheel bearings
- Ball with spacer part number 13H113. Pic 19
- Ball with built-in spacer. Part number GHB212. Pic 20
- Taper roller with spacer. Pic 21
- Taper roller with built-in spacer. Pic 22
- Taper roller with built-in spacer plus rubber O-ring. August 1996 onward. Pic 23 (Courtesy Mini Spares, Potters Bar)

DRUM BRAKE OUTER CONSTANT VELOCITY JOINTS
Refer also to drive flanges above.

Part number 17H8895
- Eighteen square splines driveshaft end.
- Austin chassis numbers A-A2S7-101 to 26590, right-hand drive.
- Austin chassis numbers

ANATOMY OF THE CLASSIC MINI

Pic 21 | Pic 22 | Pic 23 | Pic 24
Pic 25 | Pic 26 | Pic 27 | Pic 28
Pic 29 | Pic 30 | Pic 31 | Pic 32
Pic 33 | Pic 34 | Pic 35 | Pic 36

A-A2S7-26708, left-hand drive.
- Morris chassis numbers M-A2S4-101 to 24831, right-hand drive.
- Morris chassis numbers M-A2S4-25246, left-hand drive.

Part number 17H8896
- Nineteen splines on driveshaft end.

Part number 17H8600
Pic 24
- Nineteen involute splines on driveshaft end.
- Austin chassis numbers A-A2S7-26591 onward, right-hand drive.
- Austin chassis numbers A-A2S7-26709 onward, left-hand drive.
- Morris chassis numbers M-A2S4-24832 onward, right-hand drive.
- Morris chassis numbers M-A2S4-25247 onward, left-hand drive.

DISC BRAKE OUTER CONSTANT VELOCITY JOINTS
- 997cc/998cc Cooper constant velocity joint. Part number 17H8600. See 17H8600 above.
- 'S' type constant velocity joint, nineteen splines on driveshaft end, one hole drilled through joint for split pin. (Fits all with 7.5in/8.4in discs.) Part number BAU4444. Pic 25
- 'S' type constant velocity joint, nineteen splines on driveshaft end, two holes drilled through joint for split pin. (Fits all with 7.5in/8.4in discs.) Pic 26

DRIVESHAFTS
All driveshafts have nineteen splines where the shaft fits into the outer constant velocity joint, unless otherwise stated.
- 1959 eighteen spline driveshaft, part number right-hand 17H8897, left-hand 17H8898.

TRANSMISSION & LOWER STABILISER BARS

Pic 37 Pic 38 Pic 39 Pic 40
Pic 41 Pic 42 Pic 43 Pic 44
Pic 45 Pic 46 Pic 47 Pic 48

• Non Cooper 'S' driveshaft, part number right-hand 17H8601; left-hand 17H8602. Pic 27
• Cooper 'S' driveshaft. Pic 28
• Pot joint driveshaft (thick). Pics 29 & 30
• Pot joint driveshaft (thin). Pics 31-33

DRIVESHAFT CLIPS
• Outer constant velocity joint end clips. Pic 34

INNER DRIVESHAFT DRIVE FLANGE (FOR RUBBER DRIVE COUPLINGS) SLIDES ON TO DRIVESHAFT
• Grease nipple type part number 2A4360. Pic 35
• Non-grease nipple type part number 21A430. Pic 36

RUBBER DRIVE COUPLINGS
• First type of coupling (with thanks to Mervin Irvin of the 1100 club). Pics 37 & 38
• 848cc Saloon, Austin Seven Van, 997cc Cooper and 1098cc Morris 1100 (ADO16), etc. Part number 2A3718.
• 1098cc Morris 1100 (ADO16) part number 22G297.
• 1098cc Morris 1100 (ADO16) part number 22G347.
• 1098cc Morris 1100 (ADO16) part number 22A927. Pic 39

INNER DRIVE COUPLINGS (MANUAL/AUTOMATIC TRANSMISSION)
• Rubber coupling type (more than one version of this). This example fits part number 22A373. Pics 40 & 41
• Hardy Spicer drive coupling. Automatics up to approx 1973 and Cooper 'S' 1966 onward. Part number 27H7880. Pic 42
• Pot joint approx 1973 onward. Pic 43

DIFFERENTIAL OUTPUT FLANGES (MANUAL/AUTOMATIC TRANSMISSION)
Rubber coupling types (information only)
• Refer to pics 40 & 41.
• First type of rubber coupling, splined output flange, part number 2A3695.
• Second type of rubber coupling, involute spline output flange, part number 22A374.

Hardy Spicer types
• First type (round) rare, automatic 1965 onward and Cooper 'S' 1966 onward. Pic 44
• Second type (two flats machined on flange), standard automatic and Cooper 'S.' Pics 45 & 46
• Third type is very similar to second

ANATOMY OF THE CLASSIC MINI

type but has two 0.5in slots to ease separation when dismantling. Pic 47 (refer also to pic 46)
• Fourth type, output flange (knock on type, to fit pot joint sun wheel) circa 1973/74 automatic. Morris 1300 (AD016), etc. Pics 48 & 49

DIFFERENTIAL PINS
• Early 850. (Same as RWD A Series.) Pic 50
• Standard A Series pin. Pic 51
• A+ pin. Pic 52
• Demonstration pin. This is what happens when you do a lot of wheel spinning on a standard diff. (This is the worst diff pin I have ever seen.) Pic 53

DIFFERENTIAL SIDE PLATES (MANUAL TRANSMISSION)
Two side plates per vehicle.

TRANSMISSION & LOWER STABILISER BARS

- Standard non-Hardy Spicer type. Number cast into plate (22A112). Pics 54 & 55
- Hardy Spicer type. See pic 46
- Pot joint type. Number cast into plate (22G1874). Pics 56 & 57

DIFFERENTIAL SIDE PLATES (AUTOMATIC TRANSMISSION)
One side plate only per vehicle.
- Hardy Spicer type part number 88G476. Pic 58
- Pot joint type. Pics 59-61

DIFFERENTIAL SUN WHEELS (MANUAL/ AUTOMATIC TRANSMISSION)
- First rubber coupling type. Part number 22A95 plus FNZ810 slotted nut.
- Second rubber coupling type, amount of splines changed from first type. Part number 22A135 plus 13H426 nyloc nut.
- Part number 22A373 plus FNZ810 slotted nut. Pics 62 & 63
- Hardy Spicer automatic 1965 onward, Cooper 'S' 1966 onward. (Bolt type.) Pic 64
- Part number DAM6138. Pot joint type (first type) accepts thrust block. Pics 65-67
- Part number DAM3114. Pot joint type (second type) used when thrust block not fitted.

CROWNWHEELS AND PINIONS
Rather than listing the different ratios as they appeared, the crownwheels and pinions in this section are listed in ascending numerical order.
Pic 68 (A Series)
Pic 69 (A+)
- 2.760:1 This ratio was used both in manual and automatic transmissions but are not interchangeable.
- 2.95:1 A+ 998cc economy. 20-tooth pinion and 59-tooth crown wheel.
- 3.105:1 1990 onward vehicles with 12in wheels. 19-tooth pinion and 59-tooth crown wheel.
- 3.211:1 Turbo models. 19-tooth pinion and 61-tooth crown wheel.
- 3.27:1 automatic.
- 3.444:1 1275cc Cooper 'S' with 10in wheels, 998cc Mk2 Mini and 998cc Mini Clubman. 18-tooth pinion and 62-tooth crown wheel.
- 3.647:1 17-tooth pinion and 62-tooth crown wheel.
- 3.65:1 Morris 1300 and GT front-wheel drive range (ADO16) and early 1275 GT Clubman.
- 3.765:1 This ratio was used both in manual and automatic transmissions but are not interchangeable. Manual models (Minis and Coopers).
- 3.765:1 Manual, 17-tooth pinion and 64-tooth crown wheel.
- 3.938:1 16-tooth pinion and 63-tooth crown wheel.
- 4.133:1 Morris 1100 front-wheel drive range, 1962 onward. 15-tooth pinion and 62-tooth crown wheel.
- 4.267:1 15-tooth pinion and 64-tooth crown wheel.
- 4.333:1 Austin Allegro.
- 4.350:1 15-tooth pinion and 65-tooth crown wheel.

DIFFERENTIAL CAGES pre A+
- Very early 848cc Mini part number ATA7376.
- Part number BTA145. Pics 70-72

A+
- Part number DAM6027. Pics 73-75

GEARBOX CASINGS (MANUAL TRANSMISSION)
A photo of a magnesium gearbox casing can be found on page 11 of *Mighty Minis* by Chris Harvey, ISBN 094660911X. Note. With the aid of a magnifying glass you can see a circular boss to the right of the oil filter canister above the front subframe beam.

Note. N/A means not available at time of going to press.

Three-synchro gearbox casings with small double roller main shaft bearing
- Case number 2A3708 (848cc): Part number N/A.
- Case number N/A (848cc): Part number 22A76.
- Case number 22A104 (848cc): Part number 22A102.
- Case number 22A145 (848cc): Part number 22A150. Pics 76-78
- Case number 22A363 (997cc Cooper – remote): Part number 22A361
- Case number 22A363 (848cc): Part number 22A364

Three-synchro gearbox casings with large double roller main shaft bearing 'A' type gears
- Part numbers 22G66 and 22G226 were replaced by 22A1533.
- Case number N/A (848cc): Part number 22A403
- Case number N/A (848cc): Part number 22A510
- Case number 22G68 (848cc): Part number 22G66. Pics 79-81
- Case number 22G68 (1098cc – ADO16 – Remote): Part number 22G66
- Case number N/A (1098cc – ADO16 – Remote): Part number 22G226

Three-synchromesh 'A' and 'B' type gears with large double roller main shaft bearing
- Part numbers 22G66, 22G348 and 22G818 were replaced by 22A1533.
- Case number 22G68 (997cc/998cc Cooper – remote): Part number 22G66
- Case number 22G190 (1071cc/970cc Cooper 'S' – Remote): Part number 22G188. Pics 82-84
- Case number N/A (1098cc – ADO16 – remote): Part number 22G348
- Case number N/A (1098cc – ADO16 – remote): Part number 22G818
- Case number N/A (848cc/997cc/1098cc/ 998cc Cooper):

ANATOMY OF THE CLASSIC MINI

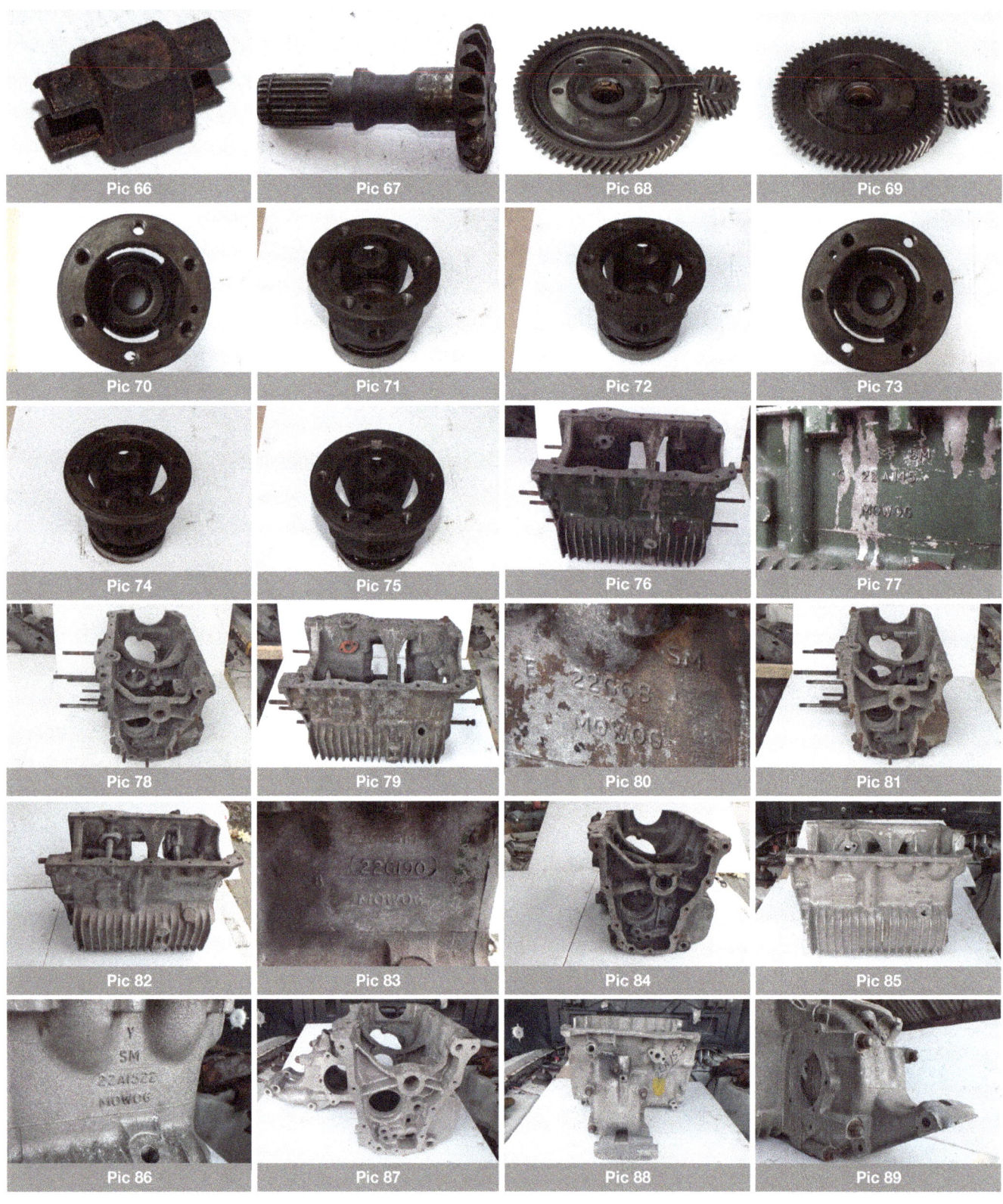

TRANSMISSION & LOWER STABILISER BARS

Pic 90 | Pic 91 | Pic 92 | Pic 93
Pic 94 | Pic 95 | Pic 96 | Pic 97
Pic 98 | Pic 99 | Pic 100 | Pic 101
Pic 102 | Pic 103 | Pic 104 | Pic 105
Pic 106 | Pic 107 | Pic 108 | Pic 109
Pic 110 | Pic 111 | Pic 112 | Pic 113

ANATOMY OF THE CLASSIC MINI

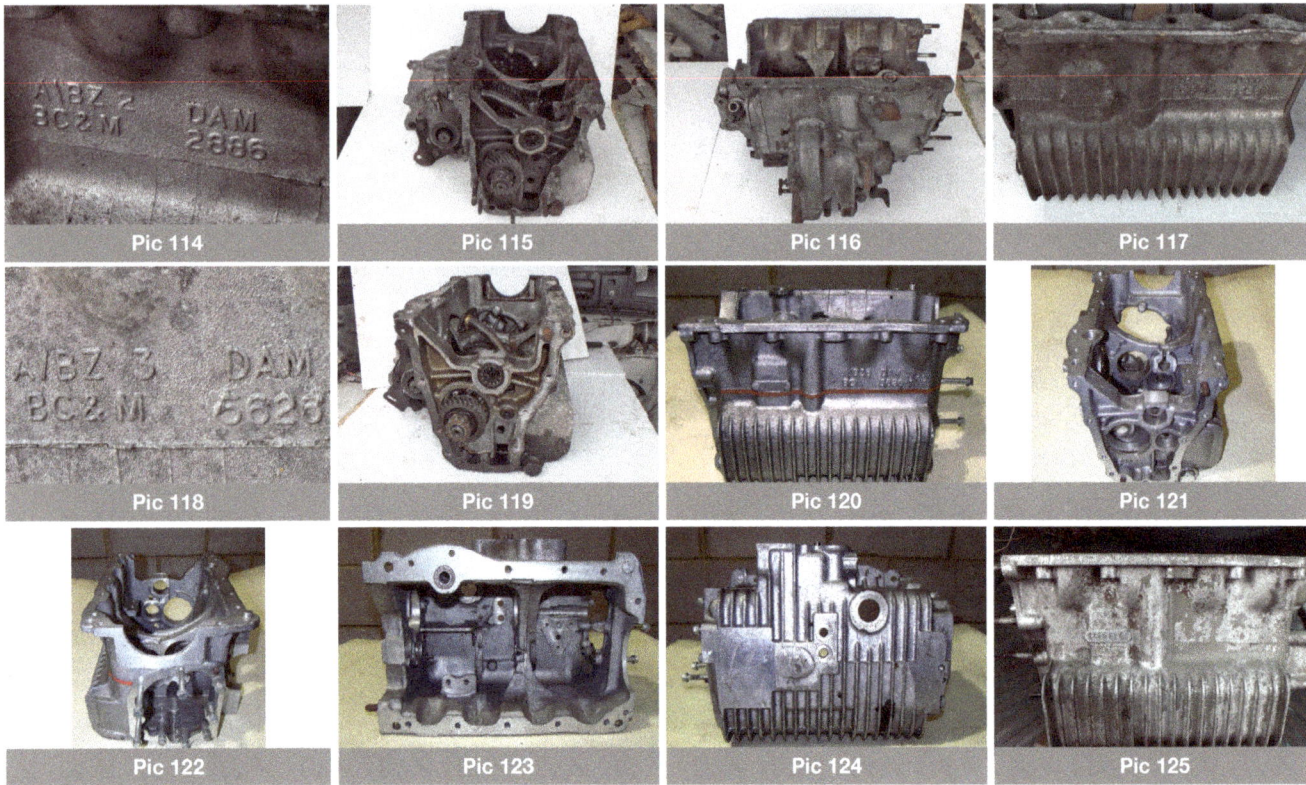

Pic 114 | Pic 115 | Pic 116 | Pic 117
Pic 118 | Pic 119 | Pic 120 | Pic 121
Pic 122 | Pic 123 | Pic 124 | Pic 125

Part number 22A1533.

Three-synchromesh 'B' type gears with large double roller main shaft bearing

- Part numbers 22G385, 22G814 and 22G883 were replaced by 22A1533.
- Part number 22A1294 became part number 22A1529.
- Part number 22A1296 became part number 22A1537.
- Case number 22A1288 (848cc/998cc): Part number N/A.
- Case number N/A (998cc): Part number 22A1294.
- Case number 22A1228 (Remote type non 'S'): Part number 22A1294.
- Case number N/A (998cc with sumpguard): Part number 22A1296.
- Case number 22A1522 (998cc Mini & Cooper 'S' – Remote): Part number 22A1529.
- Case number N/A (998cc with sumpguard): Part number 22A1537.
- Case number 22A1522 (1098cc – ADO16 – remote): Part number 22A1533. Pics 85-90
- Case number 22G333 (1275cc/970cc Cooper 'S' – Remote): Part number 22G331. Pics 91-93 Bart Theelen states three versions of the 333 casing existed.
- Case number 22G382 (848cc/998cc): Part number N/A. Pics 94-96
- Case number N/A (1098cc – ADO16 – remote): Part number 22G385.
- Case number N/A (1275cc 12G code – ADO16 – remote): Part number 22G814.
- Case number N/A (1275cc 12G code – ADO16 – remote): Part number 22G883.
- Case number 22G68 (848cc/997cc/998cc Mini & Cooper): Part number N/A.

Four-synchro gearbox casings (approximately 1967 onward)

- '22G846' cast into casing. (First Mini version.) Pics 100-103
- '22G846' cast into reinforced casing. (Second Mini version.) Pic 104
- '22G846' cast into casing. (First Morris 1100 FWD (ADO16) version.) Pic 105 This particular image shows a large circular aluminium boss, this tells me that these casings were experimented with for the next generation of rod-change gearboxes.
- Pics 106 & 107 (This particular casing has had a BMC repair to it.)
- '22G846' cast into reinforced casing. (Second Morris 1100 FWD (ADO16) version.) Pic 108
- '22G1128' cast into casing. (First version.) Pics 97 & 98
- '22G1128' cast into reinforced casing. (Second version.) Pic 109
- '22G1128' was available for both Mini and (AD016) range.
- 22G1132-22A1675 (8AC Moke, 998H-223, fitted with dynamo, sumpguard and four-synchromesh gearbox with centre gearchange.)
- 22G1338 was 22A1352 (parts book part number) (12FA/9FD/848/99H).

TRANSMISSION & LOWER STABILISER BARS

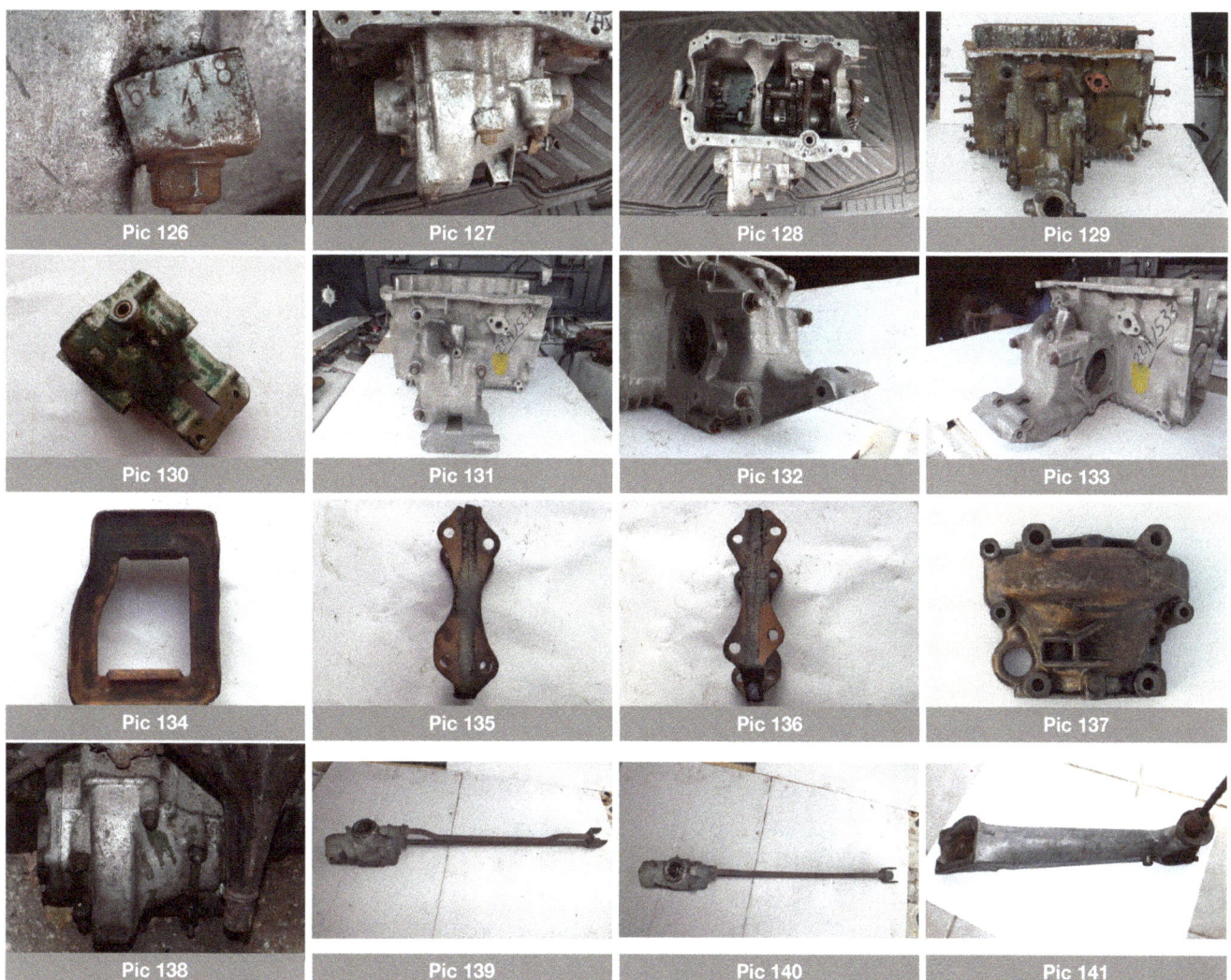

Pic 126 | Pic 127 | Pic 128 | Pic 129
Pic 130 | Pic 131 | Pic 132 | Pic 133
Pic 134 | Pic 135 | Pic 136 | Pic 137
Pic 138 | Pic 139 | Pic 140 | Pic 141

- 22G1368 was 22A1368 (parts book part number) (1098cc/12H).

Rod-change gearbox casings 1973 onward

- 22G1832 (pre A+ 1973 onward).
- DAM3220 (pre A+ small idler bearing.) Pics 110-112
- DAM2886 (A+ October 1980-onward.) Pics 113-116
- DAM4818 (A+).
- DAM5626 (A+) last of the four-speeds.) Pics 117-119
- JKD5626 (five-speed). Pics 120-124

AUTHI ROD-CHANGE GEARBOX (SPANISH)

ID'd by Bart Theelen. No number cast into casing. Pics 125-128 (Courtesy Brian Hore)

DIFFERENTIAL COVERS (MANUAL TRANSMISSION)

- Long gearlever type ('magic wand'). Pic 129
- Cooper remote type. Pic 130
- Morris 11/1300 (ADO16). Plus sandwich plate. Pics 131-136
- Rod-change gearbox, first type. (Will only accept one gear selector oil seal.) Looks identical externally to the second type of rod-change gearbox cover below. This cover will only allow one rod-change oil seal.
- Rod-change gearbox, second type. (Will accept one oil seal on top of another or oil seal leak fix kit.) Pic 137

DIFFERENTIAL COVER (AUTOMATIC TRANSMISSION)

- I believe that the pre A+ and A+ covers look the same. Pic 138

REMOTE CONTROL GEARCHANGES

When purchasing secondhand be very

ANATOMY OF THE CLASSIC MINI

Pic 142 | Pic 143 | Pic 144 | Pic 145
Pic 146 | Pic 147 | Pic 148 | Pic 149
Pic 150 | Pic 151 | Pic 152 | Pic 153

careful, the rod-change remote was also fitted to the Morris 1100/1300 ADO16

Engine size	Primary gear	Primary gear front bush	Primary gear rear bush
848cc (59 on)	22A79	22A81	22A82
848cc	22A520	22A447	22A448
848cc	22A551	22A553	22G109
997cc (61 on)	22A344	22A316	22A333
997cc	12A380	12A386	12A385
1098cc (62 on)	12A380	12A386	12A385
1098cc	22G106	22G108	22G109
1098cc	22A551	22A553	22G109
1098cc	22A1058	22G401	22G109
998cc (62 on)	22A1058	22G401	22G109
998cc	22A1493	22G401	22G109
1275cc non 'S' (67 on)	12G768	22G770	22G109
1275cc non 'S'	22A543	22A545	22G109
1275cc non 'S'	22G1053	22G770	22G109
Table 1			

vehicles, the Allegro and Mini Metro Mk1/2. I think you will find they are different in length.
- Cooper remote, plus remote mounting. Pics 141 & 142
- Morris 1100/1300 remote (AD016), plus mounting. Pics 143 & 144
- 848cc Minis with rod-change gearbox did not have reversing lights, so there was no switch fitted to the remote. Pics 139 & 140
- Rod-change remote circa 1973 onward. Mk3.5 onward. See 1990 onward for similar item.
- 1990 onward remote (engine moved forward by 0.375in). Pics 145 & 146

GEARBOX CASINGS (AUTOMATIC TRANSMISSION)

- 1098cc/998cc/1275cc part number 22A1228 became 28G263. Pics 147-149
- Gearbox casing with inhibitor switch. Pics 150-152

TRANSMISSION & LOWER STABILISER BARS

Pic 154 · Pic 155 · Pic 156 · Pic 157 · Pic 158 · Pic 159 · Pic 160 · Pic 161 · Pic 162 · Pic 163 · Pic 164 · Pic 165 · Pic 166 · Pic 167 · Pic 168 · Pic 169

TRANSFER GEARS (MANUAL TRANSMISSION)
Primary gears

The metal ring close to the gear teeth was not fitted on the early primary gears. This item is actually an oil slinger designed to keep oil away from the clutch oil seal.
22A79 Pic 153

Engine size	Primary gear	Primary gear front bush	Primary gear rear bush
848cc (1982 only)	DAM8888	DAM8887	22G109
1098cc	DAM8888	DAM8887	22G109
998cc	DAM8888	DAM8887	22G109
1275cc	DAM8890	DAM8889	22G109
1275cc economy	DAM9373	DAM8889	22G109

Table 2

22A520 Pic 154
DAM8888 Pic 155 (Courtesy Mini Spares, Potters Bar)
DAM8890 Pic 156 (Courtesy Mini Spares, Potters Bar)
Primary gear front bush, Nearest to engine block.
Primary gear rear bush, Nearest to flywheel.
No part numbers available at time of printing for 1071cc/1275cc/970cc Cooper 'S,' probably similar or same part numbers as 1275cc non 'S.'

Pre A+
See table 1

167

ANATOMY OF THE CLASSIC MINI

Engine size	Primary gear	Backing ring
848cc (59 on)	22A79	No backing ring fitted.
848cc	22A520	22A449
848cc	22A551	12G169
997cc (61 on)	22A344	22A320
997cc	12A380	12A383
1098cc (62 on)	12A380	12A383
1098cc	N/A	12A671
1098cc	22G106	12G169
1098cc	22A551	12G169
1098cc	22A1058	22G169
998cc (62 on)	22A1058	12G169
998cc	22A1493	12G169
1275cc non 'S' (67 on)	12G768	12G169
1275cc non 'S'	22A543	12G169
1275cc non 'S'	22G1053	12G169

Table 3

Engine size	Primary gear	'C' washer
848cc (59 on)	22A79	2A3597
848cc	22A520	2A3597
848cc	22A551	22A319
997cc (61 on)	22A344	22A319
997cc	12A380	12A382
1098cc (62 on)	12A380	12A382 & 12A384
1098cc	22G106	22A319
1098cc	22A551	22A319
1098cc	22A1058	22A319
998cc (62 on)	22A1058	22A319
998cc	22A1493	22A319
1275cc non 'S' (67 on)	12G768	22A319
1275cc non 'S'	22A543	22A319
1275cc non 'S'	22G1053	22A319

Table 4

A+
DAM8887 was 22G401.
DAM8889 was 22G770.
See table 2

Primary thrust washers
- 848cc part number 22A295. 1.375in tail. Pic 157
- 848cc part number 22A322. Pic 158 (Courtesy Mini Spares, Potters Bar)
- 997cc/1098cc/998cc part number 22A321. Thinner than 848cc 22A322.
- 1275cc part number 22A546 became DAM6490. Pic 159 (Courtesy Mini Spares, Potters Bar)

DU thrust washer
This washer fits behind the backing ring against the rear primary gear bush.
- 997cc part number 22A334 became part number 12A384.

Backing rings
Pics 160 & 161
- 1098cc conversion part number 12A671. Oil-fed primary to Deva bush conversion.
See table 3

Washer-thrust-primary gear-rear ('C' washer)
Pic 162 2A3597 on left and 22A319 on right
12A384 'C' washer is recessed.
See table 4

Idler gears
- Unequal length shafts. Pic 163
- Unequal length shafts, oil slinger type. Pic 164
- Three-synchro and four-synchro. (Equal length shafts.) Pic 165
- A+. Pic 166

First motion shaft gears
- Three-synchro. Pic 167
- Four-synchro and pre A+ rod-change. Pic 168
- A+. Pic 169

TRANSFER GEARS (AUTOMATIC TRANSMISSION) Primary gear
Pics 170 & 171. Pre A+ shown.
- 848cc
- 1098cc and 998cc part number 22A1064.
- 1275cc first part number 22G780, second part number 22G1010.
- A+ small bore. (for example,

TRANSMISSION & LOWER STABILISER BARS

Pic 170 | Pic 171 | Pic 172 | Pic 173
Pic 174 | Pic 175 | Pic 176 | Pic 177
Pic 178 | Pic 179 | Pic 180 | Pic 181
Pic 182 | Pic 183 | Pic 184 | Pic 185

998cc/1098cc.)
- 1275cc A+

Idler gear
Pic 172
- 1098cc, 998cc, 1275cc part number 22A1242.
- A+ idler gear.

First motion shaft gear
A Series same gear as A+ but with different angle of teeth.
 A+ Pics 173 & 174
- 1098cc, 998cc, 1275cc part number 22A1265.

LOWER STABILISER BARS
ERA turbo has two rearward facing lower stabiliser bars. Part numbers 21A2787 and 21A2569.
- Circa 1973 onward. Nearside lower rear bar. Part number 21A2787 (Mk3.5 only). Pic 175 (Courtesy Mini Spares, Potters Bar)
- Mk4 1976 onward. Offside front forward facing bar. Part number FAM2758. See KKH10013 for similar item.
- Offside lower rear bar. Part number 21A2569. Pics 176 & 177
- 1990 onward. Offside front forward facing bar. This bar is 0.375in shorter than FAM2758. Part number KKH10013.
Pic 178 (Courtesy Mini Spares, Potters Bar)

BELLHOUSING OIL SEALS & OIL SEAL GUARD
- Orange clutch oil seal. Pic 179
- Black (fuel-injection) clutch oil seal. Pic 180
- Oil seal guard. Pic 181

MANUAL BELLHOUSINGS
Bellhousing repaired by BMC dealer. Pic 182

ANATOMY OF THE CLASSIC MINI

Pic 186 Pic 187 Pic 188 Pic 189
Pic 190 Pic 191 Pic 192 Pic 193
Pic 194 Pic 195 Pic 196 Pic 197

Mk1 vehicles with three-synchro gear kits

- 848cc saloon part number 2A3676 (these were fitted to the very first Minis).
- 848cc saloon part number 22A523.
- 848cc saloon, Elf, Hornet, Austin Seven Van and 997cc Cooper part number 22A107. (Relieved for larger oil pump.)
- Part number 8G729.
- 1098cc part number 22A581.
- 1098cc part number 8G737.
- 1098cc/998cc part number 22A1183.
- 998cc part number 22G816.

Mk2 vehicles with four-synchro gear kits

- Part number 22G999 fitted with larger outside diameter idler gear bearing.
- Fitted with larger outside diameter idler gear bearing.
- Morris 1300 front-wheel drive range (breather type).

Engine size	Casting number	Part number
848cc (59 on)	N/A	2A3676 Saloon only
848cc	22A524 (*)	22A523 Saloon only
848cc	22A108 (*)	22A107
848cc	N/A	8G729
997cc (61 on)	22A108 (*)	22A107
1098cc ADO16 (62 on)	N/A	8G729
1098cc ADO16	N/A	22A581
1098cc ADO16	N/A	8G737
1098cc ADO16	N/A	22A1183
998cc (62 on)	N/A	22G816
998cc	N/A	22A1183
1071cc	22G208	N/A
Table 5 (See pics 186-195)		

Mk3 vehicles with four-synchro gear kits

- Includes Mini Clubman and Allegro
- Fitted with larger outside diameter idler gear bearing.
- Morris 1300 front-wheel drive range (AD016) and 1275 GT Clubman (breather type).

TRANSMISSION & LOWER STABILISER BARS

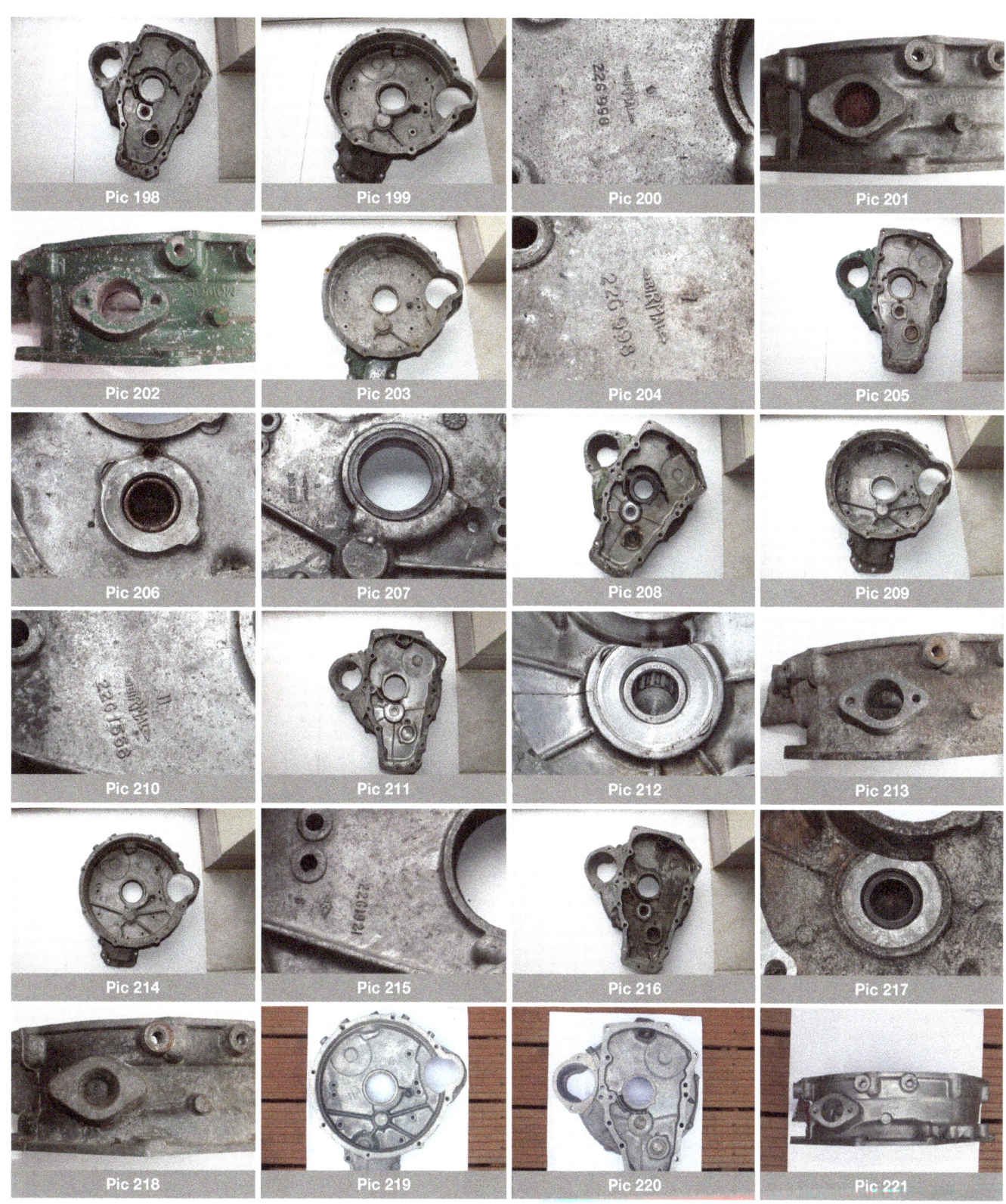

ANATOMY OF THE CLASSIC MINI

Engine size	Casting number	Part number
998cc	22G998(*)	22G999
998cc 2nd type	22G998(*)	22G999
1275cc non 'S' (67 on)	22G998(*)	22G999
1275cc non 'S'	22G1337(*)	N/A
1275cc non 'S'	22G1556(*)	N/A
Non breather	22G1921(*)	N/A
1275cc non 'S'	22G1921(*)	N/A

Table 6 (See pics 196-224)

Three-synchromesh bellhousings

Bellhousing part numbers 2A3676/22A523/22A107 were all replaced by 8G729.
Bellhousings part numbers 8G729/22A581/8G737/22A1183/22G816 were all replaced by 22G999.
See table 5
(*)Pictures for table above.
22A524: Pics 183-187
22A108: Pics 188-192

Four-synchromesh bellhousings

See table 6
(*)Pictures for table above.
998cc: Pics 193-197
998cc 2nd type: Pics 198-201
1275cc non 'S': Pics 202-206
22G1337: Pics 207 & 208
22G1556: Pics 209-213
Non-1275 (no breather hole): Pics 214-218
1275 (with breather hole): Pics 219-221

1980 onward (all A+ vehicles)

If the bellhousing has a breather boss with a large hole in the middle and two tapped holes for bolts then this is off of a 1275cc engine.
Some 1275cc non-turbo A+ bellhousings are fitted with the larger turbo first motion shaft nose bearing.

Allegro/Mini Metro/Mini and Mini Clubman plus Estate

• 1275cc breather type. Probably Allegro A+. DAM2929 cast into bellhousing. Pics 222-224
• Fitted with A+ idler gear bearing, rear raised boss on housing drilled and tapped to accept bolts for Mini Metro rear engine mount. DAM5785 (Non-breather). Pics 225-230
• Fitted with A+ idler gear bearing. DAM5785 (breather type). Pics 231 & 232

Pic 222 | Pic 223 | Pic 224 | Pic 225
Pic 226 | Pic 227 | Pic 228 | Pic 229
Pic 230 | Pic 231 | Pic 232 | Pic 233

TRANSMISSION & LOWER STABILISER BARS

ANATOMY OF THE CLASSIC MINI

Pic 258　Pic 259　Pic 260　Pic 261
Pic 262　Pic 263　Pic 264　Pic 265

- Fitted with A+ idler gear bearing (breather type), rear raised boss on housing drilled and tapped to accept bolts for Mini Metro rear engine mount. Pic 233
- Metro Turbo (breather type), fitted with A+ idler gear bearing. Also fitted with large first motion shaft nose bearing rear raised boss on housing drilled and tapped to accept bolts for Mini Metro rear engine mount. Pics 234 & 235
- Carburettor (blanking plate fitted).
- Single-point injection and twin-point injection (breather type, no blanking plate fitted), has facility for crankshaft position sensor in side of housing. Pics 236-239

ENGINE AND GEARBOX MOUNTINGS

- Manual, two per vehicle. Pic 240
- Automatic. Pics 241-243

ENGINE AND GEARBOX MOUNTING BRACKETS

- Manual 850cc Mini with pressed steel crankshaft pulley. Pic 244
- Manual 997cc Cooper onward. Plus all Morris 1100 (ADO16). Pic 245
- Automatic. Pic 246

BELLHOUSING COVERS (MANUAL)

- Pre A+. Pic 247
- A+ with hole for timing. Pic 248
- A+ with pointer shown. Pic 249
- A+. (This must have been for vehicles fitted with bracket on timing cover to do the timing.) Pic 250
- Special pre A+. Mini Cooper fitted with Formula Junior engine. Pic 251

AUTOMATIC BELLHOUSINGS

A Mk1/2 Austin Mini Metro automatic engine and gearbox will not fit in a Mini unless a lump is cut out of the subframe. (Not advisable to do this.)

Mk1 vehicles

- 848cc Mini May 1965 onward (special order only) fitted with three-synchro idler gear bearing. Also fitted to the Morris 1100 (ADO16) front-wheel drive range October 1965 onward as an option. These bellhousings would not have a breather boss cast into the top of the outside the housing. (Just below engine steady bar.)

Mk2 vehicles

- 998cc Mini fitted with four-synchro idler gear bearing. Pics 252 & 253
- 1275cc Morris 1300 (ADO16) front-wheel drive range (breather type), fitted with four-synchro idler gear bearing.

1980 onward (all A+ vehicles) Allegro/Mini Metro/Mini

- 998cc/1098cc Mini and Metro (non-breather type) fitted with A+ idler gear bearing. Pics 254 & 255
- 1275cc Allegro (breather type) fitted with A+ idler gear bearing.
- 1275cc Mini Metro (breather type), rear raised boss on housing drilled and tapped to accept bolts for Mini Metro rear engine mount. Also fitted with oil thermostat, these vehicles were fitted with oil coolers. Pics 256 & 257
- 1275cc Mini (breather type) without oil thermostat.

AUTOMATIC BELLHOUSING COVERS

- Carburettor automatic. Pic 258
- Metro automatic. Pic 259
- SPI automatic. Pic 260

CLUTCH BACKPLATES (MANUAL)

- 848cc and 1098cc part number 2A3509. Pics 261 & 262
- 997cc part number 22A274.
- 998cc part number 22A598. Pics 263 & 264
- 1071cc/1275cc/970cc Cooper 'S' and 1275cc non 'S' part number 22G270. Pics 265 & 266

TRANSMISSION & LOWER STABILISER BARS

ANATOMY OF THE CLASSIC MINI

Pic 290

Pic 291

Pic 292

Pic 293

Pic 294

Pic 295

Pic 296

Pic 297

CLUTCH DRIVEN PLATES (MANUAL TRANSMISSION, INFORMATION ONLY)

The purpose of listing all of these part numbers is to illustrate the problems that BMC had with the clutch.

848cc
- Part number 2A3666 alternative to 2A3648. Became 22A345.
- Part number 2A3648 alternative to 2A3666. Became 22A345.
- Part number 22A237 became 22A345.
- Part number 12G102 became 22A345.
- Part number 22A345.
- Part number 22A565.

997cc
- Part number 2A3648 alternative to 22A237.
- Part number 22A237 alternative to 2A3648.

1098cc
- Part number 2A3648 became 22G248 then 13H3587.
- Part number 22A237 became 22G248 then 13H3587.
- Part number 12G286 became 22G248 then 13H3587.
- Part number 22G248 became 13H3587.
- Part number 88G451 became 13H3587.
- Part number 13H3587.

998cc
- Part number 13H3555 became 88G497.

1275cc
- Part number 13H3587.

FLYWHEELS (MANUAL TRANSMISSION)

Early flywheels had an oil seal fitted to them to prevent oil from getting onto the clutch plate. (This oil seal should not be confused with the clutch oil seal fitted into the bellhousing.)
- 848cc six-spring type, part number 22A53 became 22A129. Pics 267 & 268
- 848cc six-spring type, part number 22A129.
- 848cc six-spring type, part number 22A443.
- 848cc six-spring type, part number 12A669.
- 997cc six-spring type, part number 22A327 became 12A377.
- 997cc six-spring type, part number 12A377.
- 1098cc ADO16 six-spring type, part number 12G96.
- 1098cc ADO16 six-spring type, part number 12G250 became 12A669.
- Mini/Morris 1100 ADO16 FWD range (diaphragm type) two-piece flywheel for inertia starter motor. Pics 269 & 270
- Morris 1300 ADO16 FWD range (diaphragm type) two-piece flywheel (very heavy!) for inertia starter motor. Pics 271-273
- Single-piece flywheel (diaphragm type) for inertia starter motor. Pics 274 & 275
- Carburettor (Verto type) for inertia starter motor. Pics 276 & 277
- Carburettor (Verto type) for pre-engaged starter motor. Pics 278 & 279
- Single-point (Verto type) fitted with reluctor. Pics 280 & 281
- Twin-point (Verto type) fitted with reluctor. Pic 282 (Courtesy Mini Spares, Potters Bar)

GASKET THAT FITS BETWEEN FLYWHEEL AND FLYWHEEL CENTRE
- Part number 22A130.
- Early flywheels fitted with an oil seal also had this gasket fitted.

FLYWHEEL CENTRES (MANUAL TRANSMISSION)
- Six-spring type (for 1.375in tail crankshaft). Pics 283 & 284
- Six-spring type 1098cc (ADO16) for

TRANSMISSION & LOWER STABILISER BARS

Pic 298 | Pic 299 | Pic 300 | Pic 301
Pic 302 | Pic 303 | Pic 304 | Pic 305
Pic 306 | Pic 307 | Pic 308 | Pic 309

1.5in tail crankshaft. Taper depth 1⁵⁄₁₆in.
- Six-spring type 1098cc (AD016) for 1.5in tail crankshaft. Taper depth 1⁷⁄₁₆in.
- Diaphragm type (for 1.5in tail crankshaft). Pic 285
- Verto type (for 1.5in tail crankshaft). Pics 286 & 287

SMALL OIL SEAL FITTED TO FLYWHEEL 848CC AND 997CC ONLY

Oil-fed primary gear.
- 848cc oil seal part numbers. 13H106/13H435/22A214.
- 997cc oil seal part numbers. 22A325/22A214.

CONVERTERS (AUTOMATIC TRANSMISSION)

- 848cc.
- 1098cc.
- 998cc. Pic 288 (with drain plugs) Pics 289 & 290 (without drain plugs)
- 1275cc.

- 1275cc SPI. Pic 291
- Sectioned 1275cc SPI. Pic 292

FLYWHEEL BOLTS (MANUAL TRANSMISSION)

Part number 22A326 became part number 22A747.
- Long bolt early 850 only 2A3530. Pic 293
- 848cc/1098cc 22A326. Bart Theelen advises that there were three versions of this bolt. Pic 294
- 997cc 22A436.
- 998cc/1275cc 22A747. Pics 295 & 296
- Verto DAM5922. Pic 297

FLYWHEEL BOLTS (AUTOMATIC TRANSMISSION)

Thick-headed bolt, pre A+.
- 848cc.
- 1098cc 22A1158.
- 998cc 22A1158.

- 1275cc 22A1158.

KEY, FLYWHEEL TO CRANK SHAFT (OFFSET LOCK WASHER) MANUAL TRANSMISSION

Whilst the part number listed for the 848cc is the same as other engine capacities, my own personal experience of early 848cc engines with the 1.375in crank tail is that the lock washer appears to be a lot thicker than the later 848cc with the 1.5in crank tail. The thicker washer is very similar to the lock washer fitted to the automatic engine.
Pic 298 Thick.
Pic 299 Thin part number 88G508
- 848cc 22A57.
- 997cc 22A57.
- 1098cc 22A57.
- 998cc 22A57.
- 1275cc 22A57.
- Verto part number DAM5923. Pic 300 (Courtesy Mini Spares, Potters Bar)

ANATOMY OF THE CLASSIC MINI

Pic 310 | Pic 311 | Pic 312 | Pic 313
Pic 314 | Pic 315 | Pic 316 | Pic 317
Pic 318 | Pic 319 | Pic 320 | Pic 321
Pic 322 | Pic 323 | Pic 324 | Pic 325

KEY, FLYWHEEL TO CRANK SHAFT (OFFSET LOCK WASHER) AUTOMATIC TRANSMISSION

Same as thick (offset lock washer) manual transmission.
- 848cc 22A1159.
- 1098cc 22A1159.
- 998cc 22A1159.
- 1275cc 22A1159.

CLUTCH PRESSURE PLATES (MANUAL TRANSMISSION)

- Six-spring type. Pics 301 & 302
- Diaphragm type. Pic 303
- Diaphragm type (green). Stronger spring than standard. Identified by a dab of green paint.
- Diaphragm type (blue). Stronger spring than standard. Identified by a dab of blue paint.
- 184mm GCC679. Verto type. Pic 304 (Courtesy Mini Spares, Potters Bar)
- Verto type, turbo. (Looks the same as standard Verto type but springing is upgraded.)

CLUTCH PRESSURE PLATE THRUST PLATES

- Six-spring type. Pics 305 & 306
- Diaphragm type. Pic 307
- Metro 3/1981-2/1982. Looks like diaphragm type but does not have hole in the middle. This thrust plate has a pressed dimple in the middle which is operated by a small steel plunger. Pic 308
- Verto type with plastic anti rattle sleeve. (Two parts.)
- Verto type. Pics 309 & 310

CLUTCH RELEASE BEARINGS (MANUAL TRANSMISSION)

- Large original type (fits both six-spring and diaphragm types) part

TRANSMISSION & LOWER STABILISER BARS

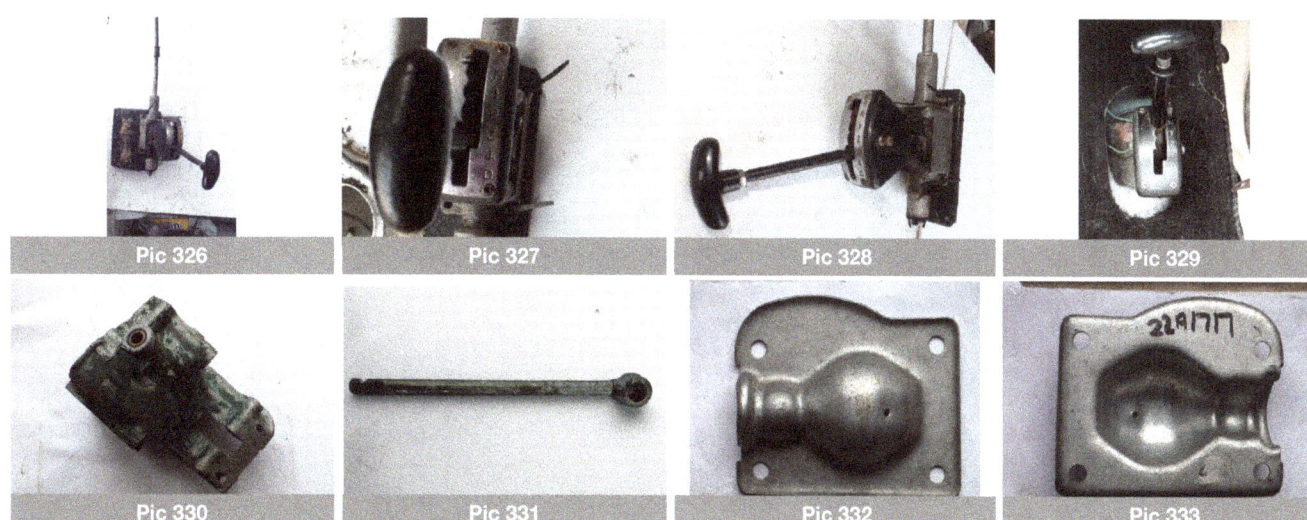

Pic 326 Pic 327 Pic 328 Pic 329
Pic 330 Pic 331 Pic 332 Pic 333

Pic 334

number 2A3653. Pic 311
- Smaller replacement for original type. Part number 22A1156. Pic 312
- Modified bearing for Mini Metro March 1981 to February 1982. Please refer to clutch plunger. (Cup that fits inside release bearing, no photo.) Pic 313
- Verto type. Part number GRB239. Pic 314

CLUTCH PLUNGERS (MANUAL TRANSMISSION)

- Six-spring type without throw out nuts part number 2A3652. Pic 315
- Six-spring and diaphragm type (with throw out nuts) part number 22A180. Pic 316
- Diaphragm type with floating thrust bearing held on by spire washer. Part number DAM1955. Pics 317 & 318
- Metro 3/1981-2/1982 DAM5262 Pic 319 (Courtesy Mini Spares, Potters Bar)
- Verto type. Part number DAM5353. Pic 320

CLUTCH ARMS (MANUAL TRANSMISSION)

- Six-spring and diaphragm type part number 2A3518 (two versions with same part number). Pics 321 & 322
- Verto type. Pic 323
- Mk2 Metro verto clutch arm is fitted with a metalastic bush.

GEARLEVERS (MANUAL)

- Straight lever. Pic 324
- First type. Cranked lever. Pic 325
- Cooper lever. Part number 22A269.
- 85H lever. Part number 22A1382. Looks very similar to cranked handle, but located differently.
- Late type gearlever (chrome). Part number 22G1190.

GEARLEVERS (AUTOMATIC)

- Four-speed. Pics 326-328
- Three-speed. Pic 329

ENGINE CODE 85H DIFFERENTIAL COVER COMPONENTS

I also believe that these were fitted to the Austin Countryman Mk2, Morris Traveller Mk2 and Mini Moke Mk2.

- Cooper remote diff cover. Pic 330
- Rod, gearshift part fits inside diff cover. Pic 331
- Gearlever. Part number 22A1382.
- Metal plate. Part number 22A1717. Pics 332 & 333
- Gearlever seat and locating pad. Part number 22A1832. Pic 334
- Spring. Part number 2A3390.
- Thrust button. Part number 2A3467.

Chapter 21
Wheels

WHEEL COLOURS
10in wheels
- Old English White.
- Rubi (Works rally cars).
- Silver.
- Matt Silver all Mk2 and Mk3 Cooper 'S.'

12in wheels
- Silver.
- Silver Grey.
- Black.
- Diamond White.
- Gun metal Grey.
- Black and Silver.
- Bright Silver (Fleck).
- Old English White.

13in wheels
- Silver.

FACTORY FITTED WHEELS
All wheels described in this chapter are of steel construction, unless otherwise stated.

3.5in by 10in
Pic 1
- Part number 2A8067.
- Riveted wheel.
- Finished in old English white.

3.5in by 10in
Pics 2 & 3
- Part number 21A559 became 21A881.
- Chassis numbers A-A2S7-82007 RHD onward, 83351 LHD onward.
- M-A2S4-6390 onward.
- Spot-welded.
- Finished in old English white.
- 21A559 embossed on the wheel centre.
- I believe the difference between 21A559 and 21A881 is the thickness of the steel used to make the wheels (21A559 made of thinner material).

3.5in by 10in (non 'S')
Pic 4
- Part number 21A881.
- Spot-welded.
- Finished in silver.
- 21A881 embossed on the wheel centre.

3.5in by 10in (non 'S')
Pic 5
- Part number 21A2744.
- Spot-welded.
- Finished in silver with 21A2744 embossed on wheel centre.

3.5in by 10in Cooper 'S'
Pics 6-8
- Finished in Old English white.
- This wheel has three lugs welded to the wheel centre for fitment of the hub cap.
- Early 1071cc Cooper 'S.'

3.5in by 10in Cooper 'S'
Pic 9 (Left: Old English White. Right: Silver, also see below.)
- Finished in Old English white.
- This wheel has three pressed in lugs to the wheel centre for fitment of the hub cap.

3.5in by 10in Cooper 'S'
Pic 10
- Wheel finished in silver.
- This wheel has three pressed in lugs

WHEELS

ANATOMY OF THE CLASSIC MINI

Pic 25 Pic 26 Pic 27 Pic 28

to the wheel centre for fitment of the hub cap.

3.5in by 10in Cooper 'S'
Pic 11
- Wheel finished in Rubi (Works rally cars).
- This wheel has three pressed-in lugs to the wheel centre for fitment of the hub cap.

4.5in by 10in Cooper 'S'
Pic 12
- Finished in Old English White or Silver.
- This wheel has three pressed-in lugs to the wheel centre for fitment of the hub cap.

4.5in by 10in
Pic 13
- Part number 21A2363.
- Rostyle wheel finished in Black and Silver.
- This wheel was standard fit on the 1969 onward 1275 GT Clubman.

5in by 10in
Pic 14
- Part number GAW113A.
- Aluminium alloy wheel fitted to the 1979 Mini 1100 Special.
- Also fitted to the Mini Sprite.

4.5in by 12in
Pics 15, 16 (non-spacered), & 17 (spacered)
- Finished in Silver.
- There were two types of this wheel.
- The cheaper version did not have a built-in spacer (usually supplied as the spare).
- The more expensive version has a spot-welded wheel spacer.

- The later wheels were finished in Black.
- These wheels were also painted Red for the specials, Red Hot and Jet Black.

4.5in by 310mm
Pics 18 & 19
- There were two versions of this wheel, dependent on whether the vehicle was fitted with disc or drum brakes.
- Denovo disc brake wheel finished in Silver.
- This wheel became available as an option in August 1974 on the 1275 GT Clubman and became standard fit in 1977.

4.5in by 12in
Pics 20 & 21
- NAM6071 cast into wheel.
- Aluminium alloy.
- Finished in Silver Grey.
- These first became available in January 1985 fitted to the Mini Ritz.
- Also fitted to Mini Chelsea.

4.5in by 12in
Pic 22
- Rosepetal aluminium alloy.
- Finished in Silver.
- These first became available in 1989 as fitted to the Mini 30 Special Edition.
- Also fitted to the Rover Special Products (RSP) Cooper.
- Wheel nut fixings in-line with spokes.

4.5in by 12in
Pics 23 & 24
- Part number RRC10301XXX cast into back of wheel.
- Stronger spoke (less sculpting on back of spoke).

- Rosepetal aluminium alloy.
- Finished in silver.
- Wheel nut fixings in-between spokes.

4.5in by 12in
Pic 25
- Rosepetal aluminium alloy.
- Finished in Silver.
- Finished in Diamond White. (October 1992 on the Italian Job special edition.)
- Finished in Gunmetal Grey. (1994 on the Monte carlo model. Also fitted to the 35th anniversary Cooper Special Edition.)
- Finished in Black and Silver. (Standard fit on the Paul Smith Limited Edition.)
- Wheel nut fixings in-between spokes.

5in by 12in
Pic 26
- Part number RRC10479MNH.
- Five spoke RFX alloy wheel.
- These first became available in June 1991 on the Mini Cabriolet.

4.5in by 12in
Pics 27 & 28
- Aluminium alloy.
- Finished in Silver part number RRC109630MNH.
- Finished in Old English White part number RRC109630NNX.
- Twelve oval shaped vent holes in wheel, commonly referred to as pepper pots.
- These first became available on Mini Seven Special Edition.

6in by 13in
Pic 29
- Aluminium alloy five spoke.
- Finished in Silver.

WHEELS

Pic 29 Pic 30 Pic 31 Pic 32

Pic 33 Pic 34 Pic 35 Pic 36

Pic 37

• These first became available in 1989 on the ERA Turbo Mini.

6in by 13in
• Part number RRC10456MMP.
• Aluminium alloy.
• Finished in Silver.
• Standard fit on the Lamm Convertible.

6in by 13in
Pic 30
• Part number RRC109640MNH.
• Rosepetal aluminium alloy.
• Finished in Silver.
• These first became available as an option and then became standard fit on the Sports pack models.

OTHER WHEELS
In the main these are wheels that are fitted to continental cars that I am aware of.

3.5in by 10in
Pics 31 & 32
• Finished in Silver.
• 24E8381 embossed on the wheel centre.
• Not known if this is a wheel for a classic Mini or a trailer.

3.5in by 10in
Pics 33 & 34
• Cooper 'S' type wheel.
• This has 'Semers' embossed on the wheel centre. Whilst this looks externally like a UK Cooper 'S' wheel the centre is positioned differently in the rim therefore the offset is different.

4.5in by 10in
Pics 35-37
• Cooper 'S' type wheel.
• Commonly referred to as reverse rims.
• These were not fitted at the factory.
• Available as an accessory only.
• Can be fitted without wheelarch extensions.

5in by 10in
• Cooper 'S' type wheel.
• Commonly referred to as reverse rims.
• These were not fitted at the factory.
• Available as an accessory only.
• These were advertised in the 1970s by a company called Radbourne.

Chapter 22
Hand-built 621 AOK & 1959 Mini 763 HKO

HAND-BUILT 621 AOK
These photographs are of 621 AOK, the very well documented pre-production 1959 Mini. Gaydon Heritage Motor Museum very kindly allowed us to take these pictures on 21st April 2010. I believe that this car was used as a 'buck,' that's to say that there are features on its bodyshell that would have been modified at the factory to cure problems with the production vehicles.

Offside front floorpan
Pic 1
- This large front floorpan has a 'X' beaten into it.
- This is the only original Mini that I have seen this on.
- Note. Two small rubber grommets.

Nearside front floorpan
Pics 2 & 3
- This large front floorpan has a 'X' beaten into it.
- This is the only original Mini that I have seen this on.
- Note. Two small rubber grommets, if you look closely you will see a large alloy blanking plug covered with sealer in-between the two rubber grommets.

Fabricated starter solenoid bracket
Pic 4
- I believe that these were fitted to the large front floorpan bodyshells only.

Offside front inner sill
Pic 5
- Drilling in inner sill. This is probably where the expanding foam was injected.

Offside 1959 front door with riveted splash shield
Pic 6
- This was a modification; hence the rivets.

Offside quarter glass
Pics 7 & 8
- Mk1 quarter glass with piano hinge.

Offside front cant rail corner piece
Pics 9 & 10
- Note. Front cant rail above windscreen is swaged. Also nearside and offside front to rear cant rail is swaged. I think this was done to help with alignment of body panels.

Nearside door kick shield
Pic 11
- Plastic kick shield with bright surround.

Welded rear bumper brackets (x5)
Pics 12-16
- When the classic Mini was originally designed it did not have an opening boot.
- Therefore, when the decision was made to add an opening boot this involved fitting external hinges.
- These five brackets were affixed to the bodyshell to allow fitting of the rear bumper to clear the external hinges.
- AOK is fitted with a three-stud rear bumper. It would have originally had a five-stud fixing bumper fitted.

HANDBUILT 621 AOK & 1959 MINI 763 HKO

ANATOMY OF THE CLASSIC MINI

Pic 25 · Pic 26 · Pic 27 · Pic 28
Pic 29 · Pic 30 · Pic 31 · Pic 32
Pic 33 · Pic 34 · Pic 35 · Pic 36

Water drain holes in gutter
Pics 17 & 18
- This would have been a recall.
- These holes would have been drilled by a dealer after car had left factory.

Front seats and seatbelts
Pics 19 & 20
- I took these pictures because I'd never seen this type of seatbelt arrangement before.

Boot stay brackets (on bodyshell)
Pics 21 & 22
- This design of boot stay bracket probably only lasted through prototype stage. I have never seen another pair like it.

Fuel tank
Pic 23
- 1959 fuel tank with no drain facility.

- Fuel tank sender held to tank by six screws.

Spare wheel well
Pic 24
- Note. Two small rubber grommets. This boot floor has been modified. It would originally have had a floor like 763 HKO. See pic 65, Bodywork chapter.

Spare wheel securing bracket
Pic 25
- First type of securing bracket.
- Later types were slightly smaller in outside diameter to cut down on material used.

1959 MINI 763 HKO
This 1959 Mini belongs to John Milicivic Senior, I believe he took this car in part exchange in the 1970s, and liked it so much that he decided to keep it.
This car has not been over-restored, and does have some incorrect parts fitted.

Offside
Pic 26
- The chrome button on the 'B' post is non-standard.
- Door is fitted with correct one hole pieces of glass.
- The trim running around the wheelarches and sill originally would have been in three pieces.
- Correct 1959 wheel trims.

Front
Pic 27
- I believe that because this car has opening rear quarter windows it should also have bumper over-riders.

Nearside
Pic 28
- The chrome button on the 'B' post is non-standard.
- Door is fitted with correct one hole pieces of glass.
- The trim running around the wheelarches and sill originally would

have been in three pieces.
- Correct 1959 wheel trims.

Rear
Pic 29
- Correct bright trim in rear windscreen rubber.
- Correct bright fuel filler cap.
- I believe that because this car has opening rear quarter windows it should also have bumper over-riders.
- Rear gutter on back panel has had two elongated holes drilled for water drainage. (This would have been when the vehicle was recalled.)

Boot
Pics 30 & 31
- Correct Austin Seven badges.
- Correct hinging rear numberplate, for use with boot left open.
- Correct bright numberplate light.

Washer jet
Pic 32 & 33
- Mk1 washer jets.

Wiper arms
Pic 34
- Correctly parked wipers.

Gearlever, dim/dip switch and heater
Pic 35
- Correct straight gearlever.
- Correct foot-operated bright dim/dip switch.
- Early recirculatory heater.

Steering column cowl
Pic 36
- Looks like a brown column cowl, would normally expect to find a black one.

Useful contacts & museums

USEFUL CONTACTS
Anstey, Mike (Birmingham area), 07956 546124
Bradford Mini Specialists (Christine, Keith, Kevin, Kim)
Hebden, Tim (Kent), 07971 549595 (Pig Shed Minis burned down!)
Hore, Brian (Didcot) aka 'The heater man', 01235 817208 – Mk1/2 specialist parts

MUSEUMS
Atwell Wilson Museum (Calne, Wiltshire) – Issigonis 9x, 1275GT on Denovos
Caister Castle Museum (Caister on Sea, Norfolk) – 1959 Mini, plus very high mileage 1071cc Cooper S
Coventry Transport Museum (The Midlands) – There is a classic Mk1 Mini on display alongside the Thrust SSC1 Land Speed Car. Without the Mini, Thrust could not have run! (Free admission)
Gaydon Heritage Motor Museum (now renamed Gaydon Warwickshire) – 621 AOK, twin Moke
Whilewebbs Museum of Transport, Whilewebbs Lane, Enfield – sectioned 850cc engines and gearboxes from colleges, plus Barry's autojumble. (Admission £4)
London Motor Museum (Hayes, Middlesex, privately owned) – Mk1 Mini 850 Automatic (white)

ALSO FROM VELOCE PUBLISHING –

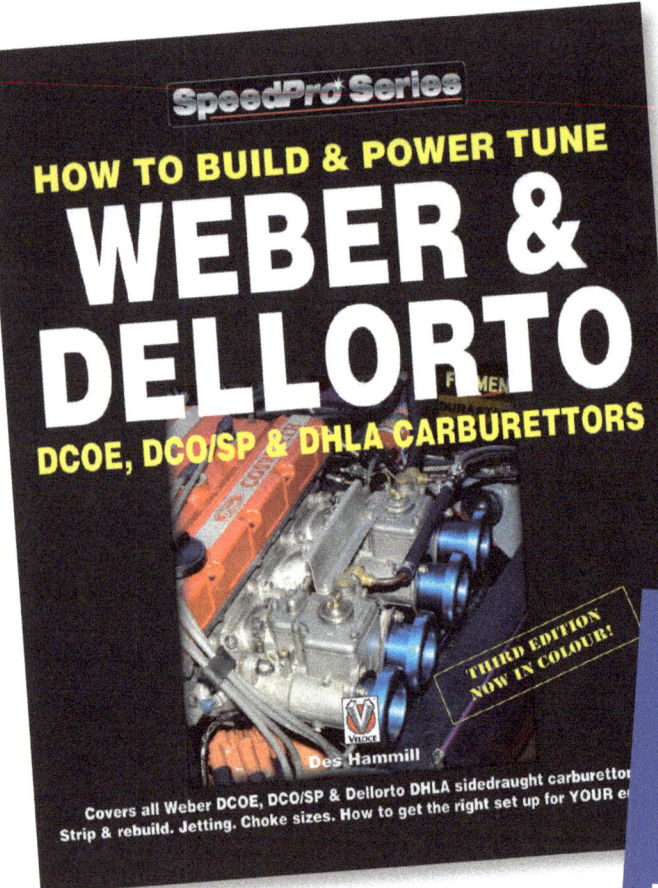

All you could want to know about the most famous and popular high performance sidedraught carbs. Covers strip and rebuild, tuning, choke sizes and much more.

ISBN: 978-1-845849-59-7
Paperback • 25x20.7cm • 128 pages
• 181 colour and b&w pictures

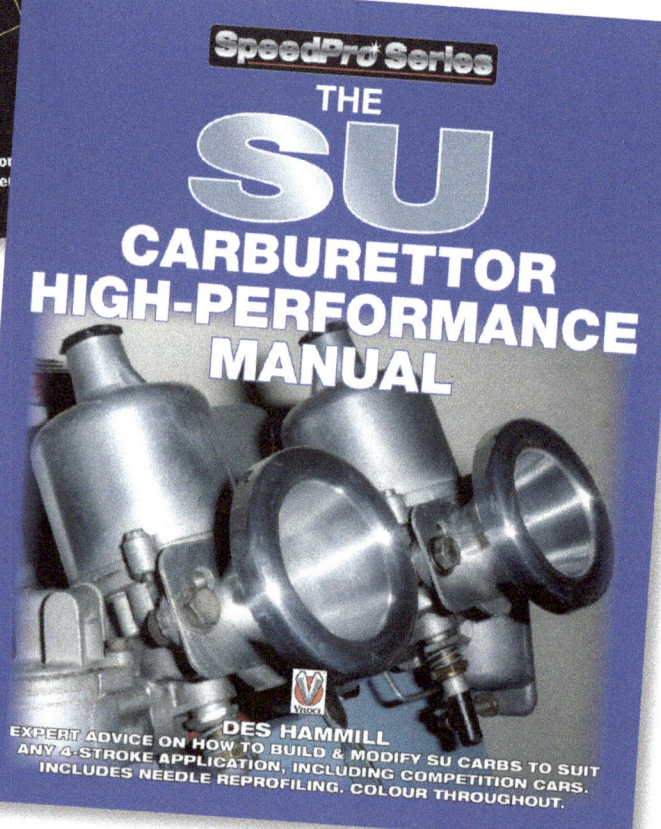

Did you know that SUs can give almost as much performance as Webers & Dellortos? Here's an expert guide to building and modifying SU carburettors to suit high-performance applications. Includes reprofiling needles & how to 'jet' SUs for almost any application.

ISBN: 978-1-787111-68-4
Paperback • 25x20.7cm • 96 pages
• 80 colour and b&w pictures

For more info on Veloce titles, visit our website at www.veloce.co.uk • email: info@veloce.co.uk • Tel: +44(0)1305 260068
* prices subject to change, p&p extra

ALSO FROM VELOCE PUBLISHING –

How to choose the right camshaft or camshafts for your individual application. Takes the mystery out of camshaft timing and tells you how to obtain optimum timing for maximum power. Applies to all four-stroke car-type engines.

ISBN: 978-1-903706-59-6
Paperback • 25x20.7cm • 64 pages
• 95 colour and b&w pictures

The complete practical guide to successfully modifying classic/retro 2-valve cylinder heads for maximum power, economy and reliability. Applies to almost every car/motorcycle (not 2-stroke) and to all road and track applications.

ISBN: 978-1-903706-76-3
Paperback • 25x20.7cm • 112 pages
• 150+ b&w pictures

For more info on Veloce titles, visit our website at www.veloce.co.uk • email: info@veloce.co.uk • Tel: +44(0)1305 260068
* prices subject to change, p&p extra

Index

621 AOK 184, 186
763 HKO 186, 187

Adaptor
  Bypass hose 60
  Oil feed pipe 139
Arches (offside & nearside rear inner) 32
Arms
  Clutch lever 179
  Rear radius 154, 155
  Steering 145, 146
  Suspension front lower 153
  Suspension front upper 152, 153
  Wiper 53
Axles (rear stub axles, suspension) 155

Backplates
  Brake drum, front & rear 33
  Clutch 174
  Disc 35, 36
Bars
  Bumper corner 43
  Front suspension 154
  Lower stabiliser 169
  Upper stabiliser 92
Baseplates (master cylinders) 119
Bearings

Camshaft 54
Clutch release 178, 179
Wheel 157
Bellhousings (manual & automatic) 169, 170, 172, 174
Bezels
  Centre speedometer 41
  Headlamp 51
  Indicator 51
  Switch carrier 53
Bins (rear companion) 14
Blocks (engine) 92-107
Bolts
  Banjo 138
  Caliper 118
  Flywheel 177
Bonnets 29, 31
Bowls (headlamp) 133
Brace (rear seat) 23
Bracket
  Column dropping 45
  Gearbox mounting 174
  Jacking 11
  Pedal box 119
  Radiator bottom 65
  Radiator top 67
Breathers (bellhousing) 37
Bulkheads (front) 20

Bumpers 41, 43

Cables
  Accelerator 124
  Choke 124
  Handbrake 36
  Heater 60, 63
Cages (differential) 161
Calipers (brake) 118, 119
Cam followers 54
Camshafts 54
Cappings (door) 47
Caps
  Fuel filler 47
  Hubcaps 51
  Oil filler 40
Carburettors 124, 125
Casings
  Filter for single carbs 125, 126
  Filter for twin carbs 126, 127
  Gearbox 161, 164-166
Centres (flywheel) 176, 177
Clips (driveshaft) 159
Colours (rocker cover) 40
Column (steering) 143, 144
Components (differential cover 85H code) 179
Converters 177

INDEX

Coolers (oil) 139
Couplings
    Inner drive 159
    Rubber drive 159
Covers
    Bellhousing 174
    Differential 165
    Front tappet chest 37
    Rear tappet chest 54
    Rocker, chrome rocker 53
    Timing 57, 59
Cowlings
    Radiator 65
Crankshafts 70-76
Crownwheels, differential 161
Cylinders
    Brake, clutch, masters 115-118
    Clutch (slave) 119
    Wheel cylinders 118

Dampers, crankshaft 87, 88
Dipsticks 136
Disks, brake 35
Distributors 89, 91
Doors 19
Drivers
    Distributor 91
    Oil pump 136
Driveshafts 158, 159
Drums, brake, front, rear 33, 35

Elbows, air intake 126
Embellisher
    Bonnet 41
    East/west box section 47
    Wheel, Clubman 53
Ends, track rod 145
Extensions, moustache 51

Facia, alloy 41
Fans, radiator
    Electric 65
    Mechanical 65
Fasteners, rocker cover 40
Finisher
    Centre speedometer 47
    Door, external 47
    Front parcel shelf 49, 51
    Rear quarter panel, external 47
Flanges
    Differential output 159, 160
    Drive flanges 156, 157
    Inner driveshaft drive 159

Floors 7, 9, 10
Flywheels 176
Frame, subframe, front, rear 148, 150
Furniture, alloy door 41

Gasket
    Flywheel centre 176
    Tappet chest 54, 56
Gauges 128, 130
Gear, timing 57
Gear changes, remote control 165, 166
Gear levers
    Automatic 179
    Manual 179
Gears
    First motion shaft 168, 169
    Idler 168, 169
    Transfer, automatic 168
    Transfer, manual 167
Glass 131, 133
Grille, rear speaker 53
Grilles, front 47, 49
Guard, oil seal 169

Handles
    Boot 41
    External door 47
    Internal door 51
Heads
    Cylinder 79, 81-83
    Oil filter 139-142
Heaters 60
Heelboards 13
Hinges
    Bonnet 31
    Boot 31
    Door 19
Hose
    Brake servo 117
Housings
    Distributor 89
    Thermostat 67
Hubs (swivel, drum, disc) 146, 147

Infill
    Front windscreen 51
    Rear windscreen 53

Joint (ball) 147
Joints (constant velocity) 157, 158

Knuckles (suspension) 152

Lamp
    Front fog 134
    Front indicator 133
    Front spot 133
    Head 133
    Rear 134, 135
    Rear, side 133
    Rear companion bin 134
    Rear fog 135
    Rear numberplate 135
Latches (internal window) 51
Lever
    Chrome gear lever 45
    Handbrake lever 36
    Handbrake lever, chrome button 51
Lids (boot) 31
Light
    Chrome numberplate 45
    Roof interior light 135
Lock (internal door lock) 51
Lockwasher
    Offset, automatic 178
    Offset, manual 177

Manifold
    Exhaust 108-111
    Inlet 111-113
Mirrors (door mirrors) 47
Moulding (external, horizontal) 45, 47
Mount (front damper) 148
Mounting
    Engine and gearbox 174
    Front subframe 148
Moustache (grille) 51

Nozzles (air vent) 60
Nuts (constant velocity joint) 156

Pads (brake) 35
Panel
    Between rear valence and valence
        and valence closing panels 31
    Boot floor and rear seat panel 14
    Closing, scuttle 25
    Front panels 27, 29
    Front windscreen panel 23, 25
    Inner door hinge panels 14
    Rear valence closing 31
    Rear windscreen panel, Elf
        and Hornet 20
    Separate outer door hinge panel 14
Pedals
    Accelerator 124

Alloy foot pedals 41
Brake 119
Clutch 119
Pieces
  Corner 25
  'T' 67
Pinion (differential) 161
Pins (differential) 160
Pipes
  Oil cooler 139
  Oil feed 138, 139
  Oil strainer 139
  Turbo oil feed 136
Plates
  Blanking plate 60
  Differential, side 161, 162
  Driven, clutch 176
  Engine, back 57
  Sandwich, thermostat 67
  Thrust, pressure, clutch 178
  Turbo oil return 142
Plugs (core) 60
Plungers (clutch) 179
Pockets (door) 47
Pods (mounting) 130
Posts (rocker) 83
Pressure (plates) 178
Pulleys
  Crankshaft 87
  Water pump 68
Pumps
  Oil 136, 138
  Petrol 123, 124
  Water 67, 68

Quadrants (handbrake) 36

Rack (steering) 144, 145
Radiator (auxiliary) 60
Radiators 63
Rail
  Lower dash 32
  Top dash 32
Rails
  Cant 25
  Drip 25
Reinforcers ('C' post) 20

Repeaters (side) 134
Retainer (balljoint) 147
Rheostat (heater) 63
Riders (over, under) 43, 45
Rings (backing) 168
Rivets (brass) 51
Rockers 83, 85, 86
Rods
  Connecting 76-78
  Push 56
Roof 25
Rubber (front windscreen) 131

Seals
  Bellhousing oil 169
  Small oil 177
Seat (balljoint) 147
Section (box, east/west) 11
Senders (fuel tank) 123
Servos (brake) 117
Shafts (rocker) 83
Shelf (rear parcel) 32
Shields (early Mk1 weather shields) 14
Shoes
  Bodyshell lifting 11
  Brake front, rear 35
Shroud (rear radius arm) 13
Side
  Bodyshell side, Elf/Hornet 17
  Bodyshell side, Mini 14, 17
Sills
  Outer 11, 13
  Separate inner 13, 14
Spacers
  Heater tap 63
  Oil filter 139
  Steering arm 146
  Water pump 68
Speedometers 129, 130
Spring (seat) 146
Springs (suspension) 151
Stops (suspension spring bump) 150, 152
Strainers (oil) 139
Strip (inner kicking) 51
Struts (suspension) 152
Surround

External door glass 45
Horn push 51
Kick panel 47

Tanks
  Fuel 121, 122
  Header 60
Taps (heater) 63
Tensioners (timing gear) 57
Toeboards 13
Tray (ash) 41
Trim
  Front inner sill 137
  Internal horizontal 47
  Rear companion bin 51, 53
  Six-piece kit (painted) 53
  Six-piece kit (stainless steel) 53
  Upper sill step 53

Valence (rear) 31
Valve
  Brake compensating 119
  Brake intensifier 149
  Reducing 119
Visor (sun) 53

Washer
  DU thrust 168
  Front upper arm thrust 153
  Primary thrust 168
  Thrust 'C' 168
Winders (window) 45
Windscreen
  Front 131
  Rear 133
Wings
  Inner, nearside 20
  Inner, offside 23
  Outer, nearside Clubman 27
  Outer, nearside, non-Clubman 27
  Outer, offside Clubman 27
  Outer, offside, non-Clubman 25
Wheels
  Differential sunwheels 161
  Road 180-183
  Steering 146

www.ingramcontent.com/pod-product-compliance
Lightning Source LLC
Chambersburg PA
CBHW040738300426
44111CB00026B/2980